MONETARY SYSTEM OF NEPAL

MONETARY SYSTEM OF NEPAL

Dr. Yadav Sharma Gaudel
Associate Professor
Tribhuvan University

ADROIT PUBLISHERS
Delhi-110 053

Published by
ADROIT PUBLISHERS
C-8/2, Yamuna Vihar, Delhi-110 053
Phone: 23266030, 23242552

Distributors
AKHIL BOOK DISTRIBUTORS
4675/21, Ganpati Bhawan, Ansari Road,
Darya Ganj, New Delhi-110 002
Phones : 23266030, 23242552
e-mail: akhilbooks@yahoo.com

ISBN : 81-87392-40-1

Layout by
Sudhir Kumar Vatsa

Laser Typeset by
Nidhi Laser Point
e-mail: nidhi_vatsa@hotmail.com

Printed in India on behalf of M/s Adroit Publishers by
Arpit Printographer, B-7, Saraswati Complex,
Subhash Chowk, Laxmi Nagar, Delhi-110 092

Dedicated To
My Grand Parents

PREFACE

Monetary system is a source of understanding the theory of the demand for and supply of money in monetary economics. This book is a revised form of the Ph. D. thesis submitted to the BHU, India in 1998. It takes into consideration of the theoretical and empirical approaches, which provide the core elements for monetary analysis.

The models developed in this book are subject to empirical tests and it is gratifying to note that their findings will be favorable in the Nepalese context. It is mainly addressed to the students of master level as a reference book on monetary economics. In addition to this, it will be of great importance to the researchers and professional for further investigation in this venture. I believe that it will also be use of all the people who are keenly interested to know monetary & financial activities in Nepal.

This book has been designed into eight chapters. The first chapter begins with introduction followed by the monetary system of Nepal. The supply of money and its components have been discussed in the second chapter. The theoretical developments of the demand for money and its determinants have been presented in the 3rd and 4th chapter respectively. The fifth chapter is concentrated mainly on quantitative analysis. The different models under the single and simultaneous equation systems have been tested empirically. With a view to discuss the role of Indian currency and to measure the currency substitution behavior of business households, the sixth chapter has been devoted as a basis of primary survey. Monetary planning as an important aspect of reliable monetary policy has been derived in the seventh chapter.

A brief outline of monetary development given in this chapter may be meaningful for implementing monetary policy. Furthermore, money supply analysis and money demand implications have been incorporated. Finally an attempt has been made to summarize the main findings and the suggestions have been given.

While writing this book, it has been taken a special care to describe the subject matters that cover the needs of teaching in Nepalese monetary economics. This book may have several shortcomings. So comments and valuable suggestion for improvement are always commendable. My senior professors of BHU and TU, several friends and colleagues of the Department of Economics in P.N. Campus had promoted from time to time to publish this book. Among them Prof. G.D. Misra, my thesis supervisor of the Department of Economics, BHU, Prof. S.R. Poudyal, Prof. B. Pyakural and Prof. G.N. Sharma of the Central Department of Economics, TU and Associate Prof. G.R. Ojha, the Department of Economics, P.N. Campus, and U.R. Khatiwada, research consultant of the NRB have been a constant source of inspiration. I am highly obliged to each one of them.

During the primary survey period, the immense help made by many friends from Mechi to Mahakali border areas of Nepal is praiseworthy. I am also happy to acknowledge with thanks every one of them.

I am deeply indebted to my parents who gave me an initiation to continue my study. Their blessing was essential for the successful completion of this book. A special thank goes to my wife Nanda and children Indira, Prakash & Pramod who created congenial atmosphere to keep on writing manuscript. Last but not least I appreciate the Mr. DK Sharma of M/s Adroit Publishers for bringing this book.

Dr. Yadav Sharma Gaudel

CONTENTS

Preface *vii*
List of Tables *xi*
Abbreviations *xiii*

1. Monetary System of Nepal **1**
1.1 Introduction 1
1.2 Different Approaches to the Definition of Money 2
1.3 Role of Money in a Developing Economy 3
1.4 Nepalese Monetary System in Historical Perspective 4
1.5 Monetary Economy and Its Management 6
1.6 Supply and Demand for Money 9
1.7 Chapter Scheme 12

2. Supply of Money in the Nepalese Economy **13**
2.1 Introduction13
2.2 Components of Money Supply 15
2.3 Money Supply Determinants 16
2.4 Money Supply Function 19
2.5 Money and Capital Markets 21
2.6 Evolution of the Financial System : A Review 26
2.7 The Nepal Rastra Bank : Its Role and Function 29
2.8 Concluding Remarks 32

3. Demand for Money in a Developing Economy **33**
3.1 Introduction 33
3.2 The Classical Approach 34
3.3 The Keynesian Approach 38
3.4 The Inventory—Theoretic Approach 42
3.5 The Modern Approach 47

3.6 Implications of the Different Approaches in the Context of a Developing Economy 52
3.7 Concluding Remarks 57

4. Determinants of the Demand for Money in Nepal **62**

4.1 Introduction 62
4.2 The Monetary Economy of Nepal : An Overview 62
4.3 Money Demand : Its Major Determinants 75
4.4 Other Determinants 87
4.5 Concluding Remarks 90

5. Empirical Evidence on the Demand for Money in Nepal **93**

5.1 Introduction 93
5.2 Data and Methodology 96
5.3 Testing Different Econometric Models in the Context of the Nepalese Economy 97

6. Money Demand and Currency Substitution in Nepal : A Case Study **129**

6.1 Introduction 129
6.2 Exchange Rate System in Nepal 130
6.3 Status of Indian Currency in Nepal 132
6.4 Empirical Analysis 135
6.5 Empirical Findings 138
6.6 Concluding Remarks 144

7. Monetary Planning and Policy in Nepal **147**

7.1 Introduction 147
7.2 Monetary Planning : An Appraisal 148
7.3 Monetary Development under the Different Economic Plans 149
7.4 Monetary Control Instruments 153
7.5 Money Supply Analysis 157
7.6 Money Demand Implications 160
7.7 Monetary Policy and its Impact on Economic Activity 161
7.8 Concluding Remarks 165

8. Summary of Findings and Suggestions **169**

8.1 Summary of Findings 169
8.2 Suggestions 173

Appendix 175

Bibliography 191

Index 209

LIST OF TABLES

2.2.1 Money Supply in Nepal
2.3.1 Determinants of Money Supply
3.6.1 Implications of the Demand for Money Theories
4.1 Average Annual Growth Rate of GDP and. Population (1966-1999)
4.2 Percentage Ratio of Gross Domestic Savings and Investment to GDP (1976-1999)
4.3 Average Annual Rate of Price and Inflation (1975-1999)
4.4 Average Annual Growth Rate of Money Stock and their Ratio to GDP (1966-1999)
4.5 Interest Rate Structure (Percent Per annum) (1965-1999)
4.6 Exchange Rate and the Devaluation of Nepalese Currency (per currency unit) (1965-1999)
4.7 Summary of Balance of Payments (1976-1999)
5.3.1 1.0 Simple Linear Model
1.1 Stability Test
2.0 Modified Linear Model
3.0 Loglinear Model
4.0 Semi-Loglinear Model
4.1 McKinnon's Hypothesis in Semi-Loglinear Model
5.1 First Difference Form (Partial Adjustment Model)
5.2 First Difference Form (Adaptive Expectation Model)

5.3.2 Simultaneous Equations Model (1966-1994)
6.2.1 Holding of Indian Currency in the Business Portfolio in Nepal, 1996
6.3.2 Business Household Demand for Money Model, 1996
7.5.1 Growth Rate of Money Supply in Nepal (1990-1999)

ABBREVIATIONS

ADB = Asian Development Bank
ADLM = Autoregressive Distributed Lag Model
BOP = Balance of Payments
C = Currency held by Public
CBS = Central Bureau of Statistics
CES = Constant Elasticity of Substitution
CGN = Claims on the Government, Net
CPI = Consumer Price Index
DD = Demand Deposits held by Public
Dh = Durbin-h Statistic
D_r = Dummy for the Rate of Interest
DW = Durbin-Watson Statistic
Er = Exchange Rate
ERI = Exchange Rate Index of NC and IC
ESS = Error Sums of Square
EXNT = Exchange Rate of NC per unit of IC
e = Elasticity
et al = And Others
6y = Elasticity of Income
6r = Elasticity of Interest Rate
FD = Fixed Deposits

F	=	F-ratio (Variance test)
F_e	=	Forward Exchange Rate
FER	=	Foreign Exchange Reserve
FERA	=	Foreign Exchange Regulation Act
FY	=	Fiscal Year
GDP	=	Gross Domestic Product
GFD	=	Government Fiscal Deficit (Exp.-Rev.)
GNE	=	Gross National Expenditure
GNP	=	Gross National Product
GR	=	Government Revenue
GRs	=	Gold Reserves
H	=	Ratio of Human to Non-human Wealth
Hc	=	Holding of Indian Currency
H^*	=	Yield on Human Wealth
HMG/N	=	His Majesty's Government of Nepal
I	=	Investment
IA	=	Interest Bearing Assets
IC	=	Indian Currency
IFA	=	Inflow of Foreign Aids (Grant + Loan)
IFS	=	International Financial Statistics
IMF	=	International Monetary Fund
ISD	=	Institute for Sustainable Development
K	=	Real Value of Bonds
ln	=	Natural Logarithm
lr	=	Lending Rate of Commercial Banks
M	=	Money Stock (Total)
M^*	=	Desired Money Balance
MABP	=	Monetary Approach to the Balance of Payments
M_d	=	Money Demand
M_1	=	Narrow Money (C+DD)
M_2	=	Broad Money (M_1+TD)
M_r	=	Reserve Money or High Powered Money

M_s = Money Supply
m = Multiplier
N = Number of Observations
N_b = Employment in Business
NC = Nepalese Currency
NCB = Number of Commercial Bank Branches
NFA = Net Foreign Asset
NIDC = Nepal Industrial Development Corporation
NPC = National Planning Commission
NRB = Nepal Rastra Bank
OLS = Ordinary Least Square
P = Price Level
P^e = Expected Price Level
P_c = Cost of Living Index
POP = Population
Pw = Wholesale Price Index
Đ$_t$ = Rate of Inflation
Đ^e = Expected Rate of Inflation
Q = Yield on Physical Assets
R = Rate of Interest
R_r = Region wise rate of interest
Re = Expected Rate of Interest
r_t-Đ$_t$ = Real Rate of Interest
R^* = Yield on Financial Assets
R^2 = Proportion of Variation
r_b = Rate Interest on Bonds
r_t = Rate of Interest on Fixed (12 month) Deposits
r' = Rate of Return
ñ = Autocorrelation Coefficient
SD = Saving Deposits
2SLS = Two Stage Least Square
T = Transaction

TC	=	Total Cost
TD	=	Time Deposits
t	=	Student t-Test
t-1	=	One Year Lag Period
t-2	=	Two Years Lag Period
T_y	=	Transactional Income
UDCs	=	Underdeveloped Countries
US	=	United States
UK	=	United Kingdom,
V	=	Velocity
W	=	Wealth
WDR	=	World Development Report
WPI	=	Wholesale Price Index
X	=	Export
Y	=	Income
Y^e	=	Expected Income
YAG	=	GDP in Agricultural Sector
YNAG	=	GDP in Non-agricultural Sector
Y_p	=	Permanent Income
Y_{pt}	=	Real GDP (at constant price)
Y_t	=	Nominal GDP (at current price)

Chapter I

MONETARY SYSTEM OF NEPAL

1.1 Introduction 1.2 Different Approaches to the Definition of money. 1.3 Role of money in a developing economy 1.4 Monetary system of Nepal 1.5 Monetary economy and its management 1.6 The supply and demand for money. 1.7 Chapter Scheme.

1.1 Introduction

Money is widely used as an economic instrument and it is clear that money plays an important role in the economic system of the country. Any definition of money, which confines to currency and demand deposits, is considered as narrow money. But some other assets like time and saving deposits at commercial banks and non-bank financial institutions, short-term treasury bills, government securities etc. are very near to money in liquidity. They are also called *quasi money* means they have a high degree of liquidity or moneyness. Thus, these assets should also be included in the boarder definition of money.

It is obvious that the total money supply narrowly defined includes coins, paper currency and demand deposits of all commercial banks. However, a broader definition of money comprises narrow money plus near money. In this regard, Chandler (1975:13) has opined that the near money is one of the determinants of community's demand function for money balances and the behavior of spending depends not only on the supply of money but also on the demand for money balances.

1.2. Different Approaches to the Definition of Money

Different writers have defined the term money. According to H.G. Johnson (1962), there are four important approaches to the definition of money.

(*a*) The Conventional Approach
(*b*) Chicago Approach
(*c*) Gurley and Shaw Approach
(*d*) The Central Bank Approach

(a) *The Conventional Approach*

This approach in concerned with definition of money as currency plus demand deposits at commercial banks. Demand deposits are the current accounts of depositors in the commercial banks. This approach is analytically better in the sense of providing the exact measure of money supply. However, it is traditional because it limits money supply within a narrow area.

(b) *Chicago Approach*

The Chicago approach led by M. Friedman defines money as a temporary abode of purchasing power. According to this approach money comprises currency and the total deposits of commercial banks. The economists of the Chicago school have argued that the time deposits can be converted into cash or demand deposits. All the deposits should, therefore, be treated as money.

(c) *Gurley and Shaw Approach*

This approach holds that money should include liabilities of the non-bank financial intermediaries. This approach presents a list of close substitutes for money. G. S. Gurley and E. H. Shaw have drawn a distinction between *outside* and *inside* money. Outside money represents wealth to which there corresponds no debt. Thus, gold coins and currency notes may be considered as outside money. However, inside money is created against private debt. It shows bank deposits and other assets generated by financial intermediaries.

(d) *The Central Bank Approach*

This approach is focused on monetary policy and it takes

money as a means of financing purchases. The Nepal Rastra Bank (NRB) as a central bank has been providing monetary data regularly in its economic bulletin since 1957. The total money supply according to NRB approach is defined by taking currency notes and coins with the public and demand deposit of all commercial banks held by the public. By adding time deposits of banks including margin deposits to money supply with the public, the total monetary resources in terms of broad money can be obtained. This broad concept of money implies that the Nepalese economy is going to be able to economize on money by substituting credit.

1.3. Role of Money in a Developing Economy

Basically, the role of money as a complement or substitutes depends upon the stage of economic development. Money may be substitute in developed economy; however, it may predominantly act as a complement in a developing economy. An important feature of a developing economy like Nepal is the prevalence of large non-monetized sector. As the economy develops, more money with monetary institutions is needed for the monetization of the economy. Thus, in the context of the developing economy, monetary development refers to the gradual transformations of the subsistence sector into a monetized sector. The role of money in this sense is crucial in determining its speeds in monetary manifestation of the growth process. The reason why money plays such of vital role in the growth process is easy to understand. *Firstly*, the use of money removes all the obstacles arising from time and space. *Secondly*, money in the growth process provides an efficient payment mechanism.

Although money is not a real factor of the growth, it acts as a catalytic agent in speeding up the process of the growth. It increases existing resources, generates new ones and channels them into productive uses. Thus, considering this role, monetary policy in developing economy like Nepal should aim at regulated expansion of money. It implies that supply of money should expand with the growth rate of GDP in the country.

1.4. Monetary System of Nepal

Monetary system of any country refers to the combined system of currency and banking. The currency system indicates legal tender money. The country as a medium of exchange and measures of value has used it. However, under the banking system, banks are to be considered not merely as dealers in money but also act as reservoirs of resources necessary for economic development. Banks can promote capital formation, encourage entrepreneurship and accelerate economic activities through monetization.

In this regard, Hanson (1965:279) has opined that monetary system includes internal and external monetary arrangements of a country. Internally, it covers standard monetary units and its division in the form of convertible, inconvertible, token and legal tender money. However, in external relationship it shows foreign exchange standard in use, such as gold standard, special drawing rights, fixed or flexible exchange rate etc. Thus, monetary system relates with transmission mechanism of monetary & banking system of the country.

It is generally believed that monetary system evolved over time from barter economy through gold, silver, copper coin to paper currency. Today, the paper currency has fulfilled the needs for a flexible money supply in the country. According to Johnson (1993), monetary system is the general mechanism for exchange of goods and services. It incorporates all the forms of exchange, namely barter exchange, full-bodied money and paper money. From the outset, monetary system of Nepal depicts the situation of dual currency system and is witnessed by the circulation of both Nepalese currency (NC) and Indian currency (IC) side by side (chapter VI). This fact shows that the IC has been used as a medium of exchange particularly in the adjoining border areas of Nepal and India. Furthermore, the Nepalese economy has to depend largely on India for importing goods and services. As a result, people in border areas, specially prefer to hold their money in terms of IC. Also the trade payment of the country as a whole shows the dominant position of IC.

Despite this, the existence of unorganized sources of credit and its influence in the rural economy is one of the major defects of the Nepalese monetary system. The other problem is the prevalence of savings gap, which cannot be bridged merely by establishing financial institutions. The next problem is that the IC is circulated in a large unknown quantity along with NC. So, monetary authority has no full and effective control over the entire monetary system. This situation, in fact reduces the capacity of the government to implement monetary policy effectively.

1.4.1 Monetary System in Historical Perspective

Though the history of modern monetary system in Nepal was not so long, it was applied under currency system in ancient period. In 5th century B.C, Licchabi king Mandev issued *Mananka* coin made of copper. This coin was considered as the first coin of Nepal. In that period, copper standards were used as a medium of exchange and measure of value. These types of coins were also circulated during Malla period in the 13th century. During that period, the trade between Nepal and Tibet was good. Due to that situation, gold was imported from Tibet and exported to India. The king Mahindra Malla issued copper coins with fixed sizes and shapes. During the time of 16th and 17th century, other Malla kings were also circulated silver coins, but the weights of those coins were not uniform. In 18th century, particularly, at the time of Rana Bahadur Shah, Gold Mohar (Asarfi), silver rupiya and other small copper coins especially *daam & paisa* were circulated in the economy. In Rana regime also, gold and silver coins were issued and circulated. Despite these, other small coins of cheap metals and the coins of British India came into existence through out the kingdom.

It is well known fact that the Nepalese monetary economy is characterized by the prevalence of dual currency system because of its open border to the south and its proximity to India in trade, religion, culture, etc. Moreover, the unique feature of equal acceptance of Indian currency (IC) in place of Nepalese currency (NC) has made possible for currency substitution in the business transaction. Keeping this fact in mind, a separate chapter (VI) dealing with the role and status of Indian currency has been mentioned in the book.

From the historical record it is known that until 1940, only metallic coins were found to be used as a medium of exchange. It was only in 1945 that the Sadar Mulki Khana (Local treasury of the government) issued currency notes. Accordingly an urgent necessity of central bank was felt to the development of banking and financial sector to manage the circulation of NC and to maintain exchange rate stability for the promotion of industry and commerce. As a result, the Nepal Rastra Bank (NRB) was set up on April 26, 1956 as the central bank of the country (NRB, 1998:36).

Prior to the establishment of the NRB, people received credit from the Nepal Bank Ltd (NBL) in Indian currency. The government employees also obtained their salaries in terms of IC. Foreign exchange reserve of the currency was also kept in Indian banks. There was no regulating agency to stabilize the exchange rate between NC and IC. Thus, challenging task for the NRB was to increase the circulation of NC by replacing the use of IC in various transactions.

The NRB issued currency notes (of Rs.1, 5, 10 and 100 denominations) for the first time in 1960. At the same time, the government also enacted Foreign Exchange Regulation Act 1954. It had prohibited foreign exchange dealing in market except by authorized dealers of the NRB (Shrestha, 1981:179). The bank then focused its attention to eliminate the dual currency system during the first decade of establishment. For this purpose, the NC circulation Act was implemented in various regions followed by the Foreign Exchange Regulation Act (1963). By the year 1966 the dual currency system was abolished and only the NC became legal tender money throughout the country.

1.5. Monetary Economy and its Management

Monetary economy as the opposite of barter economy refers to the economic system in which money is used as a medium of exchange. In a monetary economy, money is considered as a liquid asset and is used a subtle device for linking the present to the future. Despite these, the various financial institutions including central bank and the commercial banks exist in the monetary economy.

As economic development proceeds, the economy usually becomes rich in financial institutions. The demand for financial services depends upon the growth of real income in general and the pace of monetization of subsistence sector in particular. It is realized that in the early stages of development, financial institutions were not in a position to attract public preference to hold currency. However, later on the banking and non-banking financial intermediaries expanded rapidly through the increment in demand for time deposits and saving deposits. Thus, the knowledge of the appropriate definition of money and the degree of substitutability of various financial assets are essential for the purpose of policy formulation in monetary economy.

Despite the development in monetary theory, little attention has been given to the role of money and its management in underdeveloped countries. Furthermore, financial assets in these countries are limited and real assets are likely to be a close substitute for real cash balances (Adekunle, 1968: 233)[a]. In view of these considerations, it would be worthwhile to examine the monetary system in Nepal and to shed some light on integration of monetary theory with the economic development.

The Nepalese economy is characterized by the existence of a large non-monetized sector, economic instability and unorganized financial market. As the financial system is typically underdeveloped, people do not hold much money for speculative purposes. Money is largely held for commodity transactions. Bank credit is also advanced almost entirely for financing of trades and businesses. Under the these circumstances, a high proportion of total money stocks remains active, and an increase in investment outlay by the expansion in money supply tends to exert the pressure on price level.

Nepal being a predominantly agricultural and non-monetized economy, currency consists of 69.1% of the total money stock with the public (NRB, Mid -July, 2001: 2). The rural economy is characterized by the prevalence of cash over credit transactions. A large proportion of cash circulates in the economy, but it does not come into the banks accounts in the form of deposits. It is because of that there are limited banking facilities on one hand and the lack of public awareness exists on the other. Further, a desire for house building in urban areas, purchasing a piece of land for accommodation, lust for jewels, a tendency to incur huge expenditure on occasions and festivals explain the reason for currency hoarding by public. In addition to these activities, a fall in foreign exchange reserves, deficit balance of payments, increasing proportion of foreign aid in government's budget have added fuel to the fire in the investment of income in real estate or in illegal activities even though there are more opportunities of profitable and productive investment.

It is important for the monetarist to know the degree of substitutability between money and financial assets with a purpose of formulating monetary policy. To determine the assets, which are close substitutes for money and the assets that are not, one has to study the behaviours of asset holders. In the Nepalese economy, the financial markets outside the banking system are not well developed. Most of the people are not habitual of holding money for investment purposes. This type of behavior shows that the substitution between money and real assets is more important than money and financial assets.

It is observed that one of the reasons for high growth of money supply in Nepal is the increasing volume of government borrowings from the NRB. As a consequence of successive increases in overdraft to the government, pressure has been on monetary expansion. The frequent devaluation of NC as compared to foreign currency shows an upsurge of price movement and ultimately results in inflation. From this discussion, it follows that under the existing condition of Nepal, an inflationary situation beyond the control of monetary authority would accentuate the demand for substantial amount of money in purchasing real assets only.

One of the tasks of all monetary authority is to support the gradual expansion of the financial system, which links surplus and deficit spending units of the economy. The strategy for developing financial sector depends upon the effectiveness of the NRB to increase the demand for money through financial institutions. However, the process of opening and development of banking as well as financial intermediaries has been very slow since 2000 AD due to the political instability, social insecurity and economic turmoil in the country.

Monetary management implies a deliberate policy, which aims at the systematic regulation of the volume of currency and credit. The management by a central bank includes money supply that ensures the availability of credit and prices consistent with specific national objectives viz. the maintenance of a stable exchange rate & price level and the attainment of equilibrium between savings and investment.

In a developing economy like ours, the keynote of policy of monetary management may be termed as controlled expansion of money supply. It suggests that money supply has to be expanded sufficiently to match the growth of national income. Moreover, the NRB as a central bank has a responsibility to take appropriate steps to regulate money supply through credit control measures. Thus, the policy of controlled expansion in the field of monetary management is more important for the achievement of growth with stability in the economy.

1.6. The Supply and Demand for Money

The money supply and the money demand behavior of the nation depend upon the legal and institutional factors that define monetary system operating during a given time period.

Under the money supply concept, money is viewed as the most liquid of all assets that an individual prefers to hold. For an asset to be liquid, it must be either money or something else which can be easily converted with a high degree of certainty into a known amount of money (Hart, 1968:426). Further, two common features of money as the acceptable means of exchange and no interest earning to its holders have supported to recognize it in the from of liquid asset. Thus, in view of these characteristics, money is treated as a distinct object from all other assets and is generally acceptable in payment for any thing (Crowther, 1994:20).

It is generally accepted that cash and cheques drawn on banks are the means of payment for transactions and this fact leads to conclude that currency and demand deposits are the main monetary assets for their inclusion in the definition of money. However, for a proper empirical definition of money, Koot (1975) has argued that money is the sum of currency and demand deposits as well as time deposits at commercial banks.

Regarding the inclusion of time deposits, some economists have argued that time deposits are not subject to immediate withdrawal for current payment and hence the time deposits should be excluded from the definition of money. In this respect, it is true that if time deposits are not immediately withdrawn, these deposits may be used as money in prior notice (Subrahmanyam, 1977: 414). This type of controversy though remains in monetary theory, has led to the conclusion that the sum of currency and demand deposits is treated under the narrow definition of money and the time deposits together with narrow money is counted under the broad definition of money. Thus, in this perspective, money is regarded as a valuable asset because public generally accept it as a medium of exchange and use it as a store of value.

The concept of the demand for money focuses on the stock of money itself. However, as a means of payments it focuses on the process of receipts and expenditure and thereby creates the demand for money as a temporary abode of purchasing power (Handa, 1977:399). Thus, the demand for money is assigned an important role in the monetary theory. In theory, the demand for money is defined as an increasing function of income or wealth, a decreasing function of the rate of interest. Hence, the demand for money comes from the general public and the monetary authority autonomously determines its supply.

It is widely recognized that money is demanded primarily because it serves as a means of payments or a medium of exchange. If the changes in money stocks were not adequate enough to fulfill the growing needs of the economy, the level of aggregate economic activity would be restrained. On the other hand unwarranted growth in money supply would generate inflationary pressure and create unfavorable balance of payments. An understanding of the nature of the demand for money function is, therefore, vital to the process of monetary management. Further it can be established that the demand for money is a stable function of some measurable variables. It the values of these variables are known, it will then be possible to predict the demand for money and suitably adjust its supply.

In most underdeveloped countries, a substantial proportion of wealth is preserved in the form of physical and real assets. It indicates that money is held not only for transaction and precautionary purposes, but also in the convenient form of storing wealth. In this regard, if one looks monetary situation of Nepal, one can find the place made by precautionary motive is more important in the desire for money holding. People living in urban areas have a preference for holding their money either in foreign exchange accounts of joint venture banks or by purchasing urban land. This implies that most of the people do not want to invest their money in productive areas of creating employment opportunities. As a result, the gap of income and employment has been widening due to low investment in the economy. Keeping this in view, Nepal implemented a financial liberalization programme in the second half of 1980s (Tseng & Corker, 1991:14). The key reforms behind the programme were aimed at liberalizing interest rates, reducing control on credits, enhancing competition and efficiency in the financial system in the economy.

Despite these programmes, the policy for monetary planning is also related to the stability of the demand for money function. Unless the function is stable, no policy implication can be derived efficiently. Thus, a wide knowledge about the supply and demand for money is needed both from theoretical and empirical perspective specially because of their pivotal role in income, price level, exchange rate and balance of payments.

It is known that the demand for money is one of the main factors affecting the level of aggregate economic activity. It is general impression that monetary policy is oriented towards achieving economic stability. Specifically, when the effectiveness on monetary policy is under consideration, the estimation of demand for money together with money supply is an unavoidable task for economists (Liang et al, 1971:475). Thus, the estimation of demand and supply function for meaningful policy formulation in the Nepalese context would be highly appreciable.

1.7. Chapter Scheme

This book comprises of eight chapters. With the first chapter on monetary system, the second chapter presents the theoretical and empirical analysis on money supply and its components in the Nepalese context.

The third chapter shows the theoretical development of the demand for money in the classical, neoclassical, Keynesian and the modern period. It also discusses the implications of different approaches in monetary economy for the developing countries like Nepal.

The fourth chapter introduces a brief survey of the Nepalese monetary economy during the sample period (1965-99). It adduces the major determinants of the demand for money as income, interest rate, price level, balance of payments, exchange rate, and the other determinants such as population, inflation, budget deficit and the rate of monetization.

The fifth chapter analyses the various econometric models in the form of single equation, simultaneous equation system in order to obtain empirical evidences on the demand for money in Nepal.

The sixth chapter examines money demand function of the business households sector. An attempt has also been made to assess the ratio of currency substitution between NC and IC.

The seventh chapter attempts to make a design of monetary planning for achieving monetary stability in the economy. It brings together the empirical evidences for the successful implementation of monetary policy in Nepal.

The last chapter provides a brief summary of the main findings and suggestions.

Chapter II

SUPPLY OF MONEY IN THE NEPALESE ECONOMY

2.1 Introduction 2.2 Components of Money Supply 2.3 Money Supply Determinants 2.4 Money Supply Function 2.5 Money and Capital Markets 2.6 Evolution of Financial System: A Review 2.7 The Nepal Rastra Bank: Its Role and Functions 2.8 Concluding Remarks.

2.1 Introduction

This chapter traces the framework of money supply aspect to the Nepalese monetary economy. In this chapter, it has been tried to define the specification of money supply and recent changes in its composition. The term *money supply* refers to the total stock of money held by the public in spending form. Historically, the analysis of supply of money has occupied relatively less important place than the analysis of demand for money in the literature of monetary theory (Paul, 1992: 245). Money supply is generally considered as a policy determined phenomenon. According to modern view, the phenomenon of money supply shows the whole spectrum of liquidity in the asset portfolio of the individual. Thus, money supply in the modern approach has been used as a wider concept. It implies that money as a common bond generally acts to a medium of exchange, units of account, a store of value and the standard of deferred payments. It is called the most liquid asset, as it is the medium of exchange and willingly acceptable. Furthermore, saving and time deposits as well as government bonds are also liquid, but they cannot be directly and as smoothly spending as money. They will have to be converted into cash for the purpose of spending (Patnaik, 1982: 10).

In order to show the behaviour of the money supply generated by the Nepalese monetary system, money supply determinants have been determined. Further, the money supply function has been estimated for 34 years period (1965-1998). It is known that, the short-term securities with one year or less than maturity are traded in money market, while the long-term securities of more than one year to maturity are traded in capital market. Government treasury bills, commercial paper and certificate of deposits are examples of instruments that are exchanged in money market. However, the long-term securities like stocks, bonds and mortgages are bought and sold in capital market. Considering these two types of markets, a review has been made about the evolution of financial system in Nepal. Furthermore, in the perspective of financial development, the role and function of the Nepal Rastra Bank (NRB) has also been mentioned in the last section of this chapter.

Money being the most liquid asset, any change in its supply would induce the public to spend more or less either on financial assets (such as, bonds, securities, shares etc.) or on real assets like land, building, car, bus and so on. For instance, if the public decides to spend excess supply of money in purchasing financial assets, their prices would tend to go upwards, resulting in a decline in the rate of interest. The fall in the rate of interest would induce more investment affecting the gross domestic product or national income through the route of interest rate. However, in the Nepalese context the public seems to decide spend more on real assets viz. land for housing or vehicle as a consequence of increase in liquidity or money supply. From the recent past experience, it is known that with the increase in money supply, public's demand for it has also raised and consequently the people are holding all the additional supply of money without spending. The reason may be due to the insecurity of investment, non-transparent government policy towards investment, socio-economic instability and so on.

2.2 Components of Money Supply

Money supply in Nepal consists of i) notes and coins in circulation outside the banking sector ii) demand deposits of commercial banks and iii) other deposits with the Nepal Rastra Bank. The first two items are considered as the major components of money supply. Thus, money supply at any time may be composed of currency outside banks and demand deposits, which may be termed as M_1. Most economists, therefore, prefer to limit the definition of money supply to M_1 alone because of the fact that there are only acceptable liquid assets as a medium of exchange and are readily spending (Patnaik, 1982:4). Once we go beyond currency and demand deposits, and include other deposits as time or saving deposits, we may get the broad range of money supply. Thus, broad money supply, say M_2 involves M_1 plus time deposits with margin deposits also.

The following table shows money supply in Nepal for some selected years according to the definition of NRB.

Table: 2.2.1 Money Supply in Nepal

Year (Mid-month)	Money Supply (in Million Rupees) M_1	M_2	Currency/ Demand Deposits	Share of Demand Deposits (%)
1965 July	446.3	489.7	1.98	50.62
1975 "	1337.7	2064.4	2.18	45.96
1985 "	5480.0	12296.6	2.14	46.63
1995 "	32985.4	80984.7	2.14	46.64
2001 "	70776.9	214654.1	2.18	45.95

Source: Nepal Rastra Bank, Quarterly Economic Bulletin, 35 (3-4), Mid-January, 2002.

M_1 = notes + coins - cash in hand with commercial banks + demand deposits.

M_2 = money supply (M_1) + time deposits including margin deposits.

Table 2.2.1 depicts that notes and coins accounted for 2 times of the demand deposits during 1965. Even after the completion of 3 decades too, the share of the demand deposits remained

46.64%. It indicates that though the banking habit of the people is gradually increasing, the stock of currency and coins held by public has still maintained double than demand deposits.

It is generally agreed that the continuous budgetary deficit and unhealthy balance of payments position over years have witnessed continuous expansion in money supply. Moreover, the government budgetary deficit affects currency more than the demand deposits and a balance of payments deficit affects deposits more (Patnaik, 1982:9).

Despite these, the trend of monetization in non-monetized sector, the extension of banking and financial facilities in rural areas and the increment of banking habits among people have slightly effected the share of demand deposits. Thus, a gradual increase in the ratio of currency to demand deposit up to 1975 and then more or less constant ratio till 2001 indicates the sluggish growth rate in the economy.

2.3 Money Supply Determinants

It is already mentioned that the money supply under the banking system comprises of two major components. These are currency and demand deposits held by the public. Thus, the money supply, M is defined as $M = C_P + D_P$ ...(2.3.1)

The public holds h % of its money in currency (Cp) and (1-h) % in checking account deposits (Dp).

So that $Cp = hM$ ...(2.3.2)

and $Dp = (1-h)M$ ..(2.3.3).

Let K is the required reserve ratio that gives the fraction of demand deposits i.e., $RR = k.Dp$ ..(2.3.4)

The other important components of total money supply are also called reserve money. If reserve money is observed from uses side, it is called liabilities of the Nepal Rastra Bank (NRB). It can be defined as the sum of the total currency in circulation, bank reserves and non-bank deposits at the central bank. Similarly, if we analyze reserve money from sources side, it can be defined as the summation of net foreign assets (NFA) and net domestic assets (NDA) of the NRB.

Total reserve of the bank can also be divided into the sources of reserves and uses of reserves. The banks can allocate their reserves into required reserves (RR) and excess reserves (ER). In addition, some of the reserves provided by the central banks through open market operation would be finished as currency reaches in the hands of public (Cp) [Branson, 1997:272]. Both sources and uses sum is equal to total reserve (R). So, the basic reserves identity (RU+RB) is R = RR+ER+ Cp ...(2.3.5)

or $RU + RB = RR + ER + Cp$

or $RU = RR + ER - RB + CP$

or $RU = k.Dp + RF + Cp$ ...(2.3.6)

Where RU = non-borrowed reserve

RB = borrowed reserve

RF = (ER - RB) = free reserve, net.

RR = k.Dp = required reserve

Substituting the value of equation (2.3.2) and (2.3.3) into (2.3.6) we get

$$RU = k(1\text{-}h)M + RF + hM \quad \text{................(2.3.7)}$$

Solving the equation for M gives the following money supply function

$$M = RU - RF/k\,(1\text{-}h)\text{+}h = RU - RF/k\text{+}h\,(1\text{-}k) \quad \text{...(2.3.8)}$$

$$M = RU\,/\,k\text{+}h\,(1\text{-}k) - RF\,/\,k\text{+}h(1\text{-}k) \quad \text{........(2.3.9)}$$

It is clear from equation (2.3.9) that

$dM/dRU > 0$, $dM/dRF < 0$, $dM/dh < 0$, $dM/dk < 0$

The RU term in equation (2.3.9) shows the portion of the money supply determined mainly at the initiative of the NRB. It is also considered as the exogenous portion of money supply. The next term, RF gives the portion of the money supply that is endogenously determined by the banking system in response to loan opportunities and interest rates.

On the whole, the money supply rises as the NRB provides more non-borrowed reserves and declines as free reserves increase. In the same way, the money supply falls as the public preference for currency rises or the NRB increases the reserve ratio. Moreover, in the tight credit condition, when the demand for loan is high relative to the supply of non-borrowed reserves from the NRB, we would expect free reserves to be negative; otherwise it will be positive in the case of easier credit condition.

From the above discussion, it is clear that the pivot factors affecting money supply in Nepal are currencies, demand deposits, time deposits, net domestic assets and net foreign assets of the banking system. All these factors must be taken into account in order to analyze their effect on the growth of money supply as illustrated in the following Table.

Table: 2.3.1 Determinants of Money Supply

Determinants	*Mid-month 1991 July*	*1998 July*	*Percentage Change*
1. **Narrow money (M_1)**	1628.4	4516.4	177.40
Currency held by the public	1165.5	3089.3	
Demand deposit held by the public	462.9	1427.1	
2. **Net Domestic Assets (NDA)** (Dc-Co)	2156.1	7089.0	228.8
a. Domestic credit (Dc)	3449.1	11581.2	235.8
Net claims on government	1682.1	3175.3	
Claims on government enterprises	208.8	722.9	
Claims on private sector	1558.2	7683.0	
b. Net capital & other items (Co)	1293.1	4492.2	247.4
3. **Net Foreign Assets (NFA)**	1625.2	5557.3	244.1
4. **Broad Money (M_2)** (NDA+NFA) = M_1 + Time deposits	3771.3	12646.3	235.3
5. **Time Deposits**	2142.9	8129.9	
6. **Reserve Money (Mr)**	1678.7	4599.6	174.0
Currency held by private sector	1165.5	3089.3	
" " by commercial banks	95.4	289.0	
Deposits of private sector	64.9	167.0	
Deposits of commercial banks	352.9	1054.3	

Source: NRB, Quarterly Economic Bulletin, Vol. 33 (3&4) mid April-mid July, 1999.

Table 2.3.1 depicts the situation of different expansionary and contractionary factors that determine money supply in Nepal. Among the determinants of money supply, both net foreign assets and total domestic credit have exerted relatively large expansionary impact on money supply growth. However, this impact may be significantly moderated by the contractionary factors such as time deposits, net capital and other items (Gaudel, 1994:23). It is known that the net foreign asset is the difference of foreign assets and liabilities of the banking system. Any change in the net foreign assets is the direct reflection on the balance of payments of the country. In the above table, the net foreign assets witnessed an increase of 244.1 % in the mid-July 1998 compared with the same period of 1991.

The net domestic asset is the combined function of total domestic credit and the capital and other items, net. It is directly related with the former and inversely related to the latter. In accounting sense, given the net capital and other items, a rise in the net claims on government leads to an increase in the net domestic assets. It is important to note that the government has been continuing of avail overdraft facility from the Nepal Rastra Bank in substantial amount so that net credit to the government had increased by 88.8% during the review period. Thus, by analyzing these expansionary factors of money supply, it can be said that the pressure of money supply has become more elastic to the credit.

Among the contractionary factors affecting money supply, time deposit is the principal factor. The net capital and other items too play an important role to sterilize the impact of net domestic assets and net foreign assets on money supply expansion.

2.4 Money Supply Function

The behaviour of the money supply generated by any particular monetary system can be characterized by the money supply function. This function states the way in which money changes over time, showing how it responds to what factors determine it. A simple monetary system is that system in which the money supply grows at a fixed rate and depends only on its initial value M_0 and time period t. This is represented by the money supply function $M_t = M_0 (1+g)^t$ ....(2.4.1)

Here, g indicates the trend of money supply at time period t.

Actual monetary system may also be subject to certain erratic influences that cause the money supply to vary randomly. Thus, by adding disturbance term, the supply function can be represented as

$$M_t = M_0 (1+g)^t + u_t \ldots (2.4.2)$$

Here, u_t signifies a set of values that varies randomly over time and the summation of it are assumed to be zero. Sometimes, the behaviour of money supply function can be stated as

$$M_t = M_t^* + h\,(y_t - y_t^*) \quad ...(2.4.3)$$

or $$M_t - M_t^* = h\,(y_t - y_t^*)$$

In deviation form, the equation is $m_t = hy_t$ ...(2.4.4) Here, h is the coefficient of monetary feedback. This function involves positive monetary feedback when h is greater than zero and negative monetary feedback if it is less than zero. y_t is the deviation of total income from its average path y_t^*. Further m_t is the deviation of money supply at time period t from its average value m_t^*. The public demand or their economic condition depends on national income. That is why, m_t is functionally related to the deviated y_t. From the equation (2.4.4), it is clear that if money supply responses in the same direction as the changing economic condition, the system is said to be positive monetary feedback. However, in the case of negative monetary feedback, the money supply responds in the opposite direction.

One simple way to represent Nepalese monetary system involving feedback is the use of money supply equation (2.4.4) in empirical form. Taking 34 years period from 1965 to 1998, the following two deviated regression models have been applied.

That is, $m_1 =$ 0.15 y	$R^2 =$ .99	.... (2.4.4.1)
t = (100.5)***	n = 34	DW = 1.704
$m_2 =$ 0.40 y	$R^2 =$ .98	.... (2.4.4.2)
t = (53.65)***	n = 34	DW = 0.654

*** Asterisk show 1% level of significance.

The equation (2.4.4.1) states that 1% increase in GDP has a significant impact (by 0.15%) on narrow money supply. Similarly, the equation (2.4.4.2) indicates 0.4% increase in broad money supply as a result of increase in GDP by 1%. Both equations have significant t values at 1% level of significance. Durbin-Watson statistic (DW) in the case of narrow money supply equation (2.4.4.1) shows that there is no positive serial correlation problem in regression model. However, in the case of broad money equation (2.4.4.2) DW statistics shows the positive serial correlation problem. Thus, monetary system involving positive monetary feedback (i.e. $h_1 = 0.15$ & $h_2 = 0.40$)

tends to amplify economic fluctuations. In this regard, it is also argued that positive monetary feed back should be avoided because it aggravates short run economic fluctuation (Culbertson, 1972: 229). Finally, erratic variation in the money supply is not desired and is to be minimized. So, the required money supply function may be justified with the economy in which monetary feedback coefficient either becomes negative or zero.

2.5. Financial Market: Money and Capital Market

The financial market may be classified in terms of money and capital markets considering the time to maturity of the securities traded. Short-term securities with one year (or less than maturity) are traded in money market, while the long-term securities of more than one year to maturity are bought and sold in capital market.

Money Market

The money market helps investors and borrowers to manage liquid assets for short time period. It is a market for short-term transferable securities. The government treasury bills, commercial papers and certificate of deposits are examples of short-term securities that are exchanged in money market. The sale of these securities finances the working capital of business companies, industrial firms and the financial institutions. The obvious alternative instrument to bank deposits is regarded as treasury bills. The commercial paper has been purchased and sold in money market and the various borrowers turn to it as a chief alternative to borrowing from banks. The relationship between the bank rate[1] and the market rate of discount[2] is determined by the condition of the money market. All these rates bear a more or less constant relationship with one another in a perfectly developed money market. However, in underdeveloped money markets like Nepal, there is no such close relationship between the bank rate and other rates.

The most prominent feature of Nepalese money market is its dichotomy between organized and unorganized sectors. The existence of unorganized sector and its dominance in the rural economy is one of the major causes of being underdeveloped money market (Reejal, 1986: 57). Money market in the organized sector comprises the Nepal Rastra Bank and other affiliated banks as Commercial Banks, Agricultural Development Banks, Joint Venture Banks, Rural Development Banks, Postal Banks, Finance Companies, Saving and Credit Cooperatives etc. However, the structure of unorganized sector can be described as indigenous moneylenders, professional moneylenders, *dhikuti* owners, land- lords, merchants, shopkeepers, friends and relatives.

Due to the week linkage between the organized and unorganized sectors of the money market, the NRB has not yet been able to influence the unorganized rural sector through its credit policy. Thus, to make an integration of the dichotomized money market and to reduce the size of unorganized sector, the NRB has implemented the policy of extending branches of commercial banks and opening development banks in rural areas. Recently, the NRB has reduced the percentage of required reserve ratio under the new monetary policy (2002) to mop up the excess liquidity in the economy. Although the propose of the NRB is to deliver credit to the low income rural groups, the existing structure of the Nepalese money market seems to be defective for the following reasons:

Firstly, the formal credit sources are accessible only to large farmers. So, the low-income groups and rural poor should be dependent on village moneylenders.

Secondly, the credit lending procedure of commercial banks and other development banks is lengthy and tedious to the small borrowers. Furthermore, they have to face a lot of problems for completing loan sanction procedure.

Thirdly, misuse of funds in unproductive sectors may diminish the repayment capacity of the small borrowers.

Fourthly, the higher cost of lending in rural credit schemes requires intensive supervision and follows up programmes.

Fifthly, most of the credit programmes have been unsuccessful to reach at the target groups of the rural areas.

Sixthly, the credit requirement of the agricultural sector and agro-based industries are found to be high during the planting and harvesting seasons. So, the private sector has a tendency to charge the exorbitant rate of interest toward the borrowers during this period.

Lastly, the government treasury bills and bonds have been discounting only by the commercial banks. However, separate bills and bonds markets have not yet been established. Thus, the absence of well-developed organized bill markets is one more shortcoming of the Nepalese money market.

Capital Market

Capital market is the market for easy term finance. It comprises the development of financial institutions like NIDC, Sajha Cooperatives, Finance Corporation, Life Insurance Corporation, which provide long-term capital to the industry and trade. In this market, investors' handover money today in exchange for promises of money in the future. The long-term finance has two basic problems of lending. First, it increases risk. It implies that the longer the time to repayment the greater the opportunity for the borrowers to misbehave. Second, it reduces liquidity. It means that the longer the time to repayment, the less important is repayment itself as a source of liquidity (Johnson, 1993:560).

In an underdeveloped economy like Nepal, the capital market is fragmented in the sense that income categories are not well defined. The process of savings and investment also is not specialized, as it would be in advanced economies. It is known that the long- term securities, such as stocks, bonds and mortgages are traded in capital market. So, the development of a capital market is associated with the growth and operation of other financial institutions.

The increased share of fixed deposits in commercial banks can be used for creating long-term assets through the mechanism of the capital markets. In this context, the NRB may try to activate the commercial banks and industrial development corporation in terms of NIDC to foster the capital market. NIDC was established in 1959 with the objective of providing financial resources to the ongoing and new industries in the country. However, NIDC has found facing the shortage of long-term investible funds due to the lack of fund generation and the absence of long term external funding.

The capital market comprises the following items.

(*i*) Security Exchange Centre
(*ii*) Government Bonds Market
(*iii*) Number of Listed Companies
(*iv*) Market Capitalization
(*v*) Market Transparency

(i) Security Exchange Centre:

In order to develop the capital market in the economy, the security-marketing centre under the initiation of NRB was first established in 1977. Furthermore, to incorporate assets and liabilities of the security market, the security exchange centre was set up in 1981. It opened the floor for corporate share trading in 1984. Later on it was also replaced by Nepal Stock Exchange Ltd. in 1992 (NRB, 1996:47). In the beginning, the government sector was involved in trading of securities. Though the effort led to the opening of a full-fledged stock exchange in 1994, the turnover of shares in the market was found to be very low. On the whole, the security exchange centre has not yet been able to create a continuous market for share trading.

(ii) Government Bond Market:

Government bond market is an important constituent of capital in terms of value and trading. In the context of Nepal, security exchange centre has also been restricted to government bond market. That is why there is low turnover of shares in the infant capital market.

(iii) Number of Listed Companies:

Now a day there has been continuous addition in the number of listed companies. As a result of increase in the number of companies, the paid of capital of listed shares has also been gradually expanded over the years. Regarding the issue of share capital in the country, the Security Board had given authority to four organized institutions consisting of one insurance company, one hotel and the two financial companies in FY 1999.

(iv) Market Capitalization:

Initially, the market capitalization as a percentage of GNP was rather low at about 6% up to 1996 (NRB, 1996:69). Moreover, the turnover of shares was found to be very low. The main reason for being minimum ratio may be due to the psychological behavior of investors, low profitability of companies and underdeveloped primary market[3]. Besides, the transaction of share of various companies in the secondary market[4] may be done in the form of new issuance, securities transaction, market capitalization, and ultimately determining NEPSE (Nepal Stock Exchange) Index. Thus, the need for the development of capital market has been an accepted reality in the context of the Nepalese economy. So, efforts are being made to foster the activities of private sector in order to strengthen the capital market.

(v) Market Transparency:

Since early 1990s, there was a great deal of liberalization in foreign exchange to show the transparency in capital market. During the course of liberalization, Nepalese currency (NC) was made partially convertible in the current account on March 1992 and it was felt safe that currency to be fully convertible on February 1993. Though these practices were made in foreign exchange liberalization process, the lack of market transparency has been realized due to information gap in the capital market.

From the foregoing discussion it is clear that the capital market in Nepal is underdeveloped. Some major drawbacks of the capital market are listed below:

1. Absence of corporate securities is the conspicuous feature of the capital market. Most of the securities are state-owned and operated by the government. So, the financial requirements for securities are usually met by normal budgetary process.
2. Unwarranted control of price, the industrial licensing system, the harassment made by tax officials, restriction on bonus shares and the declaration of dividends coupled with the low level of private industrialization have seriously obstructed the growth of capital market.

3. The public directly holds a very small proportion of the government securities. On account of poor response of the public towards government securities, the government has made the holding of its securities by financial institutions. Furthermore, the statutory requirements for the financial institutions make them to hold certain proportion of their funds in government securities. Thus, the statutory obligation has limited the proportion of investment in the corporate securities by financial institutions.
4. The small savers and investors cannot participate in the capital market due to the lack of investment trust.
5. There existed one stock exchange centre for providing liquidity to the shares in industrial establishment in 1976. However, the active trade in shares has not yet found in the capital market.
6. The financial institutions like NIDC, ADB and the PFC are providing long-term and medium-term loans for the different activities made by the private sectors. From the national point of view, these institutions are considered as inadequate for the industrial development in the economy.
7. A notable feature of the capital market is the multiplicity of lending rates in the different account of the commercial banks and financial institutions. Thus, there exists interest rate differentiation in the underdeveloped capital market in Nepal.

2.6. Evolution of the Financial System: A Review

It is believed that the history of coinage in Nepal started from the beginning of 5th century B.C. (NRB, 1956-96:27). Most of the copper coins of that period were represented images of animals and religious symbols.

The arrival of 12th century marked a new economic history in which the silver coinage came into existence. The introduction of silver coins for the first time by Mahindra Malla as a medium of exchange widened the scope of trade outside the country. The King Jayasthiti Malla, the great ruler of medieval period (1382-95), classified the people in different castes on the basis of their occupations. Accordingly, one class of people '*Tankadhari*' means professional moneylenders came in the course of development of borrowing at the end of 14th century.

During the period of Prime Minister Ranoddip Singh (1877-85), a number of economic and financial reforms were found introducing in Nepal. The establishment of *Tejarath Adda* (1880) fully subscribed by the government was one of them. It was the government financial institution supplying credit to the public at 5% rate of interest against the security of gold and silver ornaments (Shrestha, 1981: 188). This step was taken in order to relieve the people from the exorbitant rate of interest charged by the indigenous moneylenders.

During the Prime Ministership of Chandra Shamser (1901-29) *Tejarth Adda* extended its services by opening its branches outside Kathmandu. Moreover, the installation of *Tosh Khana* as a banking agency during the regime of the Great King Prithwi Narayan Shah (1748-74) could be regarded as the first step towards initiating banking development in Nepal. Another important event during the regime of Pratap Singh Shah (1774-77) led to the development of trade relation with Tibet, where Nepalese currency was used in terms of payments.

The history of modern financial system began in 1937 with the establishment of the Nepal Bank Ltd. as the first commercial bank in Nepal. It took over the responsibilities of all the functions of the *Tejarath Adda*. Thus, the Bank became a sole institution undertaking a wide range of banking and financial activities. The bank had sufficient fund to extend its services due to the mutual cooperation between the government and the private sector. The share of capital ownership of HMG was 51% and the rest percentage (49%) was owned by the private sector. This Bank remained as the single commercial bank until the establishment of another commercial bank namely Rastriya Banijya Bank in 1966.

Until mid 1940s only metallic coins were found to be used as a medium of exchange. It was only in 1945 that the *Sadar Muluki Khana* (Treasury of the government) issued currency notes. After the establishment of this centre, an urgent necessity of a central bank was felt to the development of banking and financial sectors to manage the circulation of Nepalese currency and to maintain stability in its exchange rate.

According to the Nepal Rastra Bank Act of 1955, the NRB

as a central bank was set up in 1956. After its establishment, the development of the financial system slowly gathered momentum. Realizing the importance of industrial development, HMG/N established Nepal Industrial Development Corporation (NIDC) with the financial advice of NRB in 1959. The NRB created Agricultural Credit Fund in FY 1959/60 and handed it over to HMG/N for the establishment of the cooperative bank in 1963 (Shrestha, 2000: 68). With the equity participation of HMG/N and the NRB, Agriculture Development Bank (ADB) was set up in 1968 by incorporating the assets and liabilities of the cooperative bank.

In order to make credit available to the rural people, HMG/N had incorporated the Land Reform Saving Corporation (LRSC) in 1966. But, the LRSC could not extend rural credit to the village communities. Due to this fact it was merged into ADB/N in 1976. Then ADB became a popular financial institution for providing the rural agricultural credit in Nepal.

During the period from 1962 to 1977, a large number of non-bank financial institutions were set up, such as, Employees Provident Fund (1962), the National Insurance Corporation (1967), Nepal Insurance Company Ltd. (1968), and the Securities Marketing Center (1977). The move towards financial liberalization since 1985 encouraged the entry of joint venture and private commercial banks. Under the Finance Company Act of 1985, the Nepal Housing Development Finance Company Ltd. was established in 1992. Since 1993, the NRB authorized the Cooperative Credit Societies (CCSs) to undertake limited banking transactions. Even NGOs registered under the Societies Registration Act of 1978 were authorized by the NRB in 1995 to conduct limited banking activities. Thus, the above discussion shows that the financial system of Nepal may broadly be classified under three heads:

1. Formal Financial Institution

1.1 Banking

(*a*) Central Bank

(*b*) Commercial Banks

(*c*) Development Banks

- *(d)* Rural Regional Development Banks
- 1.2 Non-banking
  - *(a)* Finance Company
  - *(b)* Insurance ,,
  - *(c)* Provident Fund
  - *(d)* Stock Exchange Ltd.

2. Semi-formal Financial Institutions

- 2.1 Saving and Credit Cooperatives
- 2.2 NGOs with Limited Banking Activities
- 2.3 Postal Saving Offices

3. Informal Financial Institutions

- 3.1 NGOs
- 3.2 Indigenous Money Lenders
- 3.3 Merchant and Shop Keepers
- 3.4 Friends and Relatives

2.7. Nepal Rastra Bank: Its Role and Functions

2.7.1 *Role:*

The Nepal Rastra Bank (NRB) is recognized as the apex institution of the monetary and banking structure of the country. It plays a leading role in organizing, supervising, controlling, regulating and developing the monetary and financial system. The significance of the NRB lies in its function of managing the monetary system internally and externally. By nature, the NRB is closely connected with the banking system and money market of the economy. Moreover, it can regulate the monetary system in the general interest of the nation. As a bankers' bank it confines the major part of its activities to transactions with other banking institutions. It is not a profit making enterprise. So, its major concern is to promote the general economic policy of the government.

It is essential for every country to have a central bank. With this aim NRB as a central bank was incorporated on April 26, 1956. From the beginning, it constituted for regulating the issue of paper currency in circulation, achieving stability in its exchange rate and to mobilize capital for economic development. In order to achieve these objectives, the NRB is not merely confined to the role of traditional functions of the central bank. It has also played an important role in the promotion and development of monetary as well as financial system of the country.

2.7.2 *Functions:*

The NRB performs various traditional and developmental functions to meet the dynamic requirement of the nation. These functions are described in the following section.

2.7.2.1 Traditional Functions

(i) Note Issue : The sole right of note issue is the privilege that has been given to the NRB. According to the NRB Act 1956, the NRB is authorized for regulating the issue of Nepalese currency (NC). In issuing notes, the NRB has to follow rules laid down by the law. In order to inspire confidence among the people about *Nepali Rupiya* and to maintain exchange rate stability, it has to reserve the gold and other securities in fixed proportion. Thus, the note issued by the NRB is legal tender throughout the country.

(ii) Government Bank : The NRB as a central bank receives payments on behalf of the government. It is required by the Bank to lend money to the government. The Bank can also render advice to the government on financial matters. All the government funds are kept free of interest at the NRB. The Bank transacts all banking businesses of the government and carry out exchange rate, remittances and other banking operations.

(iii) Banker's Bank **:** All the other banks operating in the country are bound to keep a certain proportion of their total cash deposits as reserves with the NRB. These reserves help to control the creation of credits by commercial banks. The NRB makes loans and advances to other banks against the securities of bullion, gold and silver ornaments.

(iv) Foreign Exchange Regulation : The important function of the NRB is to keep stable external value of the domestic currency. A stable exchange rate is essential for maintaining and promoting foreign trade and encouraging the inflow of foreign investment. The Bank acts as a custodian of the nation's foreign exchange reserve, manages exchange control and external value of the Nepalese currency. Under the Banking Regulation Act 1955, the NRB enjoys extensive power of supervision, regulation and control over commercial banks and Agricultural Development Bank activities.

(v) Control of Money Supply and Credit : The next important function of the NRB is to control the supply of money and credit in the best interest of the economy. Under the credit control regulation, the NRB has to satisfy various competing claims on credit in such a way that promotes maximum output and employment with price stability and a high rate of economic growth with distributive justice. In order to perform its functions well, the NRB uses several quantitative and qualitative control instruments at its disposal.

2.7.2.2. *Developmental Functions*

Besides the traditional banking functions, the NRB also performs varieties of developmental functions in the following way

(i) Management of Public Debt : The entire management of public debt may be agreed between the government and the Bank. If there is any difference of opinion in terms of agreement, the Bank will be obliged to work on such terms that may be decided by the government.

(ii) Promotion of Commercial Banking : In order to inspire public confidence on bank deposits and thereby increase banking habit among the people of rural areas, commercial bank branches, regional rural banks and Gramin Development Banks were introduced and gradually extended during the decades of 1980s and 1990s.

(iii) Promotion of Industrial Finance : The NRB can also advance reasonable amount of loans to small-scale industries against adequate security. For providing long and medium term finance, the government financial institution in the form of NIDC has been established in 1959. NIDC from the beginning has been providing loans from its credit fund to which the NRB makes annual contributions from its profits.

(iv) Other Transactions and Publications : Despite the above functions, the Bank is also authorized to sell, purchase and rediscount bills of exchange and treasury bills; purchase and sale of government securities; makes loans and advances to cooperative societies and do all such things and duties prescribed under the Act. The NRB collects data and publishes them in Quarterly Economic Bulletin, Monthly Report, and Annual Report etc. In brief, it reviews and analyses contemporary economic policy actions in the field of money and finance.

2.8 Concluding Remarks

The supply of money at a particular point of time is the stock of money held by the public. The data about money supply reveals that the ratio of currency to demand deposits has remained more or less constant during the review period. This ratio implies that the degree of urbanization, volume of trade and ultimately the rate of economic growth is very slow in the Nepalese economy. The desired money supply Function may be justified if the coefficient of monetary feedback is zero or negative. However, in the Nepalese context the positive monetary feedback signifies the short-run economic fluctuations in the country. The existing structure of money and capital market is found to be defective. Due to the underdeveloped nature of capital market, the process of savings and investment for capital formation has not been specialized. The small amount of savings and little inducement to investment have become the main reasons for low capital formation. On the whole, the NRB has not been able to influence the prevalent unorganized sector through its traditional and developmental functions.

NOTE

1. Bank rate is the rate at which the central bank is willing to discount the first class bills.
2. Market rate is the rare of discount prevailing in the money market among the other lending institutions.
3. Primary market is the market for new long-term securities. In other words, it is called the new issue market.
4. Secondary market is the market for trading the existing long-term securities. In other words, it is also called the stock exchange.

Chapter III

DEMAND FOR MONEY IN A DEVELOPING ECONOMY

3.1 Introduction 3.2 The Classical Approach 3.3 The Keynesian Approach 3.4 The Inventory-Theoretic Approach 3.5 The Modern Approach 3.6 Implications of the Different Approaches in the Context of a Developing Economy 3.7 Concluding Remarks

3.1 Introduction

This chapter begins with a general survey of developments in the theories of the demand for money and shows their implications in analyzing the various monetary problems of a developing economy. The main concern of this chapter is to trace out the framework of money demand models through the application of traditional approaches to modern approaches, and thereby to select an appropriate approach in the context of Nepal.

For this purpose, the present chapter has been divided into five sections. The first section deals with Fisher's approach to the classical quantity theory of money and explains the Cambridge cash balance approach by Marshall and Pigous. The second section describes the Keynesian liquidity preference approach. The third section interprets the post Keynesian developments by Baumol-Tobin's inventory theoretic approach. The fourth section explains the modern approach followed by M. Friedman and others. The fifth section derives the implications of various approaches and justifies the best approach to the demand for money in order to analyze monetary problems in Nepal. The final section presents the concluding remarks.

It is generally recognized that money has the unique characteristic of being accepted as a medium of exchange. So, it is demanded for its convenience of holding means of payments. Thus, two fundamental theories of the demand for money draw the attention to the researcher in monetary economics to explain the role of the demand for money and its effect on the economic system. One is the quantity theory, which assigns an important role to money in the determination of prices and incomes by using it directly to the purchase and sale of goods and services. Thus, the demand for money in this respect is viewed as the demand for means of payment. The other is the Keynesian theory, which rejects the direct causal relationship and postulates an indirect relation by bringing money into the determination of real income or output, employment and interest rate. Hence, the demand for money is conceived in keeping view of the medium of exchange, means of payments and the store of value functions of money under the Keynesian theory (Dillard, 1979:5).

Regarding these two theories of the demand for money, it has been argued that the ideas given by quantity theorists may be more appropriate than those of Keynes for the developing economy. In connection with this argument, it would be worthwhile to start the theoretical analysis of the demand for money functions and to test them empirically (in chapter V) for their implications in the context of three decades (1965-99) of monetary experience of the Nepalese economy.

3.2 The Classical Approach

The broad outline of the quantity theory of money was made by David Hume (1752) and the satisfactory attempts at mathematical formulations were traced back to the eighteenth century. However, these two formulations of the quantity theory were fully developed in terms of the transaction version by I. Fisher (1911) and the Cambridge cash balance approach by A. Marshall (1923) and A.C. Pigou (1917) (Friedman, 1968: 433).

The classical economists believe that the demand for money

is to be determined by the total volume of goods and services transacted over a given time period. In traditional economics it is referred to as a theory of the relationship between the supply of money and the general price level (Sethi, 1992:1).

In every transaction, there is a coincidence of buyers and sellers, so that the values of sales in aggregate must be equal to the value of receipts in the economy. Keeping this view in mind, Fisher (1911) offered a consistent theory of money and emphasized its role as a medium of exchange, but he did not put it directly in a framework of the theory of demand (Patnaik, 1981: 78). The contribution made by Fisher is the formulation of the quantity theory, which can be expressed as the following identity

$$M_sV = PT$$

$$\text{Or,} \quad P = \frac{M_sV}{T} \qquad \text{.................. (3.2.1)}$$

Where M_s is the quantity of money supplied, V is the velocity of circulation, P is the price level and T is the volume of transaction. From the expression (3.2.1) it is clear that the quantity of money is determined independently of any of the three other variables. More specifically, if T and the value of V are taken as constants, one can arrive at the proposition that the price level is solely determined by the quantity of money (Laidler, 1977: 56). In this context, Fisher along with his contemporaries, held the view that it would be reasonable to include bank deposits (M'_s) and the corresponding velocities (V′) in the total supply of money. This suggestion, therefore, permits us to change the expression (3.2.1) as given below:

$$P = \frac{M_sV + M'_s V'}{T} \qquad \text{.................. (3.2.2)}$$

From this expression, it follows that the presence of deposit money does not change the link between money and price because of the normal relationship between M and M′. In Fisher's view, the matter of dispute is centred on whether to include currency in terms of money or to include deposits as well. Patinkin (1965) argued that Fisher arrived at a genuine theory by specifying a normal relationship between money (M) and near money (M′) even though critics have regarded the quantity theory as a simple truism.

Although the equation (3.2.2) does not reveal anything more than what is presented, the variables used in this equation are significant enough and more suggestive for the derivation of the theory of the demand for money (Bain, 1978: 82).It has been pointed out that the demand for money depends upon the value of transactions to be conducted in the economy and is equal to a constant proportion of these transactions. Furthermore, the supply of money is exogenously determined, so that the demand for money must be equal to its supply in the money market. Symbolically, the demand for money equation can be written as

$$M_d = KPT \quad \text{.................} \ (3.2.3)$$

Where M_d is the demand for money, K is the constant proportion of transaction, P is the price level and T is the volume of transaction.

In equilibrium, $M_d = M_s$ ....(3.2.4)

Then, $KPT = PT/V$ (from 3.2.1)

$K = 1/V$ ....(3.2.5)

Thus, from this result, it can be concluded that the velocity (V) in terms of the demand function plays an important role in linking money balances to the volume of transactions in the economy. Now, with the help of equation (3.2.5) the quantity of money demanded for nominal income (Y) and price level (P) may be expressed as

$$M_d = \frac{1}{V} PY \quad \text{.......................} \ (3.2.6)$$

This simple relationship indicates that the demand for money varies directly with the real income times the inverse proportion of velocity determined by the technical factors associated with the structure of the economy.

Considering the whole line of reasoning from Fisher's approach to monetary theory, it can be asserted that the demand for money is a constant proportion of the level of transaction. This, in turn, bears a stable relationship to the level of national income. The Fisherian transaction approach, though not originally placed in a framework of the theory of the demand for money, tends to support the statement. Nevertheless, an alternative approach to the quantity theory is the cash balance approach developed by a group of Cambridge economists.[1] This approach to the problem of the demand for money as summarized in the works of Marshall (1923) and Pigou (1917) is much more akin to the income version of the Fisher's equation (Westaway et al, 1977: 95). As far as the Cambridge approach is concerned, the more transactions an individual has to undertake the more cash he would desire to hold. To this end, the Cambridge approach is similar to Fisher's approach.

In the line of formalizing the demand for money, a group of Cambridge economists, particularly Pigou (1917) has argued that the demand for money in nominal terms is a fixed proportion of the nominal income. This can be written as

$$M_d = KPY \qquad \text{.......................... (3.2.7)}$$

where M_d is the demand for money, K is a constant, P is the general price level and Y is the nominal income. This equation seems quite similar to the Fisher's equation (3.2.6) except that the velocity (K= 1/V) in this case represents income velocity as distinguished from the velocity of circulation of money in Fisher's approach. However, the basic difference between Cambridge and Fisher's approaches is that the emphasis on the former has been given to the desire or willingness to hold money rather than ability to hold money. Moreover, keeping in view of the empirical analysis, the cash balance approach fits much more readily than Fisher's transaction approach. Therefore, the quantity theory of money as embodied in equation (3.2.7) is a theory of the demand for money, not a theory of price level or money income.

Alfred Marshall (1923), a leading neoclassical economist of Cambridge School, has made a substantial contribution to monetary theory by giving immense importance to the cash balance version of the demand for money (Roy, 1997: 18). Treating the demand for money as a stable function of income and property (or wealth), Marshall has expressed it in terms of the following equation:

$$M_d = f(Y, W) \qquad \text{........................ (3.2.8)}$$

Where Y represents community's annual aggregate money

income and W denotes the money value of wealth. Later on, the wealth variable of the demand function (3.2.8) has been ignored by the descendants of Marshall and the resulting equation becomes equivalent to the equation (3.2.7) derived earlier by Pigou.

To put it in a more formal sense, the fraction K in the Marshallian equation merely shows a reciprocal of velocity without capturing the entire range of motives for holding cash balances. However, the Cambridge cash balance (Marshall-Pigou) equation makes it clear that people want to hold a certain amount of real money balances, which is primarily determined by the real income. This implies that people are free from money illusion. Thus, the Cambridge approach in contrast to the Fisherian approach suggests those subjective factors, which are important elements in the demand for money (Johnson, 1978:62).

On the whole, this approach though simple, overlooks the influence of other important variables as the interest rate or yield on assets that lead to the development of the Keynesian theory.

3.3. The Keynesian Approach

It was left to Keynes to bring out the potentiality of the Cambridge cash balance approach in a more detailed framework of the demand for money. Keynes, of course, did not deny the validity of the quantity theory. He added some variables towards the improvement of this theory. So, his contribution to the demand for money is a detailed analysis of the factors affecting money demand function.

As can be seen in Fisherian and Cambridge approaches, money among other assets is universally acceptable as a medium of exchange. Keynes (1930)[2] by no means rejected this view and postulated the transaction demand more clearly than it was explained earlier. In the Keynesian view, the desire for money is a demand for liquidity preference. He presented three motives for holding money: transaction, precautionary and speculative motives. According to Keynes, individuals require to keep money to finance their daily purchases of goods and services, to meet unforeseen expenditure, and to hold it for making profit.

The demand for money stemming from the transaction motive is associated with the fixed technical coefficient view. It implies that money is required to bridge the gap between the receipt of income and expenditure and to meet the time interval between incurring business costs and receipts of sales (Bain, ibid: 82). The amount of money demanded for this purpose might be expected to vary directly with the level of income.

The precautionary balance is needed to provide for contingencies requiring sudden expenditure caused by accident, ill health etc. It can be used for unforeseen opportunities of advantageous purchases and to meet a subsequent liability of fixed monetary base. The size of the money balance held for these reasons is likely to be influenced by the level of income.

Considering the speculative demand for money, Keynes focused his attention on two alternative forms of holding financial assets: money and long-term bonds. He accepted that in deciding whether to hold money or bonds, investors would take account of the prospective capital gain or loss to holding bonds and the interest rate as well (Cuthbertson, 1988:13). For instance, if a capital loss on bonds is widely expected and of the interest rate not declining in the future, people might hold a large amount of money at the existing interest rate. This situation is what Keynes called the liquidity trap[3] situation. The speculative demand for money, therefore, depends upon the expected capital gains on bonds as well as on the running yield or interest rate. It is important to note that interest rate in the Keynesian system is related to the speculative motive.

The other two transaction and precautionary motives may not be ignored because of the fact that money held for one purpose is a perfect substitute for other purposes. Thus, it would be better to give equal consideration to all the motives in connection with the theory of the demand for money (Dillard, ibid: 168). To derive the total demand for money, Keynes has lumped together the transaction and precautionary demand on the grounds that both are fairly stable functions of income.

However, the speculative demand for money is especially sensitive to changes in the rate of interest. Thus, the combination of the three motives gives rise to the total demand for money in the following form:

$$M = M_1 + M_2 = L_1(Y) + L_2(R) = f(Y, R) \quad \text{............ (3.3.1)}$$

$$\text{and } \frac{\partial M}{\partial Y} > 0, \frac{\partial M}{\partial R} < 0$$

Where M is the total demand for money, M_1 is the amount of money demanded to satisfy the transaction and precautionary motives, M_2 is the amount of money required to fulfill the speculative motive, Y represents the level of income and R denotes the rate of interest. L_1 and L_2 are the liquidity functions, which determine M_1 and M_2 respectively. The equation (3.3.1) implies that the aggregate demand for money varies directly with the level of income and inversely with the rate of interest. Considering this view, Starleaf and Reimer (1967) suggested to write the money demand function as

$$M = M_1 + M_2 = L_1(Y) + L_2(R\text{-}R_e) \quad \text{............... (3.3.2)}$$

$$\text{and } \frac{\partial M}{\partial (R - R_e)} < 0$$

Where R_e is the expected normal rate of interest. M, Y, R correspond to the same meaning as in equation (3.3.1). This equation is particularly important with a view to measure the uncertainty about the future course of the rate of interest. For the purpose of empirical analysis, the Keynesian demand equation may be taken

$$M = M_1 + M_2 = L_1(Y, R) + L_2(R\text{-}R_e) \quad \text{.............. (3.3.3)}$$

$$\text{and } \frac{\partial M}{\partial R} < 0$$

This equation reflects the argument of Keynes that the transaction and precautionary demand for money may be inversely related to the rate of interest.

As a starting point in the graphical exposition, the demand for real money balances was implicitly derived by Waud (1970:439) in the complete Keynesian system. With a purpose to derive the real money balances graphically, he has suggested for taking the equilibrium condition of the money market given as under

$$M = M_1 + M_2 = KPY + PL(R) \qquad \text{.................. (3.3.4)}$$

Where M is the total money supply, which is exogenously determined by the monetary authority. M_1 is the transaction demand for nominal money balances and is equal to the constant proportion of real income or output. P is the price index. The product of KPY shows the liquidity preference for nominal money balances. M_2 is the speculative demand, which is indirectly related to the rate of interest (R). It shows the liquidity preference for real money balances. Thus, the equation (3.3.4) depicts the situation of equilibrium in the money market where the total demand for nominal and real money balances is equal to the supply of money. From this equation it is also clear that for any given interest rate, the liquidity preference for nominal money balances is proportional to the price level.

In the Keynesian approach, when the rate of interest is anticipated to fall, the demand for money is relatively low. It is so because people hold their bonds in expectation of capital gains. They want to avoid capital losses on holding bonds if the rate of interest is expected to rise. Consequently, the demand for money is relatively high. Thus, by and large, the simple form of the Keynesian demand for money function shows the relationship of transaction and precautionary balances with the level of income and the speculative balances with the rate of interest. However, in Laidler's (1977:66) opinion, the wealth variable should be included in the speculative demand on the assumption that a portion of total asset is required to hold in cash. Now, adding all these relationships the Keynesian demand function may be expressed as

$$M_d = [KY + g(R)W]P \qquad \text{.................... (3.3.5)}$$

Where M_d is the demand for money, the term KY represents the combination of the transaction and precautionary balances, g(R) denotes the negative functional relationship of money demand with the rate of interest, W shows the real wealth and the whole expression (3.3.5) multiplied by price level (P) indicates the demand for money function in real terms. The first part of this equation is similar to the Cambridge cash balance approach, whereas the second part is distinct and demonstrates the inverse relationship of the speculative demand with the rate of interest.

If people have a certain stock of money in real terms, any change in the rate of interest would have a little impact on their money balances. If monetary authorities in the economy supply more money, it would simply induce people to spend on goods and services. Hence, the demand for money is primarily based on the inelastic response of interest rate and it shows the Pigouvian real balance effect in the economy (Patnaik, 1981:92). Nevertheless, in the Keynesian framework[4] if a desire to hold cash balances were affected by the rate of interest or bond prices, an increase in the money supply by the authority would induce people to hoard idle balances rather than to spend on goods and services. This argument, therefore, indicates far-reaching consequences of the Keynesian transmission mechanism of monetary policy and its impact on the economy. This transmission procedure put forward by Dennis (1981) is derived from the elasticity of money demand function with respect to the rate of interest and investment.

On the whole, the Keynesian approach to the demand for money arrives at a conclusion completely opposite of the Fisherian approach. In Fisher's model, the demand for money being insensitive to the rate of interest is stably related to the volume of transactions in the short period. In Keynes' model, the stability in transaction demand follows Cambridge traditions, but the demand for money in aggregate could be determined by the speculative behaviours of individuals.

3.4 The Inventory-Theoretic Approach

Though the Keynesian Approach to the demand for money represents a significant improvement over the Cambridge approach, it also suffers from some inconsistencies. Thus, with a view to probing further into Keynes' theory of the liquidity preference, both Baumol (1952) and Tobin (1956) developed the inventory theoretic approach to the transaction demand for money. Notwithstanding their work being independent of each other, they arrived at similar conclusions.

Baumol (1952) took a slightly simple approach to the theory

of money demand. He used the idea that each individual wants to keep some portion of his income in the form of cash to act as a means of payment for his planned purchases. Thus, the demand for money may conceive to be determined by the minimization of total cost of transactions. The total cost comprises interest rate foregone for the money held instead of bonds and the brokerage fee involved in converting bonds into cash. The model shows that the demand for cash balances is proportional to the square root of the value of transactions and is inversely proportional to the square root of the rate of interest. Symbolically, Baumol's model[5] can be written as

$$M_d = BT^{1/2} R^{-1/2}, \text{ where } B = \sqrt{b/2} \qquad \text{...............(3.4.1)}$$

Here, M_d is the demand for transactions or cash balances measured in real terms. b is the real cost of turning bond into cash or brokerage fee. R is the interest rate. T is the real value of transactions income. This equation implies that as transaction's income (T) increases with a given interest rate (R), transaction demand (M_d) will also increase less than proportionately indicating the economies of scale in cash management. Thus, Baumol's approach in comparison to Keynes has advantages in the sense that it shows the interest elastic response in the transaction demand for money.

Further, other economists [Brunner and Meltzer (1967), Handa (1977), Ahmad (1977)] reformulated the results on the transaction demand for money originally developed by Baumol. They used it for reestablishing the validity of the quantity theory of money. They claimed on the basis of empirical findings that for large values of income or small values of fixed costs, the elasticity of demand comes to unity and there are no economies of scale in the use of money. Furthermore, the consensus from the empirical estimates seems that the approximate unitary elasticity of income in money demand is sufficient to test the validity of the quantity theory. The interest elasticity of the demand for money is low and negative.

Despite this, the application of Baumol's inventory theoretic approach has been considered as an intuitive appeal to the analysis of the demand for money. It is generally believed that inventories are kept in hand to bridge the gap between sales and purchases, and money is held to meet the interval between receipts and expenditures. Thus, Kaminow (1969) suggested applying this model in order to determine the portion of liquid assets as a means of payment and to decide the rate of net taxes as an opportunity cost of holding money.

Tobin (1958) introduced the concept of risk aversion to derive the portfolio selection in the aggregate demand for money. He formulated a model through which a desire for risk aversion and utility maximization from wealth would lead to an individual to choose a diversified portfolio of both money and bonds (Paul, 1992:224). Tobin is of the view that an individual in an uncertain situation would hold both money and bonds and he would assume to have a subjective probability distribution of future events.

Although Tobin's approach yields the conclusion akin to that of Keynes, it is superior in the sense that it reveals the rational behaviour of wealth holders in making the continuous liquidity preference function. Furthermore, it can be extended to the problem of asset choice on account of the availability of more alternatives in holding wealth portfolio. The starting point in Tobin's model is similar to Keynes and that can be presented in the form of following equation

$$M_d = f(R, W) \quad \text{..................} \quad (3.4.2)$$

Where R is the rate of interest, W is the individual's initial wealth and M_d is the demand for money. The most important characteristics of this model is that money is considered as one among various assets and it shows portfolio selection behaviour of individuals in an uncertain situation.

Regarding the portfolio selection behaviour, it is recognized that as the market rate of interest increases, an individual is willing to bear more risk by holding more bonds and less money. If the risk increases at the same level of the rate of interest, lesser bonds and more money will be held in the individual's portfolio. There is no need to limit this analysis to the case of the two extreme assets (bonds and money) only. In reality, the wealth holder is faced with a choice of various assets as cash, time deposits, short and long term bonds, stocks, shares and real capital goods (Westaway et al, ibid: 117). The demand for each asset, therefore, depends on the total value of wealth and the rate of interest on all the possible alternatives. Accordingly, the set of asset demand equations can be represented in the following matrix form.[6]

$$\underset{n\times n}{[A]}\ \underset{n\times 1}{[R]} + \underset{n\times 1}{[B]}\, W = \underset{n\times 1}{[D]} \qquad \text{.................. (3.4.3)}$$

Where [R] is the column vector of interest rates corresponding the different types of assets. [A] is the square matrix of parameters of the asset demand equations. It is expressed as a coefficient matrix of the column matrix [R]. [D] is the column vector related to the various types of assets. The level of wealth (W) is used here as a scalar of the coefficient matrix [B]. The upshot of Tobin's approach is that money is demanded not only for transaction purposes but also for asset purposes. It implies that money is non-neutral in the neoclassical sense. This result has been challenged by Levhari and Patinkin (1968) with the introduction of money balances either in the utility function or in the production function.

As regards the extension of Baumol-Tobin approach, Whalen (1968) has developed a regression model of the optimal transactions cash balances in order to relate the reciprocal of income velocity of money to the selected interest rate. The equation adopted by Whalen (1968:117)[7] can be expressed as

$$M = \left[1 - \frac{r'}{R} + \frac{r'^2}{2R^2}\right]\frac{Y}{2} \qquad \text{.................. (3.4.4)}$$

Where M is the optimal transaction cash balance, r′ is the rate of return on assets, R is the rate of interest charged on borrowed funds and Y is the volume of receipts or disbursements. Setting the partial derivatives of M with respect to r and R produces the following relations:

$$\frac{\partial M}{\partial r'} = \left(\frac{1}{R} + \frac{r'}{R^2}\right)\frac{Y}{2} < 0, \text{ if } R > r'$$

$$\frac{\partial M}{\partial R} = \left(\frac{r'}{R^2} - \frac{r'^2}{R^3}\right)\frac{Y}{2} < 0, \text{ if } r' > R$$

Of these two conditions, the first seems reasonable. In this case, Whalen has argued that an increase in the interest rate or a decrease in the rate of return on investment would increase optimal transaction balances in the economy.

For empirical estimation, dividing both sides of equation (3.4.4) by Y and simplifying the equation through the representation of coefficients a, b and c, we have

$$\frac{M}{Y} = a + b\left(\frac{r'}{R}\right) + c\left(\frac{r'}{R}\right)^2 \qquad \text{.....................} (3.4.5)$$

$$a > 0, b < 0 \text{ and } c > 0$$

From this analysis, it can be summed that the theoretical implication of Baumol-Tobin approach to the transactions demand for cash appears to be more far reaching than originally realized.

In contrast with the completely deterministic model of the transaction demand for money, studies of the precautionary demand for money were conducted with emphasis on the stochastic nature of transactions. Along this line, Miller and Orr (1966) highlighted the stochastic process in the net disbursement underlying the demand for money. Using Baumol-Tobin model, Sprenkle (1967:82) and Tsiang (1969:99) concluded that the addition of uncertainty lowers the demand for money, and thus in effect the precautionary demand is negative. However, the conclusion of Stevens (1971) differs in the sense that a firm holds larger cash balances when its decisions are made for the large payments under uncertainty conditions. Thus, in this perspective, the amount demanded for precautionary cash balances is small and positive.

To integrate the transactions and precautionary demand for money, Frenkel and Jovanovic (1980) tried to make some improvement over the previous works (Baumol, Tobin, Miller and Orr) by applying the principle of inventory management. Faig (1989:847) observed that the preceding approaches were too abstract to fully capture the usefulness of money in transactions. He suggested using seasonal fluctuation as a better proxy transaction variable in the demand for money function in order to confirm the idea that money balances are useful for relatively small transactions.

Finally, it is also important to note that in a simple version of target-threshold model under the framework of inventory theoretic approach, receipts and disbursements are assumed to be known with certainty. However, Akerlof and Milbourne (1980) introduced an element of uncertainty concerning the timing of expenditure in an extension of the target-threshold model. To sum up, the overall discussion of inventory theoretic approach tends to remove inconsistencies of Keynes' theory on the ground that people do not hold two types of money stocks (M_1 and M_2). Instead, they hold only money stock (M). It also reflects the development of subsequent literature treating the demand for money function in aggregate form.

3.5 The Modern Approach

M. Friedman (1956, 1959), leading economists of new Chicago School, restated the quantity theory in a somewhat similar manner into a theory of the demand for money. He put forth his view that the demand for money is dependent on money income and prices and that money is one of the forms of holding assets including physical and human. Thus, money in his opinion, is a durable consumer goods or capital goods held for the services it renders yielding a flow of services proportional to the stock (Peterson, 1972: 365). The demand for the stock of money is, therefore, equivalent to the demand for the flow of services.

It is argued that Friedman presented an analytical framework of the quantity theory that conveys the flavour of Chicago tradition.[8] He also attempted to clear the conceptual framework of the quantity theory with the assertion that the demand for money does not become infinitely interest elastic, but it is relatively interest inelastic (Patinkin, 1972: 886).

Although the starting point of Friedman's analysis was essentially the Keynesian, his ideas have been linked with the classical approach under the restatement of quantity theory of money. He postulated that money like any other assets yields a flow of services to the people. In his empirical analysis, he made a distinction between human and non-human wealth. He asserted that the demand for money should depend upon total wealth. Because of the illiquidity of human wealth, he preferred to include the ratio of human to nonhuman wealth.

Having discussed wealth as a scale variable of the demand for money function, Friedman then considered the yield on alternative assets[9] as an opportunity cost variable. He followed the principle of diminishing marginal rate of substitution and stated clearly that if the return on other assets increases, the demand for money holding declines. Thus, the rate of return on various assets may be taken as a relevant variable for determining the demand for money (Kavnagh and Walters, 1972: 157-50). Apart from this, the expected change in price level is also considered as an important variable of the demand for nominal money balances. In this case, Friedman explicitly recognized inflation as an expected rate of return on money and proposed it in a well-determined money demand function (Laidler, 1981:5). Thus, the demand for money function may be considered

$$M_d = f(R, H, Đ^e, W, U) \qquad ....(3.5.1)$$

Where M_d is the demand for money in nominal term. R is a vector of interest rates, which may include the return on various alternative assets. H is the ratio of human to non-human wealth. $Đ^e$ is the expected rate of change in price or inflation. W is the level of wealth. U is the disturbance term, which signifies tastes and preferences of individuals. The model is subject to some restrictions as

$$F_r < 0, F_h > 0, F_ð < 0, f_w > 0$$

With the help of restrictions imposed on specific variables of the equation (3.5.1), one can undertake these variables as potentially important determinants of the demand for money function.

In respect of model formulation, Friedman claims that the inclusion of more independent variables is a great departure from the received orthodoxy in monetary theory. But the theoretical appraisal reveals that the demand function is simply an extension of the Keynesian monetary theory (Srivastava, 1989: 193). For empirical estimation, Friedman (1959) used permanent income in terms of the weighted average of current and past levels of income instead of using wealth in the demand for money function. He considered money including all assets serving a temporary abode of purchasing power. It implies that rate of interest and current income have minor role in determining money demand. Furthermore, the expected capital gains and losses may be dropped from the demand function due to the measurement problems.

It is worth noting here that Friedman's model of the demand for money is complex as compared to other models. To make it simple, he made some changes in his original model by using bond rate of interest and permanent income without considering other variables. With this simplification, the above equation (3.5.1) then reduces to

$$M_d = f(r_b, Y_p, U) \qquad \text{..................... (3.5.2)}$$

Where r_b is the rate of interest on bonds, Y_p is the permanent income or a proxy measure of the total wealth and U is the disturbance term.

The demand for money is more likely to be the demand for real balances. Moreover, the equation (3.5.2) is homogeneous of degree one in prices, then

$$M_d/P = f(r_b, Y_p/P, U) \qquad \text{..........................(3.5.3)}$$

Where M_d/P is the demand for real balances, r_b is the bond interest rate, Y_p/P is the level of real output and U is the disturbance term.

Although Friedman emphasized the relation between money stock and the aggregate wealth, he failed to detect empirically the significant response of interest rate on money demand. Considering this issue, Meltzer (1963) further attempted to relate the demand for money to wealth rather than to income. He found a substantial contribution of interest elasticity in the demand for money. The model proposed by Meltzer (1963:223) is a general demand function. It contains the major variables consistent with the theoretical and empirical considerations. Accordingly, the demand for money function may be taken

$$M_d = f(R^*, Q, H^*, W_n) \qquad \text{.................. (3.5.4)}$$

and $f_{r^*} < 0, f_q < 0, f_h < 0, f_w = 0$

Here, M_d represents the quantity of money demand. R* is the yield on financial assets. Q is the yield on physical assets.

H* is the yield on human wealth and W_n is the nonhuman wealth which represents constraints of wealth. All the restrictions imposed on yields are negative. If this equation is homogeneous of first degree then the subscript n will drop from W. For simplicity, both yields on financial and physical assets may be combined together in one asset (R), and the others will be constant. The equation then reduces to

$$M_d = f(R)\,W \qquad \text{.................} (3.5.5)$$

Where W is the wealth and R is the interest rate. This equation (3.5.5) may turn into the familiar quantity theory of money in Cambridge form if one puts some constant term for portfolio adjustment.

Regarding the demand for money function, Gurley and Shaw (1960) expressed their opinion that money demand is affected by the different economic variables along with non-banking financial institutions. According to this approach, money is the most liquid asset and is demanded for precautionary balances against the risk of capital shortage and transactional costs. Due to this quality of money, economic agents have usually kept their cash balances in portfolio. In this approach, there is no fundamental difference between transaction demand and speculative demand for money, since both types of demand are affected by the income of capital holding, planned transaction and the current rate of interest. Moreover, the current rate of interest is the equilibrium price in the money market, which makes the equality between demand for and supply of money. The saving or surplus units in the monetary economy transfer their money balances to deficit units by the help of government bonds and banking deposits. Thus, non-banking financial institutions try to draw the idle cash balances held in the deposit account of commercial banks and they purchase government treasury bills in large quantities, which are liable to sell in the money and capital markets.

Despite these, the theoretical literature on money demand has led emphasis on money on the grounds of its capacity of reducing transactions and information costs, and saving time. In this regard, Meyer and Neri (1975:611) offered to use Keynes-Friedman model in which money demand, being a function of a modified exponentially weighted average of income, measures financial requirements. This model states that past incomes influence current expectations only through their effect on income. The interest rate is also a significant variable in money demand. Thus, the demand for money function may be expressed in linear logarithmic form

$$\ln M_t^* = \ln a_0 + a_1 \ln Y_t^e + a_2 \ln R_t \qquad \text{.......................} (3.5.6)$$

Where m_t^* denotes the desired real balances, Y_t^e is the short-run expected real income and R_t is an interest rate. To come back to the original money demand function, Meyer and Neri suggested following the expectation hypothesis about the relationship between desired and actual balances. The model based on empirical evidence, leads to support the transaction and financial motives[10] for holding real balances. It shows that the amount demanded for real balances depends not only on current or permanent income but also on real planned transactions.

Taking into account the main issues raised by Friedman in contrast to the Keynesian one, it has been argued that the stability of the demand for money is the essence of the quantity theory. However, this does not necessarily prove that quantity theory is better than the Keynesian theory (Johnson, 1978: 96). In respect of the stable relationship, the modern monetarists [Laidler (1972:127), Brunner and Meltzer (1972:845)] have believed that interest elasticity would be low, when money would be regarded as a general substitute for all other assets rather than a specific substitute for interest bearing financial assets. Friedman in his early writings argued that interest rate might play an important role in the demand for money. Later on, he contended that in practice the interest rate does not play a significant role in the demand for money function. Thus, the stability of the demand for money received an extensive attention of the monetarists for a long time.

Considering this unresolved issue, Goldfeld's (1973) survey indicated that relatively simple formulation of the demand for money yields stable (short and long run) functions. Frenkel and Johnson (1976) postulated that the existence of a stable demand for money transforms the approach from an accounting framework into a body of substantive theory. However, Lieberman (1979: 324) suggested that the omission of a measure of technical change might be an important source of instability in money demand equation.

Despite the large body of empirical evidence supporting the existence of a stable function over short and long period of time, the issue still appears to remain open (Cargill & Meyer, 1979: 322). Keeping these views in mind, Laidler (1981:15) begins with quantity theory approach used by Friedman and points out that the demand for money is an empirically stable function of some measurable variables. The inclusion of price inflation as an expected rate of return on money establishes the well-determined relationship with money demand. Thus, Laidler concentrated mainly on testing the reliability of relationship produced by monetary theories.

Summarizing the results of the prior short-run models on the demand for money functions, Akerlof (1982) gave a new outlook to those issues, which were implicit in the old approaches. In this connection, he rightly remarked that in Friedman's approach the velocity is constant. There is no attempt made in explaining the short run behaviour.

Thus, it is clear from the foregoing discussion that the demand for money function in the modern approach is stable over time in comparison to the suggestion made by early monetarists. Furthermore, empirical studies in this field have brought out the key issues to specify and test the alternative theories of money demand. To sum up, there exist marked differences among the approaches on the demand for money. These differences may shorten considerably if one tries to make empirical analysis of the demand for money function. For this purpose, chapter V has been developed and the various economic issues towards the demand for money have also been discussed and analyzed with the help of econometric tools.

3.6. Implications of the Different Approaches in the Context of a Developing Economy

Today some economists feel that the classical approach to the demand for money is traditional to some extent. It says nothing more than the statement of the formal relation between money demand and money supply. It is based upon the belief that money is neutral. It determines neither the rate of interest nor the relative volume of commodities in the real sector of the economy. It is, therefore, impracticable for predict purpose.

In spite of these criticisms, this approach is valid in the context of the developing economy where inflation is caused largely by the increase in money supply. It is argued that money is mostly demanded for transaction purposes (Bhasin, 1988: 81). The existence of some factors like frictions, political instability, market imperfections, risks and uncertainties rule out the possibility that money performs only the function of medium of exchange. So, people in developing countries generally prefer to hold money rather than to hold the other interest bearing assets. More specifically, keeping in view the low income of people with low savings, it may be more advantageous to hold money as compared to other assets.

In the Keynesian approach, the supply of money is exogenous and the demand for money is determined by the rate of interest. The implication of this analysis is that any change in the money stock has a direct and permanent influence on the rate of interest. Moreover, in the Keynesian theory, the speculative demand for money becomes infinitely elastic at a low enough rate of interest. Considering this demand, it can be said that it requires the presence of an organized securities market in which assets are continuously revalued in response to changes in the people's expectations. However, in the developing economies, money and financial markets are not well developed. So, the Keynesian argument does not permit the demand for speculation in both money and bonds. As a result, the demand for money is insensitive to the rate of interest. Therefore, the Cambridge cash balance approach appears to be better than the Keynesian liquidity preference approach.

It is believed that Keynes developed his doctrine in the background of an advanced economy and, therefore, it is not very much relevant for an underdeveloped economy like Nepal. Moreover, the absence of organized stock exchange market tends to give the impression that the Keynesian speculative approach to the demand for money becomes inoperative. Thus, the Keynesian theory as it stands may not be immediately applicable, however, the Keynesian tool as such the speculative element is always inherent in an underdeveloped economy so as prices of agricultural products related to their supplies depending on weather conditions (Prasad, 1969: 60).

The rate of interest and its structure in an underdeveloped economy is not helpful in stimulating investment. No doubt, there is a high demand for money, but it mainly arises from uncertainty and speculation in essential commodities. There is no more desire to earn from the rise or fall in prices of bonds and securities due to the underdeveloped securities and exchange markets. Furthermore, we find that there is a sharp rise in price level on the one hand and on the other there is a big push to deficit financing by the government. Thus, in view of this situation, it has been suggested to develop the subsistence economy by applying the naive model based on self-reliant policy not borrowed from abroad in the name of globalization.

Now-a-days, most South-East Asian Countries[11] are facing the pinch of economic turmoil particularly since the second half of 1997 during which currency and stock markets have plunged as a result of recession in investment. The upsurge in inflation is expected on the line of picking up the demand for food items and thereby has created food shortages and unemployment in the economy. Thus, in such circumstances, the Keynesian theory of the demand for money may be a better guide than the traditional quantity theory to observe inflation.

Despite these issues, the presence of high liquidity in an underdeveloped economy exhibits the situation of stationary equilibrium. It implies that there may be a little uncertainty about the future rate of interest. Besides, the stock and capital markets being underdeveloped, the speculative demand for money arises especially at the peak period of planting and harvesting of agriculture and thereby causes a reasonable stringency in the credit market. Moreover, in underdeveloped countries partly on account of the low level of income and partly because of high marginal propensity to consume, an increase in income is mostly spent on essential goods. As a result, the income elasticity of the demand for money approaches unity.

The most important part of Baumol's inventory theoretic approach is the square root rule whereby the demand for cash rises less than in proportion with the volume of transaction. This approach predicts that both income and interest rate elasticity of the demand for money should be less than one. In the context of developing economies, the elasticity of interest rate is extremely low and it has insignificant effect on the demand for money. This evidence shows that we are very close to the classical economic world.

As argued by Prasad and Sampath (1977:381), people in underdeveloped countries obtain cash for transaction purposes, first by borrowing it or by withdrawing it from the investment, second by withholding it from cash receipts, and the third partly by withdrawing and partly by withholding. This argument indicates that there exist significant economies of scale in holding cash balances in developing countries. Nevertheless, Baumol's approach of dealing with cash balance equation has ignored the possibility that some people might hold their wages in the forms of cash, and thus interest elasticity of money demand would become zero (Basu, 1977:404). In this regard, Johnson (1963) has recommended the possibility of keeping a block of cash by an individual out of his remuneration, investing the rest in assets and thereby reducing the interest elasticity of money demand to less than unity.

In Tobin's analysis, the interest elasticity of the transaction demand for money is important to undermine the validity of the relation between the demand and total volume of transaction. Besides, he is well aware that in highly sophisticated money and financial markets, the interest elasticity of the transaction demand for money is relevant only for big transactions. From this statement it follows that the transaction demand for money may be regarded as an approximately fixed proportion of the volume of transaction in an underdeveloped economy.

For Friedman, the problem is one of showing how a theory of the stable demand for money could be a theory of prices and outputs. Furthermore, the amount of money held in portfolios depends mainly on permanent income, which leads to a distributed lag form of the demand function. Thus, an attempt has been made (in Chapter V) to analyze the validity of the model in the context of the Nepalese economy.

The most important implication of Friedman's analysis is the nature of permanent income that is relevant to monetary policy. However, Mammen's test (1970, 1991) shows that monetary policy in underdeveloped countries can largely be based on current income. Finally, Keynes-Friedman model demonstrates that the effect of finance motive on the demand for money may be easily mitigated by the development of the banking overdraft system. In contrast, the money market in an underdeveloped economy is not well developed. So, the investor or spender should have to accumulate cash balances as a part of his preparation for planned investment or planned expenditure.

From the above discussion, it is clear that a number of empirical studies are likely to crop up in the estimation of the money demand relationship. These studies are expected to bring out the key issues to specify and test the alternative theories of money demand for their implications in developing economies. To this end, the above-mentioned theories of the demand for money are listed again in terms of their performance about income and interest rate elasticity as given below.

Table 3.6.1: Implications of the Demand for Money Theories

Money Demand Theories (M_d)	*Income Elasticity* ($\acute{o}_Y$)	*Interest Elasticity* ($\acute{o}_R$)
1. Marshall- Pigou	1.0	0.0
2. Keynes, Tobin	>0	<0
3. Baumol	0.5	– 0.5
4. Friedman	1.0	0.0

Table 3.6.1 reveals that Marshall-Pigou approach to the demand for money estimates the elasticity of income and interest rate to be one and zero respectively. The Keynesian theory generally specifies the positive sign for income and negative

sign for interest rate. Baumol's approach finds income elasticity to be 0.5 and interest elasticity to be -0.5. Tobin's estimates are equivalent to Keynes. Friedman based some of his arguments on the assumption that the interest elasticity of the demand for money is zero, but the homogeneity assumption postulates the demand for real balances and income elasticity to be one.

Thus, it may be concluded that the demand for money in an underdeveloped economy like Nepal would be a stable function of current income rather than interest rate. More specifically, the demand for real balances is expected to perform better in terms of real income. It is likely to be insensitive to the rate of interest in the context of a developing economy.

3.7 Concluding Remarks

From the analysis of various theoretical models, a number of interesting conclusions regarding the demand for money have emerged. To start with an attempt has been made to examine the demand for money theory within the framework of classical approach. To this end, the classical approach has treated the transaction demand for money as a constant function of the level of income. However, the asset demand for money arising from the store of value function has received less attention by the classical quantity theorists.

Another attempt has been made to examine the effect of interest rate on the speculative demand for money. Under the Keynesian framework, the precautionary demand for money may be added to the classical approach without making any change in its form. However, the speculative demand for money marks a complete departure from the classical approach. Furthermore, the speculative demand for money arising from the future uncertainty about the rate of interest is an important contribution of Keynes to the theory of the demand for money.

Still another attempt has been made to trace out the impact of income receipts and payments on the demand for money in the form of inventory theoretic approach. Baumol's model follows a distribution of transaction income with a view to influence the demand for money and predicts the economies of scale in money holdings. Tobin's model though yields very similar conclusion to Keynes, gives stress to the rational behaviour of wealth holder in making the choice of various assets. Whalen's model shows the extension of Baumol-Tobin's approach along the line of optimum transaction cash balances. The model draws the conclusion that an increase in interest rate or a decrease in the rate of return would increase the optimum transaction cash balances. On the whole, the essence of the inventory theoretic approach to the demand for money is the assumption of certainty in terms of the timing of income receipts from money and bonds and the brokerage fee. Thus, by making more specific and sometimes more restrictive assumptions, inventory models provide rather precise form of the demand for money functions.

Finally, Friedman has made an attempt towards the restatement of the quantity theory of money. The demand for money is placed in the selection of portfolio between money and a wide range of other financial and real assets. Friedman empirically tested the income as a stable function of the demand for money. However, the rate of interest has only a negligible effect on the demand for money. Keynes-Friedman's model deals with the problem related to the demand for desired money balances depending upon the expected income and the rate of interest. With a view to measure the finance requirements, Meltzer's model on the other hand provides the better explanation to the transaction money balances in log linear form. It does not yet provide any strong evidence for speculative money balances in the demand for money function.

To sum up, the various theoretical models discussed above are regarded as integral part of the general theory of the demand for money. The estimation of demand functions to determine income and interest rate elasticity suggests that a simple model based on quantity theory approach would perform better than the Keynesian approach in the context of a developing economy.

NOTES

1. Economists like A. Marshall (1923), A.C. Pigou (1917) D. Robertson (1936) and J.M. Keynes (1936) associated with Cambridge University developed the Cambridge equation in the

early period of 20th century. [For details, see Westaway et al. (1977)].

2. For details, see Keynes, J.M. (1930) *A Treatise on Money* Vol. I, London & New York: Macmillan.
3. It is argued that interest elasticity of the demand for money is high at low interest rate due to the speculative expectation. This situation in the Keynesian sense is called the liquidity trap. Further, because of this liquidity trap, the expansion in money supply may be absorbed into portfolios without any marked reduction in interest rate. (See, Kavanagh and Walters, 1972: 153).
4. Under the Keynesian framework of money demand, two types of speculators determine the liquidity preference. Those speculators who are pessimistic or *bearish* in expecting the future price of bonds to rise, they may prefer to hold cash rather than to hold other assets. Those who are more optimistic or *bullish* about future events in price of bonds to rise, they would prefer to hold more of income yielding assets than idle cash balances (See, Patnaik, 1981: 93).
5. To derive Baumol's model, the total cost of making transactions may be written as, $TC = bT/K + RK/2$ ... (1), where TC is the total cost, b is the brokerage fee, K is the real value of bonds, T is the transaction's value and R is the interest rate. For the purpose of cost minimization, taking partial derivative of the equation (1) with respect to K and setting it equal to zero, we have

$$\frac{\partial TC}{\partial K} = \frac{-bT}{K^2} + \frac{R}{2} = 0 \qquad ....(2)$$

$$\therefore \qquad K = \sqrt{\frac{2bT}{R}} \qquad ....(3)$$

Since money holdings over the period have an average value of K/2, the demand for money equation becomes

$$M_d = K/2 = \sqrt{\frac{bT}{2R}} \qquad ... (4)$$

Therefore, Baumol's demand equation in conventional form is

$$M_d = \left(\frac{b}{2}\right)^{1/2} T^{1/2} R^{-1/2} = BT^{1/2}R^{-1/2}, \text{ where } B = \sqrt{b/2}$$

6. In matrix form, the set of n equations can be summarized as

$$\begin{bmatrix} a_{11} & a_{12} & \cdots & a_{1n} \\ a_{21} & a_{22} & \cdots & a_{2n} \\ \cdot & & & \\ a_{n1} & a_{n2} & \cdots & a_{nn} \end{bmatrix} \begin{bmatrix} R_1 \\ R_2 \\ \cdot \\ R_n \end{bmatrix} + \begin{bmatrix} b_1 \\ b_2 \\ \cdot \\ b_n \end{bmatrix} W = \begin{bmatrix} d_1 \\ d_2 \\ \cdot \\ d_n \end{bmatrix}$$

7. It is stated that (See, Whalen, 1968: 115-18) transaction cash balances are affected by the changes in rate of return (r) on long term investment and interest rate (R) charged on borrowed funds. The average transaction cash balance for the entire period can be expressed as the sum of two components. That is,

$$M = M_1 + M_2 \qquad \text{..... (1)}$$

Where M_1 is the average cash balance held from the time period, $t = 0$ to $t = \lambda$ and M_2 is the average cash balance held from $t = \lambda$ to $t = 1$.

Here, $0 \leq \lambda \leq 1$. At $t = 0$, the firm holds λY amount of cash. This amount declines to zero when $t = \lambda$. Symbolically, the holding of average cash balance during the period form $t = 0$ to $t = \lambda$, can be expressed as

$$M_1 = \int_0^{\lambda} (\lambda - t)\, Y dt = \lambda^2 Y / 2 \qquad \text{....(2)}$$

At $t = \lambda$, the firm holds $(1 - \lambda)$ Y amount of cash as a result of its loan negotiation. This amount declines to zero when $t = 1$. Symbolically, the holding of average cash balance during the period from $t = \lambda$ to $t = 1$ can be expressed as

$$M_2 = \int_{\lambda}^{1} (1 - t)\, Y dt = (1 - \lambda)^2 Y / 2 \qquad \text{.....(3)}$$

Substituting the values of M_1 and M_2 in equation (1), we have

$$M = \lambda^2 Y / 2 + (1 - \lambda)^2 Y / 2 \qquad \text{..... (4)}$$

Now, the net profit from investment with the consideration of cost incurred in investment and borrowing may be defined as

$$\Pi = (1 - \lambda) Y r' - (1 - \lambda)^2 YR \qquad \text{.....(5)}$$

Where Π stands for net profit from investment, $(1 - \lambda)Yr'$ is the amount available for investment and $(1 - \lambda)^2 YR$ is the cost of the outstanding debt.

Taking the partial derivative of equation (5) with respect to ë and setting it equal to zero, we have

$$\frac{\partial \Pi}{\partial \lambda} = -rY - 2YR(1 - \lambda((-1) = 0$$

$$\therefore \lambda = 1 - \frac{r'}{2R} \text{ and } 0 \leq \lambda \leq 1. \quad ....(6)$$

Again substituting the value of ë in equation (4), we have

$$M = \left[1 - \frac{r'}{R} + \frac{r'^2}{2R^2}\right]\frac{Y}{2} \quad ....(7)$$

This equation indicates that transaction cash balances are optimal being a function of the ratio between the rate of return and interest rate charged. These are linearly related to the volume of receipts and disbursements.

8. The Chicago tradition of quantity theory was followed by Simons, Mints, Knight and Viner (See, Patinkin, 1972: 885).
9. The alternative assets consist of holding near monies in the form of community deposits, long term bonds, equities and real assets such as housing, consumer durables, capital equipment etc.
10. Keynes introduced the concept of finance motive which refers to balances held for planned activity in contrast to transaction balances held for actual activity (For details, see Meyer and Neri, 1975: 610-23).
11. South Korea, Indonesia, Thailand, Malaysia, Singapore, Philippines and so on (See, Bhattacharyya B (1998) "Currency Turmoil in South East and East Asia: Impact of India's Exports", *Yojana* 42(4), April, 8-10.

CHAPTER IV

DETERMINANTS OF THE DEMAND FOR MONEY IN NEPAL

4.1 Introduction 4.2 The Monetary Economy of Nepal: An Overview 4.3 Money Demand: Its Major Determinants 4.4 Other Determinants 4.5 Concluding Remarks.

4.1 Introduction

This chapter helps to understand the factors affecting demand for money. It analyses them for setting the causal relationship to test the stability of the demand for money function. For the purpose of analysis, this chapter is schematized into four sections. The first section briefly sketches the overview of the monetary economy of Nepal. The second section outlines the problems and deals with the major determinants of the demand for money. The third section entails the other determinants, which are equally applicable for the estimation of money demand function. The fourth section summarizes the findings.

4.2 The Monetary Economy of Nepal: An Overview

Nepal remains one of the least developed countries in the world with per capita income of US dollar 240 per annum (WBR, 2000)[1]. As in other least developed countries, agriculture continues to hold the first place in Nepal as a source of both income and employment. It provides employment to about 81 percent of the economically active population and generates more than 50 percent of the total gross domestic product (ADB, 1995:51)[2]. The role which manufacturing plays as a source of employment is only marginal. This is the reason why majority of the working population in Nepal is eking out a precarious living from traditional agriculture.

While taking into account the monetary system in Nepal, it shows the dualistic type of monetary economy. The urban economy is emerged in organized industries, trade and service sector. The rural economy is where the majority of the people are at subsistence level without any surplus of exchange, does not seem to have shown any remarkable sign of the improvement in the process of monetization.

If one looks historically at the monetary system of the Nepalese economy, the information shows that the two commercial banks namely, Nepal Bank Limited (1936) and the Rastriya Banijya Bank (1965) play an important role in the money market in Nepal. Though these two banks were different in their origin, they are now operating under the same rules and regulations of the Commercial Bank Act, 1964(Sharma, 1987:53). The NRB as a central bank of the country took entirely a decade since its establishment in 1956, to consolidate its power as the banker's bank and to regulate the operations of banking. By the same token, the Nepal Industrial Development Corporation (NIDC) was set up in 1959 for promoting industrial ventures and the Agriculture Development Bank was established in 1968 with a view of financing in agriculture sector.

Even though, the banking system has occupied a predominant position from the earlier days of the history of organized money market, the role of the other intermediaries too cannot be minimized. In view of this, the other special institutions like Provident Fund Corporation (1962) and Nepal Insurance Corporation (1968) were also established for mobilizing savings in the economy (Basyal, 1994:36). After that in 1984, the process of financial liberalization started with the establishment of the first joint venture banks, viz. Nepal Arab Bank Ltd. and then followed by the Nepal Indosuez Bank (1986), Nepal Grindlays Bank (1987) and others. The total number of such banks reached to nine in FY 1996/97(Economic Survey,

HMG, FY 1996/97)[3] Nepal then committed to follow the liberal marked oriented economic policies. As a result, the banking and financial institutions adopted liberal and flexible approach in their functioning. On the whole, the Nepalese monetary system in the organized form consists of the Nepal Rastra Bank and its sister institutions-commercial banks, agriculture development banks, joint venture banks and private banks together with 430 bank branches (NRB, 2001). These are mostly concentrated in urban areas of the country. It indicates that organized monetary system has not become popular to attract private initiative particularly in rural areas of Nepal.

4.2.1 Gross Domestic Product

As the gross domestic product (GDP) of a country reflects the situation of economic development, the National Income Accounting should be scientific and reliable. When the country moves towards development, new activities come into existence in the economy and they should be incorporated in National Income Accounting in order to make national income or GDP more realistic (The Eighth Plan, 1992-97, HMG, 1992:50). In this perspective, National Planning Commission, HMG, Nepal made some improvement first in GDP series in FY 1974/75, then revised it in FY 1993/94 and prepared the amended series from FY 1984/85 (Economic Survey, HMG, FY 1994/95:16). Thus, National Income Accounting provides a wide view of the entire Nepalese economy and reveals clearly the basic changes in the past and suggests the trend for future. Keeping this in mind, the average annual growth rate of GDP and population for the period 1966 to 1999 in Table 4.1 has been presented.

Due to the absence of GDP estimates prior to the FY 1964/65, the annual growth rate of nominal and real GDP has been computed from the FY 1965/66 onwards. The trend analysis of GDP shows that the average annual growth rate in nominal GDP was 13.2 %and the real GDP was 3.8 % during the period of 34 years from 1966 to 1999.

While taking into account the population and real GDP growth rates, it can be observed that during the period of 34 years the average annual growth rate of population was 2.2 %

Table: 4.1 Average Annual Growth Rates of GDP and Population (FY 1965/66-1999/00)

Year+	*Nominal GDP (%)*	*Real GDP at 1974/75 Price (%)*	*Population (%)*
1966-67	9.8	2.6	1.65
1971-75	14.4	1.8	2.07
1976-80	7.3	2.4	2.07
1981-85	13.8	5.0	2.66
1986-90	17.5	4.7	2.66
1991-94	17.8	5.1	2.08
1995-99	11.5	4.7	2.24
Total Average	**13.2**	**3.8**	**2.2**

Sources: Appendix-A and Statistical Pocket Book, CBS, Nepal, 2000
+ The year represents fiscal year (FY 1965/66 is equivalent to 1966)

whereas in the real GDP it was merely 3.8 %(Table 4.1). It indicates that the per capita income is very low because of the low growth rate in GDP compared to high rate of population growth. The economic development in Nepal, therefore, seems to be remarkable and the country herself stands among the poorest nations of the world.

4.2.2 Savings and Investment.

In the context of low per capita income along with the pressure of the population, consumption as a ratio of GDP has increased, resulting in low level of gross domestic savings and investment in the economy.

Table 4.2 depicts the average annual growth rate of gross domestic savings and investment, their percentage ratio to GDP and the gap of savings and investment from 1976 onwards. As evident from Table 4.2, during the period of 24 years from 1976 to 1999, Nepal had a very low level of gross domestic savings ratio (12.2 %) to GDP and large savings gap (19.3%)due to negative resource balance in the economy. The average rate of investment relative to savings was also maintained (16.0%) at low level. Furthermore, the poor domestic savings rate (12.8%) incited continuing heavy reliance on external resources for investment [Economic Survey, FY 1992/93]. In addition, the

Table 4.2: Percentage Ratio of Gross Domestic Savings and Investment to GDP (FY 1975/76-1998/99)

Year+	*Average Annual Savings (%)*	*As a Percentage of GDP*	*Average Annual Investment (%)*	*As a Percentage of GDP*	*Average Annual Savings Gap (%)*
1976-80	9.6	12.1	12.6	16.7	30.4
1981-85	21.4	10.8	19.5	19.5	21.0
1986-90	7.3	10.5	13.9	20.7	22.8
1991-94	37.8	13.0	23.9	22.8	9.5
1995-99	9.8	14.5	10.1	25.3	13.0
Total Average	**17.2**	**12.2**	**16.0**	**21.0**	**19.3**

Source: Appendix-B + The year represents fiscal year.

gross domestic savings declined due to excessive liquidity and the lack of alternative opportunities to mobilize meager savings.

To increase the quantum of savings, there must be the reduction in aggregate consumption expenditure. Moreover, in matters of savings, it is found that the government adopted ?Consumerist Oriented Approach? which crunched the resources available in the economy (The Times of India, Nov.10, 1995). It is, therefore, envisaged that the government should have followed the ?Savings Oriented Approach? in order to curtail the consumption and efforts should have been made to continue the raising rate of gross domestic savings in the Nepalese economy.

4.2.3 *Price and Inflation*

The consumer price index (CPI) has been used to reflect the price situation in Nepal. A general view of the price level as measured by the change in consumer price index shows, on an average, a progressive escalation from 1975 to 1999(Table 4.3).

Table 4.3 shows an erratic fluctuation in average consumer price index, ranged from 54.4 to 355.7 during the past 24 years. The corresponding figures about average inflation rate ranged from 6.7% to 11.7% during the same period. This trend indicates

Table 4.3: Average Annual Rate of Price and Inflation (1975-1999)

Year	*Average Consumer Price Index (1984=100)*	*Average Inflation Rate (%)*
1975-79	54.4	6.7
1980-84	83.4	10.8
1985-89	135.4	10.5
1990-94	232.1	11.7
1995-99	355.7	8.0
Total Average	**172.2**	**9.5**

Source: Appendix-C

that the inflation during each successive period was very closely and invariably associated with shortages of supply in Nepal.

In this context, the Institute for Sustainable Development (ISD) for Nepal Rastra Bank has observed that the devaluation of Nepalese currency (Nov. 1985, July 1991) and trade-transit impasse between Nepal and India (March 1989- Jan. 1990) combined with sharp increases in government administered prices must have had their own share in price escalation process in Nepal (ISD, 1994:99)[b]. This analysis exhibits the influence of international prices, which have a significant bearing on domestic prices. Further, price rise in abroad works as a cost push factor through increased prices of imported manufactured goods, which constitutes an integral part of the Nepalese economy.

With regard to inflation, it is argued that inflation is like a *"Tooth-Paste"* once out, it is hard to push back into tube (The Economist, 1995:94). Any way, Nepal is not free from such type of problem and is facing the challenge for taming the higher speed of inflation.

4.2.4 Monetary Situation

The monetary system of Nepal is directly concerned with the issue of narrow money (M_1), broad money (M_2) and reserve money (M_r). The narrow money (M_1) consists of currency in circulation plus demand deposits, whereas broad money (M_2) comprises M_1 plus time deposits (quasi money) and reserve money (M_r) includes net foreign assets plus net domestic assets of Nepal Rastra Bank.

Historically, the first Nepalese currencies or coins were found so far date back to Lichhavi period of the Fifth Century A.D. (Rawat, 1947:129). Since then different coins made from copper and silver have been found issued by several ruling chiefs of Lichhavi and Malla period. However, *"Rupee"* coins (equivalent to Double Mohars of Malla period) were introduced since the time of King Prithvi Narayan Shah, the Great (Sen, 1977:95). During the Second World War, the price of silver surged up so highly that the silver coins disappeared from the market due to more profits by the activities of hoarding, melting and exporting. It was, therefore, with twin objectives of fulfilling the scarcity of coins and to control malpractices. The Muluki Khana (Treasury of HMG) issued currency notes of one Rupee in 1945 (Rawat, 1947:ibid). It is important to note that before this, only metal coins were used as medium of exchange.

It was only in 1956, thc Nepal Rastra Bank (NRB) as a central bank of the country set up under the NRB Act, 1955 and started with its monopoly power of notes issue in 1959. However, it could not play any pivotal role of the central bank up to 1966 (Ojha and Rajbahak, 1945:47). In July 1957, the NRB started to publish the total money stock figures in its bulletin on regular basis. However, in the absence of GDP data prior to 1965 and other financial infrastructure, an attempt was made to evaluate the performance of Nepalese monetary economy only after 1965 onwards.

Table 4.4 indicates that the average annual growth rate of narrow money (M_1) remained the highest (21.1%) from 1986 to1990 and the broad money reached to the maximum (22.0%) during 1991 to 1994. In the case of reserve money (high powered money) also, the largest growth rate was observed during the period from 1986 to 1990.

In comparison to money stock, the average annual growth rate of GDP showed a minimum of 7.3% to a maximum of 17.8% during the period of 34 years (1966-1999). Besides, the pace of monetization (i.e. M_1/GDP and M_2/GDP) was also observed more elastic (e>1) in each year - interval except in 1971 to 1975.

Table 4.4: Average Annual Growth Rates of Money Stock and Their Ratio to GDP (1966-1999)

Year	*Nominal GDP (%)*	*Narrow Money M1 (%)*	*Ratio M1/ GDP*	*Broad Money M2 (%)*	*Ratio M2/ GDP*	*Reserve Money Mr (%)*	*Ratio Mr/ GDP*
1966-70	9.8	11.4	1.2	14.8	1.5	13.2	1.3
1971-75	14.4	12.2	0.8	16.4	1.1	11.2	0.7
1976-80	7.3	16.4	2.2	20.8	2.8	16.0	2.2
1981-85	13.8	14.2	1.0	18.4	1.3	16.1	1.2
1986-90	17.5	21.1	1.2	20.8	1.2	22.1	1.3
1991-94	17.8	19.0	1.1	22.0	1.2	19.7	1.1
1995-99	11.5	12.4	1.1	17.0	1.5	13.0	1.1
Total Average	**13.1**	**15.2**	**1.2**	**18.6**	**1.5**	**15.9**	**1.3**

Source: Appendix-D

These statistical figures, therefore, support the argument that heavy government borrowings (or overdraft) from the NRB to finance budget deficits and the increment in net foreign assets (NFA) were the principal causes of monetary expansion in Nepal (Gaudel, 1994:19).

In a developing country like ours, it is suggested that the rate of monetary expansion should be equal to the growth of domestic output and the pace of monetization should be equal to unity. Judged by these criteria, the monetary system of Nepal seems to be highly volatile and inflationary.

4.2.5 *Interest Rate Structure*

The most important syndrome of Nepal is its monetary dualism. It implies that there is coexistence of two money markets namely organized within the same economy. The organized money market consists of commercial banks, agriculture development banks and other financial institutions. Their activities though expanding rapidly in recent years, are confined to few urban centers only. The unorganized money market consists largely of indigenous moneylenders (Sahukars, Mahajans etc.), traders, landlords and dhikuti owners (savings cooperatives), provide the bulk of credit requirements to the semi-urban and rural areas. The participants of unorganized money market, therefore, are generally outside the control of the Nepal Rastra Bank.

This type of dualism also prevails in the interest rate structure of the Nepalese economy. In the organized sector, the NRB as a central bank is authorized to fix nominal interest rate to be charged or offered by the commercial banks. The nominal interest rate in the organized money market thus has been under the control of central bank (Pant, 1983:16). In the unorganized sector, interest rates are determined by the monopoly market condition. There exist a few creditors or indigenous moneylenders in relation to a large number of borrowers. So, the interest rate charged by them has always been exorbitant (24% to 60%) in comparison to the interest rates of organized sector (Shrestha, 1965:79).

Table 4.5: Interest Rate Structure (percent per annum) (1965-99)

Year	*Commercial Banks*					
	Deposit Rates on				*Lending Rates on Commercial Loans*	
	Savings		*Fixed*			
	Nominal	*Real**	*Nominal*	*Real**	*Nominal*	*Real**
1965	1.5	–9.3	3.5	-7.3	6.0	–4.8
1970	4.5	6.6	6.0	8.1	9.0	11.1
1975	6.5	–10.2	9.5	-7.2	15.0	–1.7
1980	8.0	–1.7	12.0	2.3	16.0	6.3
1985	8.5	4.4	12.5	8.4	17.0	12.9
1990	8.5	–1.2	12.0	2.31	8.0	8.3
1994	7.0	–2.0	9.0	0.0	13.5	4.5
1999	5.8	–6.9	7.3	-5.4	11.0	–1.7

Source: The NRB, Quarterly Economic Bulletin (Various Issues)
* Real interest rates have been derived by taking the difference of nominal interest rates and inflation rates. (Appendix-E).

From the year 1966, there occurred a new thinking about the interest rate policy that the high interest rate on bank deposits is necessary to mobilize savings for economic development.

Accordingly, many changes have been taken place on the deposit rate structure of commercial banks from 1966 onwards (Reejal, 1986:35). Nepal adopted a new approach of high but flexible interest rate policy in April 1975. Since then it tried to follow the prescription of maintaining positive loan and deposit rates as argued by real money theorist (Pant, 1983:ibid).

In this context, Table 4.5 shows that the adjustment made by the monetary authority towards higher rate of interest on savings and fixed account of commercial banks offered an inducement to save more in bank deposits. Similarly, the loan rates on commercial banks showed an upward movement over the past several years from 1965 to 1990. Further, it was stated that the interest rates in organized money market were administrated and regulated not only on deposits and loans of commercial banks but also on the securities issued by the government until 1989 (Khatiwada, 1994:4). Particularly, since May 1986, the Nepal Rastra Bank decided to deregulate interest rate policy in the context of financial liberalization (NRB, 1997:54). As a result, the interest rate on savings and fixed deposits was found reduced since 1994. Moreover, it also gave an advice to commercial banks to reduce the existing gap between deposits and lending rates assigned by them to stimulate the investment. However, the policy of independent interest rate too did not materialize. (The Eighth Plan (1992-97), HMG, 1992:674).

While considering the real rate of interest from 1965 to 1999, the trend did not give any consistent pattern to analyze the impact of interest rates in the economy. Although there is a little scope to generalize on the basis of ISD's conclusion, the erratic movement in the real interest rate has caused capital outflow and the deficit balance of trade in the country (ISD, 1994: 79)[a]. From this analysis it may be inferred that the long run trend of interest rate in Nepal does not reflect the opportunity cost of holding money for speculative purposes. Low interest rate policy seems to encourage unproductive expenditure and to discourage savings mobilization.

4.2.6 Exchange Rate Regime

There was virtually a stable rate of exchange between the Nepalese Currency (NC) and Indian Currency (IC) for the period of 57 years from 1876 to 1933 (Reejal, 1986: 48). However, since 1933 onwards, the exchange rate between these two currencies started to oscillate and the value of NC vis-à-vis IC depreciated continuously except in 1956 and 1957. This reflected the attitude of the people to accumulate IC and eventually created the shortage of IC in the market. It is also important to note that after the political change in 1951, the government of Nepal took a number of measures to stabilize exchange rate between NC and IC and also to unify national currency in the country. In spite of this, NC did not seem to have replaced IC to any noticeable extent. As a result, IC occupied a strategic role in the Nepalese monetary economy (Shrestha, 1965: 40-47).

In 1962, the Foreign Exchange Regulation Act (FERA) was introduced in Nepal to regulate all types of transactions in terms of foreign currencies. Since then in 1967, the value of NC in terms of US dollar was started to fix with the International Monetary Fund (IMF) (Reejal, ibid: 50). If one observes the exchange rate of NC in terms of US dollar, one can find frequent devaluation of Nepalese Rupee vis-à-vis US dollar. But this was not followed in the case of Indian Currency (Table 4.6).

Table 4.6: Exchange Rate and the Devaluation of Nepalese Currency (1965-1999)

(Rs. per Currency Unit)

Year (Mid-July)	*US Dollar*	*Devaluation of NC/$ (%)*	*Indian Currency (IC)*	*Devaluation of NC/IC (%)*
1965	7.6	—	1.59	—
1970	10.1	32.9	1.35	–15.1
1975	10.5	4.0	1.39	3.0
1980	11.9	13.3	1.45	4.3
1985	17.6	47.9	1.45	0.0
1990	29.1	65.3	1.68	15.9
1994	49.1	68.7	1.60	–4.8
1999	68.2	38.9	1.60	0.0

Source: NRB, Quarterly Economic Bulletin, 36(1&2), Mid-January, 2002: 70.

From Table 4.6 it is evident that the prevailing exchange rate system of NC against convertible currencies(i.e. US $) was replaced by a flexible exchange rate regime based on the concept of ?Currency Basket System? in the early 1980s. As a result, there had been an unbalanced movement in the exchange rate of NC vis-à-vis convertible currencies. In the case of IC, unlimited convertibility was allowed at the prevailing fixed rate of exchange (Sharma, 1993:14,1994:77[a]).

After the restoration of multi-party democracy in Nepal in 1990, the elected democratic government committed to bring about structural changes in the economy by initiating many reform measures. With effective from March 1992, the government adopted partial convertibility of the Nepalese currency against convertible foreign currencies. At the same time, Nepal had to make corresponding adjustment in NC's exchange rate in order to avoid broken cross rate difference between IC-dollar and NC-dollar, when India devalued IC vis-à-vis convertible currencies during 1991 (Thapa, 1993:29)[a]. In view of the favourable economic indicators of the Nepalese economy, the government felt safe to take decision of full convertibility of current account transaction and announced the decision in February 1993 (Economic Survey, FY 1992/93; 97). Above all, looking at the problem from the global concept of trade liberalization, the movement towards full convertibility of currency on current account transaction might be preferable for generating exportable surplus in the Nepalese economy.

4.2.7 Balance of Payments Situation

The balance of payments is a comprehensive summary of systematic annual records of international transactions during a given time period (Sethi, 1992: 711). Though the history of foreign trade in Nepal is long, the data relating to the balance of payments (BOP) has been received only from the FY 1974/75 (NRB, 1997:12). From the beginning, there is a growing problem of trade deficit due to low volume of exports compared to imports. The difficulty is that the major exportable items of the country are primary agricultural products, whereas the imported items are the manufactured consumer goods. Nepal is thus facing this critical situation, falling exports to keep pace with the fast growing imports in each year. If this situation persists in the economy, it is most likely that there may be a heavy pressure on balance of payments position of the country (Shrestha, 1990: 90).

While turning to the BOP on time series basis, Nepal has faced continuous current account deficit since the past fiscal year 1979/80 (Table 4.7). Besides, imports exceeding exports tremendously causes a huge trade deficit in the balance of trade account. This situation, if not checked, would ultimately lead to internal instability due to adverse balance of payments in the economy (Shrestha, 1993:2).

Table 4.7: Summary of Balance of payments (FY 1975/76-FY 1999/00)

(Rs. in million)

Particulars	*1975/76*	*1979/80*	*1984/85*	*1989/90*	*1993/94*	*1999/00*
a. Trade Balance	**–812.9**	**–2403.0**	**–5022.2**	**–13186.6**	**–31312.7**	**–58779.1**
b. Services, Net	284.3	873.2	1079.5	2752.9	17476.5	26445.7
c. Unrequited Transfer, Net	588.6	1188.2	2093.7	2790.1	6809.0	23368.2
d. Current Account Balance	**60.0**	**-341.6**	**-1849.0**	**-7643.6**	**-8027.2**	**-8965.8**
e. Official Capital, Net	145.8	577.3	1270.2	5888.8	10723.3	8485.4
f. Misc. Capital Item, Net	152.4	209.3	287.2	4404.4	3587.2	14928.8
g. Overall Balance	**358.2**	**26.4**	**-866.0**	**2649.6**	**6283.3**	**14448.4**

Source: NRB, Quarterly Economic Bulletin (Various Issues)

Table 4.7 presents that the balance of payments position of Nepal continued to look favourable since the FY 1985/86. However, an increase in the trade deficit coupled with increase in income from net services and net transfers contributed to the decline in current account deficit from FY 1975/76 to FY 1999/00. Under the capital account, net official capital recorded a significant growth from FY 1985/86 and the increment in miscellaneous capital items resulted all along in a surplus overall balance of payments. From Table 4.7, it is clear that after reaching to the maximum limit of adverse balance of payments (Rs.-866.0 million) in the FY 1984/85, the economy gained continuous surplus in the balance of payments. This trend indicated the unsatisfactory result due to excessive current account deficit even if there was surplus in the overall balance of payments.

Regarding the widening gap of trade deficit in Nepal, the Institute for Sustainable Development for NRB observed that the country has utilized the outstanding loan very often during the last 25 years since FY 1974/75 specially to tide over the short-term need of Indian currency. Besides, a large part of the current account deficit has also been financed by purchasing IC (ISD, 1994: 76)[a]. From this statement it is evident that service receipts and unrequited transfers are still inadequate to match the trade deficit in Nepal. Moreover, the deficit on current account balance shows the depletion of foreign exchange reserves in the economy. This explains the extent of the problem of BOP, which is serious and indicates the need to find the durable solution. In brief, the analysis of balance of payments shows the chronic problem of trade deficit mainly due to very week performance of exports over imports and the problem of current account deficit is almost met with the inflow of net official capital.

4.3 Money Demand: Its Major Determinants

In this section an attempt has been made to understand the determinants of the demand for money in general and to select the major determinants, which are applied for the specification of the demand for money function in the context of Nepal. From the various studies of the demand for money discussed in chapter III it is clear that money is pronounced as a means of exchange in views of classical economists. Particularly, in Fisher's equation the level of income is found as a major determinant of the demand for money. The Cambridge economists notably, Marshall and Pigou have concentrated on the fraction of income that can be held in the form of money. They have concluded that the level of income mainly determines the demand for money.

Keynes' liquidity preference theory is considered as a

remarkable refinement over the classical theory signifying the demand for money as an act of performing medium of exchange and a unit of account. This theory suggests that the aggregate demand for money generated by the transaction and precautionary motives is positively related with the level of income, while the speculative motive signifying the demand for money is inversely related to the rate of interest. Baumol-Tobin's theory as a reviewed approach of the Keynesian theory gives rise to a conclusion that the transaction demand for money above certain level is negatively correlated with the rise in interest rate. So, it is not merely a direct function of the level of income but also an inverse function of the rate of interest (Srivastava, 1989: 190). Further, Tobin's analytical framework indicates that the public holds diversified portfolio in order to lessen the risk in the case of uncertainty. Thus, a rise (fall) in the interest rate may cause readjustment in the portfolio selection in favour of bond (cash) holdings on account of the reduction in risk.

Friedman, reformulating classical and Keynesian theories of the money demand has recommended that the current income is not appropriate determinant due to its erratic fluctuation in each year. For this purpose, he has argued that the concept of permanent income as a proxy for wealth together with other explanatory variables as the nominal/expected rate of return on bonds and equities and the expected rate of change in price as a representative of the expected return on real assets should be included as determinants in the demand for money function (Singh, 1984:87).

Taking into account of this broad concept in the demand for money function, Friedman concluded that the rate of interest is not as influential as the permanent income or wealth in determining the demand for money. Thus, the review of all foregoing studies reveals that the income is found to be a significant determinant of the demand for money. In some studies, the rate of interest is also found to be a significant factor affecting the demand for money.

In the absence of developed financial market in developing countries, the real income determinant has always been significant scale variable in the demand for money function. For instance, in India the studies by Singh (1984,1990), Chakraborty and Kulkarni(1991) and Barari (1996) have shown that the income is one of the major determinants of the demand for money. However, interest rates in both short-term and long-term are found to be insignificant factors affecting the demand for money. In Nepal, such studies have received some considerations only after 1980s. Hence, whatever studies are available today are of rather recent origin. The first attempt in this field was made by Poudyal (1989) for the period 1975-87 and then very recently by Khatiwada (1997) covering a period of 21 years from 1976 to 1996. In their studies, the aggregate real income is found as a major determinant for both narrow and broad definitions of the demand for money. The rate of interest though having right sign is found to be insignificant in the former study. The coefficient of price level in terms of implicit GDP deflator in the latter has produced biased result.

The efforts made so far in this direction have been limited to only two studies. Thus, in this perspective an overview of the Nepalese monetary economy described in previous section 4.2 is helpful to indicate the demand for money for transaction purposes. It also shows the evidence of the high ratio of narrow money to the total money stock during the sample period from 1965 to 1999. The insignificant influence of the rate of interest on the demand for money may be attributed to the less developed money and capital markets in the economy. Moreover, the lack of speculative motive also seems to be responsible for the insignificant effect of the rate of interest on money demand.

4.3.1 Problems in Selecting the Major Determinants

At the outset, it should be noted that the major determinants of holding money balances may not be identical and all the determinants cannot be measurable. Furthermore, in Nepal due to the coexistence of non-monetized and monetized sectors, it is difficult to select the major relevant determinants. For instance, if income is to be taken as the main factor determining the money demand function, a problem still remains of selecting

GDP or GNP at market price or at factor cost. Similarly, it becomes problematic to find out a representative rate of interest in the midst of a large number of short-term and long-term interest rates existent in the unorganized financial market of the economy. In addition, the inclusion of two types of interest rates as the explanatory variable accentuates the problem of multicollinearity in the demand for money function.

In spite of the above-mentioned problems, there are numerous factors that cannot be included in the demand for money and their relative importance does not remain the same all the time. Among the determinants, which are likely, to have a systematic influence on the demand for money and the actual contribution of each of them cannot be easily ascertained. Thus, considering the availability of data and their limitations, some of the major determinants are specified in the following form:

4.3.1.1 The Income Level

The relationship between the demand for money and aggregate income is one of the central themes in the theory and practice of monetary economics. This issue is deeply rooted in the literature on money demand mostly for developed economies. It has received inadequate attention in developing countries. There is, therefore, much scope for investigation of appropriate scale variable in the estimation of the demand for money function in Nepal.

While using income or wealth as a scale variable, it is noteworthy that Friedman (1959) has made a distinction between two concepts of income, that is, measured income and permanent income. The measured income refers to the concept of income usually formulated in national income accounting and the permanent is a long-run concept, which can be measured in terms of the stock of wealth. Regarding this issue, some economists emphasizing on the transaction motive of holding money hold the view that the level of monetized income[4] would be the major determinant of the demand for money. But, some others have given stress to the asset motives of holding money and preferred wealth or permanent income as the major determinant.

In the developed countries like USA and UK, there is a general agreement [Meltzer (1963), Walter (1965), Laidler (1966a), Chow (1966), Starleaf &Reimer (1967), Laidler and Parkin (1970)] that the use of permanent income or wealth rather than the use of current income is an appropriate determinant. However, Latane (1960), Courchene and Shapiro (1964)have applied measured income in the place of permanent income. Likewise, in an examination of the post- war quarterly data, Goldfeld (1973), Arango & Nadiri (1981) have found a more stable demand function for narrowly defined money with current income in preference to wealth.

In the context of developing countries, most of the empirical studies have found taking measured income as the major determinant of the demand for money instead of wealth or permanent income. One of the main reasons for not including wealth is the absence of data in the non-monetized economy. As pointed out by Laumas (1978) and Hwang (1994), the relevant concept of income in the study of the demand for money is that portion of the total income, which can be derived from the monetized (non-agriculture) sector of the economy. Several studies in India [Gujarati (1968), Bhattacharya (1974) Sampath & Hussain (1981), Deadman & Ghatak (1981)] have chosen current income as the major determinant. In this regard, it is believed that the stock of money is exogenously determined and the nominal income is a major factor influencing the demand for money. However, Trivedi (1980:63) is of the view that the demand for money function is formulated in terms of wealth constraint proxies by permanent income or in some cases by the measured real income also. Thus, permanent real income is considered as a relevant determinant of the demand for money.

Despite these, the use of gross national product (GNP) as a scale variable might not be applicable in developing countries (Mookerjee, 1984:50). This is because, the developing economies are characterized by a dual economic structure composed of large non-monetized sector and a small-monetized sector. In regard to this, Bomberger and Makinen (1980) have also suggested to use gross national expenditure

(GNE)[5] as a scale variable for explaining the demand for money in open countries. Thus, the general agreement in the specification of the demand for money function observed from the various studies shows that some measure of income or wealth must be incorporated as a major determinant. But the inclusion of both income and wealth variables may be problematic due to multicollinearity.

While considering this in the Nepalese context, the studies by Poudyal (1989), Sharma (1987) and Khatiwada (1997) have found significant and stable relationship between the gross domestic product (GDP) and the stock of money holding. For all types of money, GDP has emerged as the principal determinant of the money demand. Regarding GDP, it is also stated that in a predominantly agricultural country like Nepal, the share of non-monetized income is supposed to de higher owing to the existence of a subsistence level of farming and the prevalence of barter system in factor payments. Besides, the lack of adequate data on wealth or permanent income and monetized income precludes employing ideal scale variable in the money demand function. Moreover, the choice of scale variable for the empirical study covering a longer periods back has to be confined in nominal or real GDP rather than in GNP figures[6]. Thus, aggregate income or GDP is regarded as the most important definition of income and it should be introduced as a chief determinant by avoiding monetized income in the context of our economy.

4.3.1.2 The Interest Rate

The interest rate is considered as the second major determinant of the demand for money. Its significance works as a Keynesian phenomenon in the demand for money balances. It is observed from the Keynesian liquidity preference theory that the demand for real money balances is a function of the two determinants as the bond rate of interest and the level of real income. The negative impact of variation in the first is called the liquidity or the Keynesian effect and the positive response of the second is called the income or Wicksell effect (Siebke, 1977: 148). This framework does not furnish the fact that over the longer period nominal interest rate becomes relatively more important than bond rate of interest[7].

The linkage of money and interest rate plays a vital role in monetary transmission mechanism[8]. However, the relationship between money and the nominal rate of interest has been a controversial issue in monetary theory (Blejer, 1978: 529; Pathak, 1981: 12). It is clear from Blejer's study that when money stock is increased at a rate higher than the rate of growth in money demand, the excess liquidity so created induces an increase in the demand for alternative financial assets, and consequently raises the price level. The interest rate, therefore, tends to be depressed until the demand for real cash balances raises enough to eliminate the discrepancy in the money market. As pointed out by Crockett and Evans (1980: 549), the opportunity cost variable in the demand for money function is usually an interest rate for a financially developed economy. But in developing countries, it is widely accepted that an interest rate is, in practice, an unsatisfactory measure of the opportunity cost of holding money.

Basically, there are two reasons for interest as an irrelevant determinant in the demand for money function. In the first place, the financial markets outside the banking system are not well developed. So, the possibility of substitution between money and other financial assets is scanty. Secondly, a more practical objection is that the observed interest rates are pegged by monetary authorities and remain unchanged for long period. Thus, there is insufficient variation in interest rate to enable its influence on money demand function.

There has been some disagreement over whether or not the interest rate is the relevant opportunity cost variable of the demand for money. Regarding the choice of the interest rate variable, the Keynesian theory supports that the long-term interest rate is the better indicator of the opportunity cost of holding money than short-term debt instruments. This view has led some economists to conclude that the models using a narrow definition of money and long term rate of interest would yield the highest interest elasticities.[9] Those with a broad definition and short term rate of interest would yield the lowest elasticities.[10] Some studies by Heller (1965) for the United States and Fisher (1968) for the United Kingdom indicate inability to find a significant role of interest rates on money demand.

Despite these conflicting views, a large number of empirical studies such as, Laidler for UK (1971), Teigen for USA (1964), Clinton for Canada (1973), Bhattacharya for India (1979) have proved the significant effect of a unique interest rate on the demand for money. However, a study by Lee (1967, 1969) employing the interest rate differential between time deposits and various other assets has revealed the better results in the demand for money function. A few studies [Friedman (1959), Laidler & Parkin (1970)] have also failed to establish a significant negative relationship between the rate of interest and the money demand, Thus, the role of interest rate variable in the demand for money function has remained clearly in dispute. In the Nepalese context, there exist varying degrees of the unorganized market rate of interests and the financial market is almost in a rudimentary stage. So, in such circumstances the choice of particular rate of interest as an appropriate determinant is really difficult and more impracticable.

Regarding the choice of the rate of interest, it is believed that time deposit rather than other deposits is more responsive. This implies that a change in interest rates on interest bearing assets can lead to a change in the demand for holding cash balances. Furthermore, as pointed out by Saravene (1971), Subrahmanyam (1977), an attractive rate of interest paid on time deposits would be an effective tool to change the saving habits of those people who do not come to deposit in banks and channel their savings in the unorganized sectors of the economy.

In the Nepalese context, the above condition may not be applied where a large proportion of population remains at subsistence level. An increase in income of the people can be held in the form of cash for the fulfillment of their basic needs. Holding their income on savings and time deposits for interest earning purposes would become luxury (Thapa, 1997:56). Moreover, the interest rate in the organized sector has remained administered for a long time and the other interest rates prevailing in unorganized sector are not recorded officially. The use of Treasury bill or government bond is also irrelevant because of its inefficiency to change public asset portfolio. Due to this fact, the market of government bond yield rate has been restricted to the banking system only. Thus, it is evident that in the absence of alternative financial assets, the interest rate on time deposits may be taken as a relevant determinant for the estimation of the demand for money in Nepal.

4.3.1.3 The Price Level

The relationship between money and price has remained a matter of debate among economists of the different era. The classical full employment equilibrium model has shown direct and proportionate relationship between money and prices. The Keynesian underemployment equilibrium structure has emphasized the partial effect of money on price level. The monetarists have renewed the classical framework. They argue that the rate of change in price level or inflation is purely a monetary phenomenon and has significant effect on money demand (Singh, 1995:425). Moreover, the monetarist version holds the view that the demand for money like other assets depends upon its own return in terms of the rate of interest and return on its substitutes in the form of price of physical assets. If these assets serve as alternative to holding money, an increase in their prices would cause a shift from money or bonds to real assets. Thus, there is an inverse relationship between money demand and price changes. In view of this, the inclusion of the price level as a separate determinant seems reasonable in the demand for money function.

For the empirical analysis, a large number of studies have been conducted to test the theoretical propositions provided by the classicists, Keynesian and monetarists in developed countries. The very little work in this respect has been done in the case of developing countries. Prior to the derivation of the demand for money, it is to be decided on the use of appropriate price level in order to deflate the stock of nominal money balances. To that extent, the relevant price index as suggested by Barrow (1970) would be the customer price index if the aggregate demand for money were dominated by household's behaviour. In this regard a number of researchers adopted different techniques for measuring the price variable. Cagan (1956) and Khan (1985) used the wholesale price index. Hamburger (1966), Spencer (1985) and Friedman (1992) applied the GNP deflator. The NNP deflator was introduced by Meltzer (1963). Feige (1967) had chosen the general price index as a separate determinant in the demand for money function. In spite of these measures, Frenkel (1977:659) put forward a composite price index[11] consisting of the wholesale price index and the cost of living index. While making a choice between these two indices, he preferred the cost of living index.

The empirical studies on the behaviour of prices in Nepal have also shown contradictory results with regard to the relationship between money stock and prices. The studies by Pant (1978) and Sharma (1987) have exhibited a weak association between prices and money but the studies of Khatiwada (1994, 1997) have revealed a good relation. Furthermore, in our economy there is no availability of statistics about general price index and the wholesale price index so far the choice of the appropriate price index has been confined to the consumer price index or the GDP deflator. Besides the GDP deflator as the most general measure of prices may be inappropriate due to its limited area of covering domestic output only. For this reason, the consumer price index (CPI) may be preferable as a measure of the opportunity cost of holding money. In some cases, it would be an imperfect indicator due to the poor quality of data in most of the underdeveloped countries. Thus, in this context, the inflation rate computed from both the CPI and the GDP deflator might be the ultimate choice for measuring the relevant determinant.

4.3.1.4 *The Exchange Rate*

One more factor determining the money demands is the exchange rate of the domestic currency vis-à-vis the currencies of foreign countries. During the period under study, there has been marked depreciation of NC as against with foreign currencies. For this purpose, it is essential to include exchange rate as one of the relevant determinants in the demand for money. The theories dealing with the demand for money can be empirically integrated with foreign exchange reserve of the country. Its need is particularly important to fulfill the discrepancy between desired and actual reserves. Some studies by Clark (1970), Frenkel (1974), Edwards (1984), Biswas & Saunders (1990) have shown that the reserve movements in the economy respond both to differences between the desired and actual reserves and to the situation of monetary disequilibria. This analysis, therefore, suggests that the amount of desired reserve depending upon the country's scale (income) is an important factor in determining the demand for money.

It is worth noting that in an open economy, the stock of foreign currency held by banks and residents plays a significant role in money demand. Moreover, in the context of Nepal, the NC is substituted for IC although the monetary authority has pegged IC's rate, including it in the currency basket system. As far as the domestic money is held as a substitute for foreign exchange, the specification of the demand for money function should include the anticipated change in the exchange rate or the expected rate of inflation and thereby incorporating it as a determinant in the demand for money function. It is evident from the previous section (4.2.6) that Nepal has had a fixed exchange rate regime for a long time particularly with IC. Even after including it in a basket of foreign currencies in 1986, the exchange rate of NC as against with IC has still remained fixed. However, the rates with respect to other convertible currencies have been fluctuating for a long period. If we observe the exchange rate during the study period (1965-99), there appears frequent discrete revision in it. Altogether it was 6 times exchange rate adjustment with US dollar and 7 times with Indian rupee since 1966 to 1994.Besides, the exchange rate of the other currencies like pound sterling, Dutch mark and Japanese yen have been floating since 1972 onwards (NRB, 1995: 58-59).

In a system of fixed exchange rate and at the embryonic stage of financial market, it is not easy to absorb the monetary shocks created by the excess reserve flow in the economy. For this purpose, it has been formally adopted managed floating exchange rate regime in Nepal to adjust the exchange rate for domestic monetary shocks. However, the adoption of this system along with discrete revision in exchange rate would not be effective to absorb the monetary fluctuations. Thus, by and large it can be inferred that the application of fixed exchange rate system rather than managed floating exchange rate seems reasonable to include as a determinant in the demand for money. Apart from this, the existence of foreign exchange deposits in the joint venture banks and the possibility of a large degree of currency substitution between NC and IC in the entire Nepalese economy argue for the inclusion of the exchange rate as a return variable in the demand for money function.

4.3.1.5 The Balance of Payments

The balance of payments as a monetary phenomenon has been extensively explored in developing countries due to high rate of inflation and growing deficits in balance of trade accounting. Since the balance of payments (BOP) often acts as a critical constraint in economic activities, it is useful to examine the monetary approach to the balance of payments (MABP) [Johnson (1973),Swoboda (1976), Zecher (1976) and Wilford & Wilford (1978)] in the context of the small and open economy. The core of this approach has relied on Walras law according to which the excess demand for goods and services, money and securities altogether equals to zero. Furthermore, as pointed out by Aghevli (1975: 42) and Salam (1995: 70), the balance of payments is always reduced to zero if there is equilibrium in goods and bond markets in the economy. Thus, from this approach it follows that the excess demand for money is always zero when balance of payments is in equilibrium condition. An excess money demand (money supply) could be alleviated by an inflow (outflow) of foreign reserves, thereby creating surplus (deficit) in the balance of payments. It shows that the balance of payments is substantially a monetary phenomenon through which both demand for and supply of money functions will be determined.

In an open economy like ours, there exists a free mobility of the labour and capital particularly from India. The effects of monetary shocks are not only confined to national income and price level but also have an effect on the balance of payments. Thus, it is relevant to examine the MABP in the Nepalese context because of the following two reasons:

Firstly, Nepal has had fixed exchange rate regime for a long time. *Secondly*, Nepal has comprised of the small monetized and large nonmonetized economy. Its openness to India can be reflected in terms of trade, capital flows and labour mobility. The MABP, therefore, provides a convenient framework for the analysis of monetary disequilibrium in the economy.

While taking into account the balance of payments in Nepal, it is evident (Table 4.7) that there has been a continuous surplus in the balance of payments since 1986.It has a direct impact on money stock in the absence of active and regular sterilization policies of the Nepal Rastra Bank. The financial market in the economy is also narrow and rudiment. Due to these circumstances, the NRB has not yet been able to neutralize the expansionary effect of BOP surpluses on money supply. Thus, in such a situation, the analysis of BOP through monetary approach as a determinant in the demand for money would be expected to restore the monetary equilibrium in the Nepalese economy.

4.4 Other Determinants

Despite the aforementioned determinants, the other determinants are equally applicable for the analysis of the demand for money. These are briefly discussed below:

4.4.1 *Inflation*

Ghatak's study (1981) has shown that inflation is an important determinant under the hypothesis of monetarism and structuralism. The monetarist's model reveals that excess stock of money is the root cause of inflation. It can be derived by the conventional money demand function. The structural model, however, has presented several approaches in connection with the specific features of developing economies.

Basically, the two indices-the consumer price index (CPI) and the implicit GDP deflator may be used to measure the rate of inflation in developing countries. However, Joshi and Saggar

(1995: 94) have observed that wholesale price index (WPI) is widely used in order to measure the inflation because of its wide coverage of commodities. Its computation is said to be based on a well reporting system. It is also important to note that as WPI is affected by the change in administered prices, the choice of CPI has been used here to measure the rate of inflation as an additional determinant of the demand for money in Nepal. As far as the influence of opportunity cost variable in the demand for money is concerned, Lahiri's study (1991) examines the process of monetary accommodation of inflation to the money demand behaviour. In a study, Kamath (1984) has argued that the demand for money function is best formulated in terms of inflation rate as the opportunity cost of holding money. The use of time series data during the sample period (1965-99) under study reflects the view that inflation in Nepal is a continuous process beginning with an initial slow build up prior to the 1970s, picking up momentum (16.7%) in 1975 and running into galloping price rise (21.1%) in 1992 (see, Appendix-C). This trend shows that a persistent rise in price level has created a sustainable type of double-digit inflation in the economy. Thus, the inclusion of inflation rate as a determinant plays an important role in the estimation of the demand for money in Nepal.

Regarding the appropriateness of opportunity cost variable, it is also hypothesized that the long-run expected rate of inflation[13] exerts a separate negative effect on the demand for money. In this context, various studies [Cagan (1956), Adekunle (1968)[b], Shapiro (1973), Melitz (1976) and Frenkel (1977)] have asserted that the inclusion of expected rate of inflation does not differ from the interest rate in the sense of increasing cost of holding money. However, this issue as argued by Trivedi (1980) had added more significance for a developing country like Nepal due to the following reasons:

* There is a wide divergence of interest rates in the organized and unorganized markets.
* The interest rate is pegged in the organized market by the monetary authority.
* Rudimentary type of financial market has created a paucity

of the financial substitutes for money.

All these factors, therefore, tend to support that the appropriate opportunity cost variable would be the expected rate of inflation rather than interest rate in developing countries.

4.4.2 Population

Among the several determinants of the demand for money function, population factor also seems to exert its influence on its estimation. This factor is important in the sense that it is closely related with per capita GDP. While using the population as a deflator in the demand for money function it has been argued [Friedman (1959), Laidler (1966)[a], Khan (1974)] that per capita real money holding and real income rather than aggregate values should be used for its correct specification. In Jacobs' study (1974), the alternative specifications of the demand for money function depending on aggregate data deflated either by population or by price are equivalent when data are dominated by time trend. In White's study (1978), population deflating can be ignored only when the real income elasticity of the demand for money is around unity. Even if the data are not purely in time series but cross-sectional, money demand at that situation may be estimated either using population or price as a separate determinant.

4.4.3 Budget Deficit

Budget deficit as a determinant may be included in the demand for money function because of its monetary implications. In Nepal, there is a tendency of persistent budgetary deficit in each fiscal year and most of it is financed by issuing paper currency and thereby monetizing the fiscal deficit. As a consequence, there is always price hike inflation in the economy. In this respect, Aghevli and Khan (1978) argue that inflation has an instantaneous impact on government expenditure, while revenue takes time to adjust with rising prices due to bureaucratic delaying. Hence, it is relevant to say that the introduction of a budget deficit variable in the demand for money function plays a vital role in correcting monetary disequilibrium in the Nepalese economy.

4.4.4 Rate of Monetization

It is known that the rate of monetization would be higher if the nonmonetized sector is larger and more efforts are geared up to develop it. Thus, in a large unorganized economy of Nepal, the additional amount of money is demanded in the process of transformation of nonmonetized income into monetized one. Furthermore, as pointed out by Lodha (1988), the aforesaid conventional determinants of the demand for money are insufficient and somewhere inapplicable due to slow speed of monetization in developing countries. Thus, in such a situation, the degree of monetization in terms of proxy variable like the number of bank branches or the per capita bank branches may be included as a determinant in estimating the money demand equation.

In this regard, Aghevli (1975:46) has also claimed that the demand for money can be specified taking velocity of money as the indicator of monetization and the development of banking facilities for financial intermediation. Thus, in the wake of financial intermediation, a rise in the number of bank branches not only increases the demand for money by familiarizing people with the advantages of monetized transaction (or cheque payments), but also induces a shift in balances from currency to deposits by making banking services more accessible. From this discussion, it follows that the rate of monetization is an important determinant contributing to the rise in demand for money.

4.5 Concluding Remarks

To sum up, the overview of the Nepalese monetary economy discussed above exhibits a large non-monetized sector. Our economy being open has low gross savings, price instability, transmitted inflation from outside, inelastic response of interest rate on savings and investment, sluggish growth of national income, import oriented trade and the continuous deficit on trade account balance. Thus, in this connection, an analysis of determinants derived in section (4.2) seems reasonable to overcome these hurdles through the estimation of the demand for money function in order to maintain the monetary stability in the economy.

In brief, a number of factors emerged as determinants of the demand for money function can be listed under the major determinants as national income, interest rate, price level, exchange rate and balance of payments and the other determinants can be counted as inflation, population, budget deficit and the rate of monetization. Thus, from the overall analysis, it may be concluded that the national income or GDP is an important determinant of the demand for money in Nepal. The analysis of prices in an open economy framework reveals that foreign prices and imported inflation have greater impact on the price movement in Nepal. Furthermore, to eliminate the excess demand for money generated from inflation, the balance of payments should react to change in domestic prices and it should be zero to restore monetary equilibrium in the economy. On the whole, the rise in income changes in price level or inflation and the rate of monetization are likely factors contributing jointly in the variation of the money demand.

NOTES

1. WBR refers to the World Bank Report, 2000.
2. ADB represents Asian Development Bank, 1995.
3. 1. Nepal Arab Bank Ltd. (1984), 2. Nepal Indosuez Bank Ltd. (1986), 3. Nepal Grindlays Bank Ltd. (1987), 4. Himalayan Bank Ltd. (1993), 5. Nepal SBI Bank Ltd. (1993), 6. Nepal Bangladesh Bank Ltd. (1994), 7.Everest Bank Ltd. (1994), 8. Bank of Kathmandu (1995), 9. Nepal Bank of Ceylon Ltd. (1996), [see, *Banking and Financial Statistics*, 32, NRB, Mid-Jan. 1997]. Economic Survey [HMG/N, FY 2001/02: 52-53] reports that out of the total 430 bank branches established in five development regions in Nepal, a large number of bank branches (187) were established in the central development region. Among the bank branches of this region 83 (44.4%) branches were concentrated only in Kathmandu Valley.
4. Monetized income refers to the monetized ratio times income (see Bhattacharya, 1974:502-10).
5. Gross national expenditure (GNE) is defined as the sum of gross national product (GNP) and the net import (X – M′). That is, GNE = GNP + X – M′.
6. Gross national product (GNP) figures in Nepal were available

only from the fiscal year 1974/75 onwards.

7. The bond rate of interest may be taken as a sum of the real rate of interest and the anticipated rate of inflation.
8. Monetarists vindicated their emphasis on interest rate as a link with transmission mechanism. The sketch of the mechanism given by Friedman and Schwartz seems to offer changes in interest rates as the avenue through which money stock changes in real asset (Johnson, 1972:75).
9. The highest interest elasticity on the basis of narrow definition of money was derived by Meltzer (1963), Brunner and Meltzer (1964), Courchene and Shapiro (1964), Laidler (1966)[b] and Courchene and Kelly (1971).
10. The lowest interest elasticity with broad definition of money was also tested by Laidler (1966)[b].
11. Composite price index can be computed in the form as

    $P = P_w^{\delta} P_c^{1-\delta}$

    Where P is the price deflator (composite price index), P_w is the wholesale price index, P_c is the cost of living index, δ and (1 – δ) are the corresponding weights of the wholesale price index and the cost of living index (see, Frenkel, 1977: 660).
12. The premium (or discount) on a forward contract for foreign exchange is approximately related to the interest rate differential. That is,

    $$\frac{Fe - Se}{Se} i - i^*$$

    Where Fe is the forward exchange rate, Se is the spot exchange rate, *i* is the domestic interest rate and *i** is the foreign rate of interest on comparable securities for the same maturity [for details, see Sargent & Wallace, 1973: 328-50].
13. In Lefton's view, when both short term and long term expected rate of inflation are used in the regression model, the demand for money is found to be positively related to the contemporaneous rate and negatively related to the permanent rate of inflation. Contemporaneous rate is the short rate, which can be approximated empirically by a simple moving average of the rate of change in implicit GDP deflator over two successive quarters. Permanent rate of inflation is expected to occur over a longer time period and it can be approximated by an exponentially weighted average of past annual rate of change in the implicit GNP deflator (for details, see Lefton, 1974: 274-75).

CHAPTER V

EMPIRICAL EVIDENCES ON THE DEMAND FOR MONEY IN NEPAL

5.1 Introduction

This chapter is devoted to examine the theories and empirical evidences of the demand for money function. It determines the stability of the function for the successful implementation of monetary policy in Nepal. A large number of studies on the demand for money in the developed economies especially in USA [Meltzer (1963), Goldfeld (1973), Laidler (1977), Feige & Pearce (1979)], and UK [Laidler & Parkin (1970), Artis and Lewis (1976), Haque (1989)], have assessed some issues on the appropriate definition of money, the relevant scale variable (income or wealth) and the choice of suitable variable to represent the cost of holding money. However, these issues have not been tested as required for the countries with developing economies (Arize, 1985: 289).

A number of researches have been conducted on the estimation of the demand for money in developing countries. Mahajan (1980), Deadman & Ghatak (1981), Beswas & Saunders (1990) have emphasized on the appropriate choice of the scale and opportunity cost variables, and the proper functional form of the demand for money equation.

Despite of sufficient literature on theoretical and empirical aspects of the demand for money, this topic retains its controversial character (Shahi, 1977:357). The relationship between money and income has been conclusively established. However, the association of money and interest has remained inconclusive. The systematic and detailed studies of the demand for money for the developing countries are a few and they are inappropriate with respect to methodologies, data, models and time periods (Sampath & Hussain, 1981:17). As a result, no such study has explored all-important issues involved in the demand for money. Most of the studies are hampered by the limitations of the availability of data. In view of the above, we intend to analyze some important issues related to the demand for money permitted by the available data of the Nepalese economy.

Regarding the selection of income or wealth as a scale variable in the demand for money function, income is used as an appropriate determinant in the developing economies. For instance, Adekunle (1968), Wong (1977) and Aghevli et al (1979) used the current income, whereas fry (1978), Mangla (1979) and Khan (1982) have resorted to permanent income in the money demand equation. Further, in developing countries, the major proportion of the population lives near the subsistence level so that the more attention could be focused on current income rather than permanent or future income (Perera, 1988:19). In the context of Nepal, permanent income cannot be observed directly. So, one is forced to use the current income in terms of GDP (Poudyal, 1989:31). With regard to the interest rate as an opportunity cost variable in the demand for money function, neither the theory provides any clear cut indication nor empirical studies provide strong evidence in support of either short term or long term rate of interest. Thus, as a rule of thumb, the interest on fixed deposits of one year has been selected as a proxy for the opportunity cost of holding money.

It is argued that in developing countries, substitution between money and real assets is more important than money and financial assets. The relevant opportunity cost of holding money would be the expected rate of inflation rather than interest rate (Khan, 1982:263). In the case of Nepal, the series on wholesale price index are not available for a relatively longer period. Further, it may not be possible to generate expected rate of inflation as weighted average of the past rates. Thus, in such a situation, inflationary expectation may be replaced by the rate of change in consumer price index.

Apart from these variables, some others such as the number of bank branches, fiscal deficit of the government, size of the population etc. are also expected to exert influence on the demand for money. Thus, to measure the impact of these variables including the above-mentioned variables, we have specified different models of the demand for money function in the next section.

Money stock in general is defined so as to include total currency outside banks and the demand deposits with commercial banks. In fact, there is no unanimity among economists on the monetary components to be embodied in the empirical definition of money. Some economists have favoured narrow concept of money (M_1) which constitutes currency held by the public plus demand deposits at the commercial banks, while many other have associated with the broad concept of money (M_2) including time and saving deposits in the components of narrow money (Pathak, 1981:12). Beyond this, Friedman and Schwartz (1970) have provided a strong statement that choosing a definition of money is primarily an empirical issue. They have further argued that the demand for high-powered money or reserve money (M_r) should be more stable than the demand for other monetary aggregates. Following this statement, Lothian (1976:60) has proposed a solution that a suitable definition of money is the high-powered money. It comprises of total currency outstanding along with banks and the other private deposits at the central bank alone. High-powered money is called the reserve money in the sense that it is a portion of the total deposits, which always yields monetary services without earning interest rate. In this way, several definitions of money have been employed in the course of testing the theories of the demand for money. As far as the Nepalese economy is concerned, this empirical study has been confined to the definitions of narrow, broad and reserve money only.

5.2 Data Methodology

In this study, time series data have been employed for the period of 1965 to 1994. The data on money stock and consumer price index were compiled from various issues of the Quarterly Economic Bulletins published by the Nepal Rastra Bank. The national income aggregates represented by GDP series were obtained from the International Financial Statistics-Year Books, the National Planning Commission Secretariat of HMG, Central Bureau of Statistics and the Economic Survey (various issues) of the Ministry of Finance, HMG, Nepal. Since we have used annual data throughout this study, the adjustment of the desired and actual money balances has been assumed to be instantaneous and so that it has fully been adjusted within a year.

Before empirical tests are carried out, it may be plausible to say something about the data problems associated with the estimation of the demand for money. Indeed, econometric research works in Nepal are very few due to the lack of availability of the reliable data. Beside, the appropriate series on monetized income or wealth, government bond yield rate, wholesale price index are not available. So, they are excluded from the estimation of the demand for money.

There are no quarterly series on GDP data and even the national figures from expenditure side are available only from the fiscal year 1974/75 onwards. Besides, there are no suitable price indices to convert the nominal money balances into real balances. On account of these problems, the data on nominal money stock were taken from the annual averages of the end of the month figure and the nominal GDP were converted into real terms by using implicit GDP deflator.

Regarding the use of interest rate variable, Poudyal (1989:40) has argued that the use of Treasury bill rate is preferable in the case of narrow money, while in the case of broad money time deposit rate is preferred. The issue of Treasury bill in Nepal though started from 1962, has not yet become market oriented. So, the ownership of it by the public is almost negligible. At this juncture, 12-month time deposit rate for all types money has been chosen as a relevant interest rate variable and it has been included in the demand for money function. Therefore, the existing inadequacy of statistical information in Nepal has forced to limit the study on annual data on the specified variables only.

In this study, the various specifications of the demand for money functions as per restrictions imposed by the data problems have been tried. The ordinary least square (OLS) method has been applied to the simple linear, loglinear, semi-loglinear and first difference form under the single equation system. In addition, to analyze the issue of simultaneity in relation to the demand for money, the two stage least square (2SLS) procedure under the simultaneous equation system has been employed by assuming the equality between demand and supply functions in the money market.

Having discussed the issues with regard to the selection of appropriate variables included in the demand for money function in section 5.1 and the data problems with methodology in section 5.2, it is necessary to develop the appropriate specification of the model that can be estimated and best fitted in the context of the Nepalese economy. Thus, in section 5.3.1 various specifications of the models under the single equations system are examined and the results of the empirical works are discussed including Chow test of the stability and McKinnon's hypothesis. The section 5.3.2 consists of formulating a system of the demand for and supply of money equations and estimates of the results by using OLS and 2SLS procedures. It draws inferences about the importance of the simultaneity by comparing the results of these two methods. Finally, the summary of the empirical findings from the different models is given in section 5.4. The data and the sources are shown in the Appendix.

5.3 Testing Different Econometric Models in the Context of the Nepalese Economy

The multinational study by Lewis and Breen (1975) has provided a basic guideline for developing different models in the context of the present study. Based on it, the following propositions have been made:

1. The marginal propensity to hold money with respect to income or income elasticity is greater than unity.
2. The interest rate coefficients and elasticities are negative.
3. The negative price coefficient justifies the hypothesis of existence of money illusion on money demand behaviour.
4. The increase in the number of banks is the most important factor contributing to the rise in demand for nominal and real balances.
5. Dynamic adjustments are not rapid in the least developed countries[1].
6. The other variables as inflation, interest bearing assets, foreign exchange reserves etc. used in the demand for money function are less successful in the developing countries.

On the basis of these propositions, it can be expected that the demand for money in Nepal is likely to be a stable relationship of a few pivotal variables as income, interest rates, price level and the number of bank branches.

5.3.1 Single Equation System

1. Simple linear model

There exist a number of empirical studies [Bhattacharya (1974), Laumas (1978), Aghevli & Khan (1978)] on the demand for money in developing countries. The simple model applied in these studies is in the linear form. It includes income and interest rate as the appropriate explanatory variables to explain the demand for money. Besides, Laidler and Parkin (1970) consider that the demand for money would adjust almost immediately to and increase in aggregate money income as a result of rise in population or price level. They suggested that where permanent income plays no role, the price level is included as a separate explanatory variable. Thus, we can formulate the following simplified version of the linear model as

$$M_t = \alpha_0 + \alpha_1 Y_t + \alpha_2 r_t + \alpha_3 P_t + \alpha_4 NCB_t + U_t \qquad ....(1)$$

Where M_t is the nominal money stock, which represents the demand for money at a time period t, Y_t denotes gross domestic product at current prices, r_t is the rate of interest on one year fixed deposits of commercial banks, P_t is the price level represented by the consumer price index, NCB_t is the number of commercial bank branches and U_t is the structural disturbance term which is assumed to have zero expectation.

The parameters are expected to be $\alpha_1 > 0$, $\alpha_2 < 0$, $\alpha_3 > 0$, $\alpha_4 > 0$

The equation (1) is regressed for the full period (1965-94) and the two sub-periods (1965-74) and (1975-94). It takes alternative definitions-narrow, broad and reserve concepts of money. The results are summarized in Table 1.0

5.3.1 Regression Results Under the Single Equation System

Table 1.0: Simple Linear Model

Full Period: (1965-94) Annual data

Eq.	*Dependent Variable*	*Constant*	*Coefficients of independent variables* Y_1	r_t	P_t	NCB_t	*Statistic* R^2	*SEE*	*F*	*DW*
1.1	M_{1t}	623.61	1.46	-.03	-.56	.13	.999	275.8	5323.1	1.97
			***	***	***	***				
			(10.84)	(-2.56)	(-3.31)	(2.85)				
1.2	M_{2t}	1403.75	1.63	-.03	-.73	.12	.998	915.9	2869.7	1.57
			***	*	***	*				
			(8.93)	(-1.72)	(-3.20)	(1.98)				
1.3	M_{rt}	770.93	1.59	-.03	-.70	.13	.998	390.0	2697.2	2.89
			***	*	***	*				
			(8.44)	(-1.83)	(-2.95)	(2.05)				

Full Period: (1965-74) Annual data

Eq.	*Dependent Variable*	*Constant*	*Coefficients of independent variables* Y_1	r_t	P_t	NCB_t	*Statistic* R^2	*SEE*	*F*	*DW*
1.4	M_{1t}	-88.23	.05	-.10	.41	.64	.998	36.9	102.21	1.56
					**	**				
			(0.21)	(-1.02)	(2.60)	(3.20)				
1.5	M_{2t}	-604.89	.03	-.07	.49	.62	.991	57.9	136.80	1.91
					**	**				
			(0.12)	(-.80)	(3.62)	(3.55)				
1.6	M_{rt}	-13.99	.10	-.15	.32	.72	.987	33.7	92.84	1.50
						**				
			(0.39)	(-1.40)	(1.93)	(3.41)				

Full Period: (1975-94)										Annual data
Eq.	*Dependent Variable*	*Constant*	*Coefficients of independent variables*				*Statistic*			
			Y_1	r_t	P_t	NCB_t	R^2	*SEE*	*F*	*DW*
1.7	M_{1t}	877.93	1.55	-.02	-.64	.11	.99	332.1	2735.3	1.95
			***		***	**				
			(8.59)	(-1.58)	(-3.06)	(2.71)				
1.8	M_{2t}	2601.08	1.73	-.02	-.83	.11	.99	1116.2	1472.9	1.60
			***		**	*				
			(7.06)	(-1.22)	(-2.91)	(1.98)				
1.9	M_{rt}	885.55	1.68	-.01	-.78	.11	.99	481.4	1343.9	2.94
			***		**	*				
			(6.55)	(-0.97)	(2.61)	(1.97)				

Note: Figures in parentheses below the parameters of each equation indicate t values.

* Significant at 10% level.
** Significant at 5% level.
*** Significant at 1% level.

R^2 : The degree of explanation of the dependent variable.
SEE : Standard error of estimates.
F : F statistic for the joint significance of all coefficients.
DW : Durbin-Watson statistic for the presence of autocorrelation.

Table 1.0 presents the regression results obtained from the different equations of the demand for money for the full period and sub-periods. As can be seen from Table 1.0, each of the estimated equations for the full period (1965-94) confirms a priori notion in terms of both sign and magnitude except in price variable. The coefficient of income plays a dominant role in all types of the demand for money equations and satisfies the first proposition mentioned in section 4.3. The interest rate variable on the other hand seems to be significant at 5% level for M_{1t} equation only. Similarly, the price level with the negative sign and the number of bank branches with the expected sign are found significant at 1% level. The negative price coefficient with less than one magnitude in all demand equations implies that there is an indication of the presence of money illusion in money demand behavior in Patinkin sense.

Thus, a reduction in money demand may be due to

presumption of the public towards the increment in future price expectation. From the statistic, it is clear that the percentage of variation explained by the regression R^2 is 99% for all the demand equations. Again, the size of the F statistic in all cases is significant at 1% level. The DW statistic above the upper limit of indecision for M_{1t} definitions shows the absence of autocorrelation. Thus, evaluating the entire statistic, it can be inferred that the income variable appears to be the most appropriate determinant in all money demand equations.

Turning to the sub-period (1965-74) and taking the result as a whole, the striking fact is that all variables except the number of bank branches in equations (1.4 to 1.6) are insignificant with proper sign even though the values of R^2 and F statistic are very high. The coefficient of income though having correct sign, is not significant in either equation. The result may be due to either the lower degrees of freedom or the use of old GDP series from 1965 to 1974. Likewise, for the sub-period (1975-94), all variables appear to be significant except the coefficient of the rate of interest. This coefficient of interest rate having right sign suggests that the speculative demand for money is being insensitive to the rate of interest.

In comparison to the results for all the three periods, we note that in terms of the t-statistic, the models in the full period (1965-94) perform better than sub-period. Judging the overall performance of the equations for the two sub-periods and the whole period, we conclude that M_{1t} definition of money is the best definition in the context of the Nepalese economy.

1.1 Stability Test

It is interesting to note here that the stability of the demand for money function is of crucial importance to the effectiveness of monetary policy. Thus, with a view to test the stability in the demand for money function, one of the popular tests[2], known as Chow test (1960) has been applied and presented in Table 1.1.

With regard to the stability test of the demand for money, Clinton (1973) and Foot (1977) in Canada, Artis & Lewis (1984) in the United Kingdom have observed that money narrowly defined has a stable demand function but the inclusion of broad definition of money results in instability. Thus, in order to make use the Chow test for our study, we have estimated the individual demand functions by segregating the entire sample period in the two sub-groups (1965-74) and (1975-94). The F value has been calculated by using Chow's formula[3]. The results are summarized in Table 1.1.

Table 1.1: Stability Test

Money demand equations	*ESS_1 (1965-94)*	*ESS_2 (1965-74)*	*ESS_3 (1975-94)*	*F value*
M_{1t}	190958.62	6802.74	1654342.54	0.58
M_{2t}	20976210.95	16772.99	18686673.53	0.49
M_{rt}	3802555.51	5678.03	3475970.97	0.37

Critical value: F .05 (5.20)=2.71

As for the stability test, the result in Table 1.1 shows that there is not any definition of money for rejecting the null hypothesis at 5% level of significance. It is because of the fact that F-value is found below the critical value for M_{1t}, M_{2t} and M_{rt} definitions of money at 5% level of significance. Thus, Chow test for the three alternative definitions of money strongly suggest that the structure of money demand relationship in Nepal has remained stable over the sample period. And there is no need to choose appropriate definition from narrow, broad as well as reserve concepts of money for testing the stability in the context of Nepalese economy.

2. Simple Modified Model

A convenient model for examining the demand for nominal and real money balances may be specified as

$$M_t/P_t = \beta_0 + \beta_1 Y_{pt} + \beta_2 r_t + \beta_3 \pi_t + \beta_4 (POP)_t + V_t \qquad ...(2)$$

Where M_t/P_t is the demand for real money balances represented by the real money stock, Y_{pt} is the real income denoted by the real GDP at constant prices, r_t is the rate of interest on 12 month fixed deposits, $ð_t$ is the rate of inflation proxied by the rate of change in consumer price index, $(POP)_t$ is the size of the population which is used (in Table 2.0) for calculating the per capita nominal money balances and V_t is the disturbance term.

The expected signs of the parameters are

$$\beta_1 > 0, \beta_2 < 0, \beta_3 < 0, \beta_4 > 0$$

The results are summarized in Table 2.0 and discussed below

Table 2.0: Regression Results

Modified Linear Model (1965-94)

(Annual data)

Equation	*Dependent Variable* / *Constant*	*Independent Variables*		*Statistic* R^2	*SEE*	*F*	*DW*
	Nominal balances						
2.1	$M_{1t}/POP=$ -27.93 (9.82)***	$1.02Y_t/$ POP (-1.75)*	$-.02r_t$ $-.01P_t$ (.12)	.998	18.3	4178.9	1.81
2.2	M_{2t}/POP $= -120.18$ (9.19)***	$1.20Y_t/$ POP (-1.57)	$-.03r_t$ $-.19P_t$ (-1.43)	.997	56.5	2640.95	1.54
	Real balances						
2.3	$M_{1t}/P_t=$ -25.46 (40.97)***	$1.01Y_{pt}$ (-.82)	$-.02r_t$ $-.04\eth_t$ (-1.83)*	.990	2.5	831.23	1.76
2.4	$M_{2t}/P_t=$ -108.92	$1.0Y_{pt}$ $-.007r_t$	$-.02\eth_t$	.993	5.9	1161.34	1.82

Note: Figures in parentheses and asterisks have the same meanings as explained in Table 1.0.

Table 2.0 reports on the results pertaining to nominal (per capita) and real money demand equation for both narrow and broad definitions of money. The linear formulation with M_{1t}/POP as the dependent variable provides the best fit with income and interest rate variables significant with the expected sign. But the inclusion of price variable in equation (2.1) and (2.2) has not made a significant impact on the demand for both narrow and broad definitions of money.

The coefficient of real income equation (2.4) is unity, suggesting the assumption of classical model that the demand for nominal money balance is proportional to the price level.

The inclusion of inflation rate (or price expectation) in the real demand equation for narrow money also turns to be significant at 10% level with the expected sign. For the statistic, all four equations give a high R^2, significant F values for nominal per capita and real money balances. The DW statistic except in equation (2.2) is closed to 2, revealing the absence of autocorrelation.

As stated in the overall estimates of the nominal per capita and real money demand functions for both definitions of money, the income coefficient is highly significant at 1% level. The coefficients of interest rate as well as inflation are significant at 10% level for narrow definition of money only. Thus, from this analysis it is obvious that there is virtually no difference in the explanatory power of regression R^2 between M_{1t} and M_{2t} definition of money though the former one performs better in terms of t scores of parameters. Hence, it is quite possible to say that the modified linear models do not adequately represent the money demand behaviour in the Nepalese context. The error in specification might be the reason for the statistical insignificance and unexpected algebraic sign of the price coefficient.

3. Loglinear Model

In Laidler's (1977) words, it is quite remarkable that positive real income elasticity, a negative opportunity cost elasticity and unit price elasticity would be well-determined variables in the demand for money function. Thus, Hoffman and Rasche (1991: 665) have focused their attention on the long run income and interest elasticity estimates for the US economy. Nyong (1993: 89) tried to solve the problems raised by Heerden (1981) on the income and interest elasticities of the demand for money in South Africa. He came to the conclusion that the elasticity of income is less than unity and the interest rate elasticity is neither significant nor confirm to an expected sign. Keeping these facts into consideration, an attempt has been made to estimate the elasticity of demand for money in Nepal with respect to the income, interest rate, price level etc.

Accordingly, the appropriate form of the demand for money

TABLE 3.0 : REGRESSION RESULTS

Loglinear Model (1965-94) (Annual data)

Eq.	*Dependent variable*	*Constant* *Independent variables*	*Statistic* R^2	*SEE*	*F*	*DW*
3.1	$\ln M_1$	= -2.60 + 0.72 ln YAG - 0.07 ln r + 0.33 ln IA (7.20)*** (-2.03)* (2.78)***	0.993	0.11	1303.35	1.14
3.2	$\ln M_2$	= -2.34 + 0.53 ln YAG - 0.04 ln r + 0.50 ln IA (6.25)*** (-1.44) (4.98)***	0.995	0.11	1807.25	0.91
3.3	$\ln M_1$	= -0.25 + 0.80 ln YNAG - 0.02 ln r + 0.22 ln IA (16.37)*** (-1.40) (3.81)***	0.998	0.06	4945.48	1.76
3.4	$\ln M_2$	= -0.47 + 0.62 ln YNAG - 0.002 ln r + 0.39 ln IA (16.08)*** (-0.14) (8.34)***	0.999	0.05	7934.94	1.20
3.5	$\ln M_1/POP$	= -2.07 + 0.60 ln Y/POP - 0.03 ln r + 0.22 ln P + 0.21 ln IA (4.11)*** (-1.15) (1.23) (2.07)**	0.996	0.07	1487.14	1.42
3.6	$\ln M_2/POP$	= -1.73 + 0.31 ln Y/POP - 0.008 ln r + 0.33 ln P + 0.37 ln IA (2.69)** (-0.35)(2.30)** (4.66)***	0.997	0.07	2371.51	1.22
3.7	$\ln M_1/P$	= -8.32 + 0.58 ln Y_p - 0.02 ln r + 0.42 ln POP (3.40)*** (-0.27) (2.06)**	0.980	0.07	424.75	1.47
3.8	$\ln M_2/P$	= -7.96 + 0.19 ln Y_p + 0.02 ln r + 0.80 ln POP (1.84)* (0.61) (6.56)***	0.993	0.06	1236.06	1.50
3.9	$\ln M_r$	= -21.91 + 0.64 ln Y_p + 0.17 ln IA + 0.02 ln FER + 0.18 ln GFD (9.98)*** (2.65)** (0.69) (2.33)**	0.997	0.07	2266.06	1.72

Note : Figures in parentheses and asterisks have the same meanings as explained in Table 1.0.

function may be specified as

$$M_t = \delta_0 Y_t^{\delta 1} r_t^{\delta 2} P_t^{\delta 3} IA_t^{\delta 4} e^{ut} \qquad .....(3)$$

For empirical estimation, the equation (3) can be expressed the following loglinear form:

$$\ln M_t = 1n\delta_0 + \delta_1 1nY_t + \delta_2 1nr_t + \delta_3 1nP_t + \delta_4 1nIA_t + U_t \qquad ....(3)'$$

Where M_t is the demand for money, Y_t is the income, r_t is the rate of interest, P_t is the price level, IA_t is the interest bearing assets consisting of fixed deposits and saving deposits of the commercial banks and U_t is the disturbance term used for representing the other relevant explanatory variables.

The coefficients are expected to be

$$\delta_1 > 0, \delta_2 < 0, \delta_3 < 0, \delta_4 > 0$$

The regression results are summarized in Table 3.0 using M_1, M_2 and M_r definitions of money. Prior to the discussion of different categories of the demand for money function, it would be worthwhile to know whether the inclusion of various variables cause any difference in the estimated demand function.

It may be seen from Table 3.0 that the elasticity of income in all equations turns out to be less than one, indicating economies of scale in the management of cash balance. The income elasticity estimated from the agricultural sector (YAG) in equation (3.2) is 0.53 for broad definition of money and this elasticity is near to Baumol-Tobin's prediction (0.5). However, the highest income elasticity (.80) is obtained from the non-agricultural sector (YNAG) in equation (3.3) for narrow definition of money. Furthermore, it can be observed that the coefficients of agricultural and non-agricultural income in the case of M_1 and M_2 definition of money are statistically significant at 1% level with the expected sign. The coefficient of non-agricultural income is greater than that of the agricultural one. It suggests that non-agricultural income has greater impact on the demand for money function. This is because the business households or community and private institutions hold the stocks of both narrow and broad money engaged in various non-agricultural activities in Nepal.

The rate of interest (r) on both types of narrow and broad definitions of money, though having expected sign, is not statistically significant in explaining the variations in nominal or real money balances. Out of the eight estimates of the interest rate elasticities, only one in equation (3.1) is found to be significant at 10% level of significance. All these indicate a negative sign except in one equation (3.8), where the population variable (POP) is included explicitly in the demand for broad real money balances. From these estimates, it can be concluded that the estimated parameters lie numerically between the highest value of .07 and the lowest value of .002. This indicates very little influence of rate of interest on the demand for money. To search an appropriate determinant of money demand, interest-bearing assets (IA) considered by Laumas (1978: 615) have been included as a measure of the opportunity cost of holding of money. For M_2 definition of money, the maximum elasticity of (IA) is .50 in equation (3.2) and for M_1 definition of money it is .33 in equation (3.1). It shows that the fixed and saving deposits may not be considered as luxury assets.

The price variable (P) in equation (3.5) has a significant effect on narrow money (M_1) with positive sign and for broad money (M_2) in equation (3.6) has the same sign with a magnitude significantly different from zero. This elasticity has unexpected sign and has no indication of homogeneity condition in the demand for money function.

For the influence of population (POP), it is found that an increase in the size of population would enlarge the attractiveness of money balances. The elasticity of population in equation (3.7) and (3.8) indicates the expected sign and is statistically significant at 5% and 1% level. The value of R^2 is extremely high and F statistic exceeds its critical value by a large margin for all estimated equations.

With reserve money (M_r) the demand equation (3.9) is estimated in logarithmic form, using the real income (Y_p), interest bearing assets (IA), foreign exchange reserve (FER) and the government fiscal deficit (GFD) as explanatory variables. For the inclusion of GFD in the demand for money function, Aghevli & Khan (1978) and Krishnamurti (1984) have pointed out that in developing countries, there is a tendency of persistent budgetary deficits and issuing currency notes by the central bank finances most of it. Thus, the process of automatically monetizing deficits has an effect on the demand for reserve money. In equation (3.9), the real income variable is highly significant at 1% level and the other two variables IA and GFD are statistically significant at 5% level. The coefficient of FER is statistically insignificant, suggesting its negligible role to be played in determining the demand for reserve money.

A close examination of the overall results reported in Table 3.0 reveals that the income elasticity of the demand for money is positive and significantly less than unity. This result, therefore, suggests that money has the characteristic of essential good in Nepal. The argument for the opportunity cost elasticity is not justified by the rate of interest because of its insignificant t-value in almost estimated equations though it has the expected sign. Rather, the inclusion of interest bearing assets in the demand for money function as an argument of the opportunity cost elasticity gives a statistically good fit in all equations. Finally, the statistical tests suggest the importance of alternative assets in Nepalese economy.

4.Semi-Loglinear Model

From the above discussion it is clear that the interest rate is not an appropriate argument for the opportunity cost of holding money. As mentioned by Frenkel (1977) and Wong (1977), the expected rate of inflation serves as the true opportunity cost of holding money for developing economies. On the basis of this judgment, it can be argued that in a situation of rising prices, nominal interest rate may not be the proxy for the opportunity cost of holding money.

The rate of inflation in Nepal has been in double digits for fifteen years out of thirty years of the sample period. However, the rate of interest in saving deposits during this period remained more or less the same (see, Appendix-E). Therefore, it would be desirable to include the rate of inflation as the best opportunity cost variable in the demand for money function. It is important to note that the rate of inflation is negative in some of the years of the sample period creating problems in estimating the loglinear model. In this case, semi-loglinear model is appropriate and is applied for those variables, which were found negative. Thus, the model is specified in the following form:

$$\ln M_t/P = \varnothing_0 + \varnothing_1 \ln Y_{pt} + \varnothing_2 \ln r_t + \varnothing_3 \eth_t + U_t \quad ....(4)$$

where M_t/P is the demand for real money balances, Y_{pt} is the real income represented by the real GDP, r_t is the rate of interest, $\eth_t$ is the rate of inflation proxie by the rate of change in consumer price index and U_t is the disturbance term.

The parameters are expected to be

$$\varnothing_1 > 0, \varnothing_2 < 0, \varnothing_3 < 0$$

The results obtained from the different regression equations for M_1,M_2 and M_r definitions of money are presented in Table 4.0.

Table 4.0: Regression Results

Semi-Loglinear Model (1965-94) (Annual data)

Equation	*Dependent Variable*	*Constant*	*Coefficients or independent Variables*			*Statistic*			
			$\ln Y_{pt}$	$\ln r_t$	$\eth_t$	R^2	SEE	F	DW
4.1	$\ln M_{1t}/P$	-11.49	.92	.11	-.06	.98	.07	434.34	.45
			(24.58)***	(2.93)***	(-2.66)**				
4.2	$\ln M_{2t}/P$	-17.09	.83	.23	-.03	.98	.10	488.83	.65
			(23.52)***	(6.25)***	(-1.26)				
4.3	$\ln M_{rt}$	-33.8	.95	.07	-.005	.99	.11	1355.86	1.56
			(44.25)***	(3.31)***	(-.35)				

Note : Figures in parentheses and asterisks have the same meanings as explained in Table 1.0.

From Table 4.0, it is apparent that the income elasticity of the demand for money (M_1, M_2 and M_r) is less than unity, lying within the range of 0.83 to 0.95. It reveals that money does not appear to be a luxurious commodity in the economy. Comparing the t-values of the real income variable (Ypt) in the equation (4.1) with its counterpart in the other two equations suggest the real income as a significant factor in determining the demand for money. The interest rate elasticity in all the three equations is statistically significant with incorrect sign. In this respect, Cooley & Leroy (1981 :825) have argued that a positive coefficient, particularly a significantly positive would be considered as a fact-raising question about the validity of the theory. The result, therefore, seems to justify the inappropriateness of the semi- log model in relation to the interest rate variable.

Crockett and Evans (1980), Driscoll and Lahiri (1983) and Metwally and Rahman (1990) have pointed out the static price expectation or inflation in developing countries as an appropriate determinant in case of the annual data used to estimate the demand for money. Thus, the rate of inflation is included in this model as an additional determinant in case of the annual data used to estimate the demand for money. Thus, the rate of inflation is included in this model as an additional determinant of money demand. As for the inflation rate is concerned, it is significantly negative at 5% level in equation (4.1) but in other equations, it is found insignificant with expected sign. This indicates some support for the existence of exceptional effect in the demand for money and the public may sacrifice liquidity for hoarding goods and physical assets to get rid of inflation.

The values of R^2 and F statistic suggest goodness of fit, but the DW statistic in all estimated equations put forward the evidence of positive serial correlation. To deal with the problem, an attempt has been made to re-estimate the demand for money equation in the first difference form by using autoregressive lag scheme in section 5. Further, to measure the impact of physical assets, Mckinnon complementarily hypothesis including real rate of interest has been employed as an alternative approach to the demand for money.

4.1 McKinnon's Hypothesis

Mckinnon (1973)[4] came out with an alternative suggestion when monetary theories became inappropriate for explaining the dominance of real money balances in the operation of capital market in developing nations (Sampath & Hussain, 1981:31). Applying McKinnon's hypothesis, Fry (1978) found a little evidence in a search for complementarities in the demand for money function. Thus, with the help of this hypothesis it has been attempted to determine the demand for money in Nepal, using annual data for the period 1975-94.

The demand for money in real form may be expressed as

$$M/P = f(Y_p, I/Y, R-\pi) \quad ....(4.1)$$

where M/P is the real money demand, Y_p is the real income, I/Y is the ratio for gross investment to income and R- π is the real rate of interest.

Thus, we can estimate the demand for money function, using both definitions of money in the semi-loglinear form:

$$\ln M_1/P = \gamma_0 + \gamma_1 \ln Y_p + \gamma_2 \ln I/Y + \gamma_3(R-\pi) \quad ....(4.1.1)$$

$$\ln M_2/P = \gamma_{0'} + \gamma_{1'} \ln Y_p + \gamma_{2'} \ln I/Y + \gamma_{3'}(R-\pi) \quad ....(4.1.2)$$

The regression results pertaining to the above equations are given below in Table 4.1.

Table 4.1 : Regression Results McKinnon's Hypothesis in Semi-Loglinear Model (1975-94)

(Annual data)

Equation	*Dependent Variable*	*Constant*	*Coefficients or independent Variables*			*Statistic*			
			$\ln Y_{pt}$	$\ln r_t$	$ð_t$	R^2	SEE	F	DW
4.1	$\ln M_1/P$	-10.64	.86	.12	.09	.99	.06	225.46	1.38
			(11.59)***	(1.55)	(2.42)**				
4.2	$\ln M_2/P$	-13.69	.77	.22	.10	.98	.08	266.14	1.15
			(11.20)***	(3.18)***	(2.84)**				

Note : Figures in parentheses and asterisks have the same meanings as explained in Table 1.0.

Table 4.1 reveals that the coefficient of income elasticity for both money demand functions is less than unity and statistically significant at 1% level. Similarly, the coefficient real interest rate for both cases is significant at 5% level. However, for M_1 definition of money the elasticity of investment to income is not statistically significant though it is highly significant at 1% level for M_2 definition of money.

On the whole, all the estimated parameters have proper signs as suggested by Mckinnon. The overall explanatory performance of the model is better than the other conventional models. Furthermore, the empirical findings imply that money and physical assets are complementary rather than substitutes in the context of our economy. Thus, the general conclusion derived from this discussion is that Mckinnon hypothesis is clearly justified by the availability of annual data.

5.0 Autoregressive Distributed Lag Model

The conventional models discussed so far assumed the instantaneous adjustment of actual stock of money to its desired level. But in actual practice, this may not be true and only a part of the money balances may be adjusted to the desired value over a given time period. The basic notion is that the people do not adjust their money holdings instantaneously due to some reasons like inertia, ignorance, delay in decision-making etc. Thus, to capture the sluggish adjustment of money holdings towards desired level, some empirical attempts [Feige (1967), Starleaf (1970), Solvin & Suskha (1975), Laumas and Mehra (1976)] have been made with the distributed lag formulations. The lag structure is assumed to be in geometric form and is reduced by the method of Koyck transformation. In this respect, both partial adjustment and adaptive expectations models have been applied to justify the use of distributed lags.

5.1 Partial Adjustment Model

A convenient framework for examining the adjustment of actual stock of money balances to its desired level is Nerlovian partial adjustment model. Following this, Chow (1966) has argued that the application of partial adjustment model would make it possible to distinguish between the long run (or equilibrium demand) and short run demand functions. Jumping ahead to the modern era and accepting the views of some adherents [Valentine (1977), Milbourne (1983), Fair (1987) and Habibulla (1990)], we can postulate the desired level of the demand for money function, which may be expressed in loglinear form:

$$\ln M_t^* = \ln a_c + a_1 \ln Y_t + a_2 \ln P_t/P_{t-1} + U_t \qquad .....(5.1.1)$$

where Mt* is the desired or long run demand for money represented by the nominal money balances, Y_t is the aggregate

TABLE 5.1 : Regression Results
First Difference Form (Partial Adjustment Model) : 1966-94

(Annual data)

Eq.	*Dependent variable*	*Constant* *Independent variables*	R^2	*SEE*	*Statistic* *F*	*DW*	*Gh*
5.1.4.1	$\ln M_{1t}$	$= 0.66 + 0.15 \ln Y_t + 0.009 \ln r_t + 0.84 \ln M_{1t-1}$	0.998	0.05	5376.07	2.35	1.29
		(1.18) (0.85) (6.70)***					
5.1.4.2	$\ln M^{2t}$	$= -0.42 + 0.07 \ln Y_t + 0.02 \ln r_t + 0.92 \ln M_{2t-1}$	0.999	0.03	15932.3	2.38	1.09
		(1.28) (2.16)** (15.62)***					
5.1.4.3	$\ln M_{1t}/P$	$= -0.33 + 0.30 \ln Y_{pt} + 0.03 \ln r_t - 0.11 \ln Pt/Pt\text{-}1 + 0.71 \ln M_{1t}/P\text{-}1$	0.991	0.05	682.02	2.41	1.40
		(2.68)** (1.13) (-5.04)*** (6.18)***					
5.1.4.4	$\ln M_{2t}/P$	$= 1.82 + 0.10 \ln Y_{pt} + 0.04 \ln r_t - 0.09 \ln P_t/P_{t-1} + 0.89 \ln M_{2t}/P\text{-}1$	0.998	0.03	2938.98	2.41	1.17
		(2.03)* (2.74)** (-7.93)*** (14.83)***					

Note : Figures in parentheses and asterisks have the same meanings as explained in Table 1.0.

nominal income denoted by the national GDP, r_t is the long term rate of interest proxies by the 12 month fixed deposit rate, P_t/P_{t-1} is the ratio of current year to the previous year consumer price index. It has been used as a proxy variable for the expected rate of inflation. U_t is the disturbance term.

Since the desired demand is not directly observable, we have to make an adjustment in the above equation (5.1.1) through the partial adjustment mechanism. Symbolically,

$$\ln M_t - \ln M_{t-1} = \lambda (\ln M_t^* - \ln M_{t-1}) \qquad ....(5.1.2)$$

where λ is the coefficient of adjustment with $0 < \lambda$ 1.

Combining the equation (5.1.1) and (5.1.2) and rearranging the terms , we have

$$\ln M_t = \lambda \ln a_0 + \lambda a_1 \ln Y_t + \lambda a_2 \ln r_t + \lambda a_3 \ln P_t/P_{t-1} + (1-\lambda) \ln M_{t-1} + \lambda U_t \qquad ....(5.1.3)$$

For the estimation purpose, we may write the equation (5.1.3) in the following form :

$$\ln M_t = A_0 + A_1 \ln Yt + A_2 \ln r_t + A_3 \ln P_t/ P_{t-1} + a_4 \ln M_{t-1} + V_t \qquad ....(5.1.4)$$

where $A_0 = \lambda \ln a_0$, $A_1 = \lambda a_1$, $A_2 = \lambda a_2$, $A_3 = \lambda a_3$, $A_4 = 1 - \lambda$, $V_t = \lambda U_t$

The regression results based on the short-run demand function (5.1.4) are presented in Table 5.1.The data from the equations 1 and 2 reveal that short- run elasticity of income is statistically insignificant even though the interest rate elasticity in the second equation is found significant with inappropriate sign. The coefficient of lagged money stock variable in both equations is highly significant at 1% level. The adjustment coefficient (λ) ranges from .08 to .16. It implies that the actual money holding adjusts quite slowly towards the desired level at an annual rate of 16% for narrow money (M_{1t}) and 8% for broad money (M_{2t}).

It is observed that the estimated DW for M_{lt} is above 2 and lies in the acceptance region. But for M_{2t}, it falls in the zone of indecision indicating the test to be inconclusive. Furthermore, the DW statistic in autoregressive model, using annual data is not appropriate. Thus, in order to detect the presence of the first order autocorrelation, the Durbin- h test[5] has been applied. The use of Dh statistic in both equations shows the evidence that there is no problem of the first order serial correlation. Considering the overall results, we come to know that in equation first and second no matter what definition of money stock and interest rate are used, the lagged money stock variable is always significant. The adjustment coefficient in both M_{1t-1} and M_{2t-1} variables suggests the results consistent with Goldfeld (1976) and Santomero & Seater (1981) who found the lower speed of adjustment in the nominal partial adjustment model.

While comparing these equations with the third and fourth of the real partial adjustment models, we find better results including the expected rate of inflation as the opportunity cost variable. The coefficient of real income shows its better influence on narrow definition of real money balances in comparison to the broad definition. However, the coefficient of interest rate for both equations appears significant with inappropriate positive sign contributing to financial deepening in the Nepalese economy as suggested by Tseng and Corker (1991:11). The expected rate of inflation is negative and significantly different from zero. It suggests that the expected rate of inflation in addition to the rate of interest in ADL model is a significant determinant of the real money balances.

On the basis of various statistic employed, these equations appear quite satisfactory in terms of R^2 and F values. The adjustment coefficient in both equations ranges from .11 to .29, implying that about 11% for broad money and 29% for narrow money of the discrepancy between the desired and actual real money balances can be eliminated in a year. This type of slow adjustment in the short-run money demand function may be due to the presence of bottlenecks hampering the quick adjustment of money demand. Durbin h Statistic is rather small in both equations, leading to the acceptance of hypothesis of no first order serial correlation.

The comparison of statistical results obtained from all four equations mentioned above indicates the superiority of real partial adjustment model. Thus, it can be inferred that the equations with real partial adjustment are more appropriate for the estimation of the short run money demand functions.

With regard to the experiment of the first order difference

form of the demand for money, Artis and Lewis (1979), Haque (1989) and Boughton (1991) supported the hypothesis that if there is high degree of autocorrelation in the error of equation, the standard error of the regression will not be meaningful. So, the best fit for estimating the ADL model occurs when the short rate is excluded. Keeping these views in mind and following the ideas proposed by Gujarati (1978: 272), we estimated the long-run elasticity of the demand for money function. Dividing the coefficient of income, interest rate and expected rate of inflation in the third and fourth equations by the adjustment coefficient and dropping lagged dependent variables, we have

$$\ln M_{1t}/P = -1.14 + 1.03\ln Y_{pt} + .10\ln r_t - .38\ln P_t/P_{t-1} \quad \text{....(5.1.4.5)}$$

$$\ln M_{2t}/P = 16.54 + 0.91\ln Y_{pt} + .36\ln r_t - .82\ln P_t/P_{t-1} \quad \text{....(5.1.4.6)}$$

These estimates of long-run income elasticity of both narrow and broad real money balances are higher than that of short run real money balances. Moreover, the long-run income elasticity corresponding to the M1definition of money is greater than unity. It is a fairly standard result in developing countries in conformity with the observation made by Aghevli et al (1979: 790). However, the magnitude of income elasticity in M2 definition provides the validity to arguments of Paul (1992) and Barari (1996) that the real income elasticity in developing countries is declining in recent years. Thus, on comparing with the income elasticity of these two equations, it can be concluded that Nepalese people prefer narrow real money balances rather than broad one both in short and long run.

5.2 Adaptive Expectations Model

Adaptive expectations model as a rationalizing way of Koyck model has been used here to determine the future course of price in the demand for money function. This model is based on behavioural hypothesis, which states money demand function in the following form:

$$M_t = b_0 + b_1 Y_t + b_2 r_t + b_3 P\ddot{y}_t^e + U_t \quad \text{....(5.2.1)}$$

where M_t is the demand for money (nominal balances), Y_t is the aggregate nominal income (nominal GDP), r_t is the rate of interest (on fixed deposits of CBs), $P\ddot{y}_t^e$ is the expected price level and U_t is the disturbance term.

TABLE 5.2 : Regression Results
First Difference Form (Adaptive Expectations Model) : 1966-94

(Annual data)

Eq.	*Dependent variable*		*Constant* / *Independent variables*	*Statistic* R^2	*SEE*	*F*	*DW*
1	M_{1t}	=	$-72.95 + 0.14\ Y_t - 0.03\ r_t + 0.002\ P_t + 0.60\ Y_{t-1} + 0.009\ r_{t-1} + 0.26\ M_{1t-1}$	0.999	167.5	9439.8	2.76
			(1.25) (–3.30)*** (0.36) (4.41)*** (1.02) (2.11)**				
2	M^{2t}	=	$-147.86 - 0.19\ Y_t - 0.02\ r_t + 0.002\ P_t + 0.74\ Y_{t-1} - 0.007\ r_{t-1} + 0.46\ M_{2t-1}$	0.999	493.4	6486.25	1.77
			(–1.46) (–2.07)** (0.38) (4.67)*** (–0.62) (4.28)***				

Note : Figures in parentheses and asterisks have the same meanings as explained in Table 1.0.

Since, the expected price is not directly observable, it is supplemented with the hypothesis, known as adaptive expectations. It is important to note that expectations are seldom fully realized. There is usually a gap between actual price and expected price. On the basis of this discrepancy, the adaptive expectation employed by Friedman (1959) may be stated as

$$P_t^e = P^e_{t-1} + \delta(P_t - P^{-e}_{t-1}) \quad ....(5.2.2)$$

where δ is the coefficient of expectation and such that $0 \leq \delta \leq 1$.

Substituting the equation (5.2.2) into (5.2.1), we have

$$M_t = b_0 + b_1 Y_t + b_2 r_t + b_3[P^{-e}_{t-1} + \delta(P_t - P^e_{t-1})] + U_t \quad ...(5.2.3)$$

To eliminate P_t^e in equation (5.2.3), lagged (5.2.1) by one period, multiplying it by the coefficient of decay (1- ä), subtracting the product from (5.2.3) and making some algebraic transformation, we have

$$M_t = b_0\delta + b_1 Y_t - b_1(1-\delta)Y_{t-1} + b_2 r_t - b_2(1-\delta)r_{t-1} + b_3\delta P_t + (1-\delta)M_{t-1} + V_t \quad ....(5.2.4)$$

where $V_t = U_t - (1-\delta)U_{t-1}$

Now, the equation (5.2.4) contains all the variables in observable form. The regression results derived from the estimating equation (5.2.4) are summarized in Table 5.2.

The results obtained from both equations (Table 5.2) seem to indicate that current income (Y_t) does not provide a better explanation of the money demand when lagged dependent variable is introduced in the model. This conclusion is consistent with Motley's (1967) view in order to analyze the path of dynamic equilibrium. The coefficients of lagged income and current interest rate yield significant t-values for both M_{1t} and M_{2t} equations.

By taking into account the views of Villanueva (1971), Goldfeld (1973) and Trivedi (1983), the actual rate of change in price level or inflation ($\dot{P}_t$) as an empirical measure of the price expectation has been included in M_{1t} and M_{2t} equations. However, in practice, this variable does not underline the role of price expectation. This yields insignificant t- values in both the demand for money functions. Thus, the evidence of appropriate lagged interest rate variable shows the non-monetized environment of the Nepalese economy. In this respect, partial adjustment mechanism mentioned in section 5.1

performs better than price expectation one.

Despite these, lagged values of the money stock variable for M_{1t} and M_{2t} equations are significant at 5% and 1% level respectively. The estimated coefficients of the lagged money stock variables indicate the annual completion of 74% adjustment between desired and actual holdings for narrow money balances and 54% adjustment for broad money balances. Thus, from these results it may be concluded that lagged income to be a better scale variable than current income. However, the current rate of interest in spite of its lagged rate performed as a better opportunity cost variable in the short-run demand for money.

It is worth noting here that the lagged income appeared significant in both M_{1t} and M_{2t} equations. It manifests the presence of lag pattern or the response of expected income in the economy. Thus, to measure the influence of lagged income in the demand for nominal money balances, Almon polynomial lag technique has been applied in the following section.

5.3 The Almon Polynomial Lag Model

The Almon polynomial lag as an alternative approach to the Koyck distributed lag model has been used here to find out the response of lagged or expected income variable in the demand for money function. With the Almon technique (1965), money demand is regressed on the construction income variable on the basis of the degree of polynomial and length of the chosen lag. Here, the second-degree polynomial with the three previous periods has been selected for the purpose of analysis. However, with this method the empirically derived lag coefficients due to their insignificant t-values[6] (for details, see Notes) do not allow us to conclude whether the partial adjustment or adaptive expectation phenomenon is correct and applicable for the estimation of short as well as long run money demand function. Thus, from this analysis it may be inferred that the Almon technique does not provide better result as compared to the partial adjustment and adaptive expectations models although it overcomes some of the problems associated with the Koyck model theoretically.

5.3.2 Simultaneous Equations System

Thus, so far, we are concerned with the estimation of various parameters in order to find the relationship under the single equation system. The unidirectional relationship may not be meaningful if we find more than one equation to understand the multiple influences among the variables. Thus, in these circumstances, if one applies OLS procedure to estimate the parameters of each equation without considering other equations of the system, the estimates so obtained may not be only biased but also inconsistent (Gujarati, 1978: 336).

This section is confined to examine the problem of simultaneity in the estimation of the demand for money function. One of the important ways of looking at the simultaneity problem in money demand studies is to formulate a system consisting of demand for and supply cf money equations. The second step is to estimate the parameters by using single (OLS) and simultaneous (2SLS) equations method. The final step is to draw inferences about the importance of the simultaneity factor by comparing the relative performance of these methods (Kamaiah, 1984: 346). In this regard, the attempt made by Cooley and Leroy (1981) was totally inadequate. So, they were not convinced by their current attempt to compute a money demand equation. Carr and Darby (1981) considered the two equations system for eight industrial countries and recognized that OLS method would yield inconsistent results.

Needless to say, the demand for money is not an observable variable. So, the empirical estimation of the demand for money requires explicit specification of the supply of money function. In view of this, we can formulate the simultaneous equation model as:

$$M_d = \alpha_0 + \alpha_1 Y_t + \alpha_2 r_t + \alpha_3 P_t + U_t \quad ....(1)$$
$$M_s = \alpha_0 + \beta_1 Y_{t-1} + \beta_2 rt + \beta_3 GFD_t + V_t \quad ....(2)$$
$$M_d = M_s = M_t \quad ....(3)$$

Equation (1) is the demand for nominal money balances, where Y_t represents nominal income (or GDP), r_t represents nominal rate of interest and P_t represents the price level. V_t is random variable whose mean value is expected to be zero. Equation (2) is the supply of nominal money balances, where

TABLE 5.3.2 : Regression Results Simultaneous Equations Model (1966-94)

(Annual data)

Eq.	*Method*	*Depend. var.*	*Const.*	*Coefficient of independent variables* Yt	Yt-1	rt	Pt	GFDt	*Statistic* R^2	F	DW
1	OLS	Md	–246.97	1.32	—	-0.01	-0.32	—	0.997	3253.05	1.50
				(13.54)***		(-0.63)	(-3.14)***				
	2SLS	Md	–300.24	1.47	—	0.008	-0.48	—	0.998	14340.8	2.13
				(29.85)***		(1.03)	(-9.32)***				
2	OLS	Ms	–3574.96	0.14	1.03	—	—	-0.18	0.998	3995.15	0.79
				(0.69)	(5.04)***			(-4.23)***			
	2SLS	Ms	–3566.52	0.18	0.99	—	—	(-0.18)	0.998	3964.4	0.78
				(0.53)	(2.96)***			(-4.13)***			

Note: Figures in parentheses and asterisks have the same meanings as explained in Table 1.0.

Y_{t-1} is the lagged GDP which indicates previous period income. GFD_t is the fiscal deficit. V_t is the random variable. Equation (3) is the equilibrium condition, which makes equality between demand and supply in the money market. Thus, the system has two structural equations with one identity. As suggested by Bhattacharya (1974) and Aghevli (1975), the 2SLS method is employed to overcome simultaneous equations bias.

For the purpose of estimation, the system of equations (1) to (3) is undertaken for using OLS and 2SLS methods into two phases. In the first phase, OLS method is applied directly in the individual equation to obtain the parameter estimates. In the second phase, both demand and supply equations are brought under the reduced form to determine the identification of an equation in the system. The application of the rule of identification (rank and order condition)[7] reveals that both estimating equations are over identified requiring the use of 2SLS procedure. Thus, we have estimated both demand and supply equations in the system given above and the results thus obtained are presented in Table 5.3.2.

It is apparent from Table 5.3.2 that in the demand equation (M_d), the income (Y_t), interest rate (r_t) and price level (P_t) are introduced as major determinants. The coefficient of income in both OLS and 2SLS methods is correct and statistically significant at 1% level. However, the coefficient of interest rate appears to be insignificant with the right sign in OLS but it is presented incorrectly in 2SLS with the wrong sign. Likewise, in both OLS and 2SLS procedures, the coefficient of price variable seems to be significant with the negative sign. It implies that money is considered as a consumer's durable and the demand for it declines as a result of increase in prices. Regarding the positive sign of the rate of interest in both demand and supply equations, it is expected from Poloz's (1980: 411) statement that the shocks arisen in the real side of the economy would cause national income and the rate of interest to move in the same direction. Thus, one can expect the resulting simultaneous equations bias of two parameters to be of the same sign.

The coefficient of Y_t in the supply equation (M_s) is insignificant with correct sign in OLS as well as in 2SLS. One possible reason for the insignificance of Y_t may be the high degree of correlation between Y_t and Y_{t-1}. The coefficient of GFD_t is statistically significant with the negative sign indicating an increase in the deficit of the government budget to have adverse impact on the money supply in the country. In addition to this, in terms of the statistical evidences (R^2, F value & DW statistic), it may be inferred that there is no risk if money demand function is estimated independently. However, this finding may be considered as tentative at macro level due to implicit assumptions of the simultaneous equations model and the small-scale experiment on the relevant determinants of the money demand. Furthermore, in respect of the measurement of the extent of the bias (difference of OLS & 2SLS estimates), the analysis of the money demand has indicated that earnest pursuit of the money stock targets may give rise to positive bias (180.0%) in the interest rate. Considering this variability in the magnitude of the bias, it can be suggested that it is desirable to monitor the situation carefully by the NRB as a central bank in order to regulate the money market effectively. Thus, a comparison between OLS and 2SLS estimates of the parameters indicates that 2SLS provides better results in all estimates except in interest rate. Furthermore, it removes the problems of OLS biasness and autocorrelation in the demand for money functions.

5.4 Empirical Findings

The major findings from the empirical analysis of the demand for money models are summarized as follows:

1. The demand for money in Nepal over the sample period 1965-94 can be best interpreted by the income as a scale variable and the expected rate of inflation and interest bearing assets as opportunity cost variables.
2. Chow test is conducted to investigate the stability for the three alternative definitions of money in the demand function. From the test of stability, a stable relationship is maintained in all definitions of money.
3. The overall results of the linear models conclusively point out the superiority of narrow (M_1) definition over the broad (M_2) definition of money. The coefficient of income, interest

rate and price level together with the value of R^2 and F statistic on M_1 demand function are by and large higher than M_2 function. DW statistic also falls in the acceptance region in almost M_1 equations. This fact seems to indicate that M_1definition of money demand is more appropriate than M_2 definition providing the evidence of non-monetized economy.

4. The income elasticity of the demand for money is positive and significantly less than unity in all loglinear models suggesting that money is not a luxury asset in Nepal. It also supports the approach of Baumol and Tobin implying that there is a significant economy of scale in holding money balances.
5. The interest rate coefficients of the demand for money in linear models and interest elasticity in loglinear models are found to be low, statistically insignificant with appropriate sign and justifying the second proposition mentioned in section 5.3. However, the results obtained from fitting semi-loglinear model and ADL model show an inappropriate significant relationship of the interest rate elasticity.
6. The price elasticity is positively significant for broad money in the case of loglinear model in spite of its absolute negative coefficient in the simple linear model and simultaneous equation system. This contradictory result as suggested by Johnson (1972: 291) indicates the price instability in the economy and thereby creates uncertainty and money illusion on the part of public behaviour.
7. Mckinnon's hypothesis performs significantly better than other conventional semi-loglinear models in explaining the demand for money function. The empirical findings from this hypothesis imply that money and physical assets in Nepal are more complementary rather than substitutes.
8. There exists a lower degree of demand adjustment in the short-run demand for money function in ADL model. It suggests that there are several bottlenecks in the economy to eliminate the discrepancy between desired and actual money balances. The application of partial adjustment model seems appropriate to determine the short-run and long run money demand functions. The Dh test has performed better indication of autocorrelation.
9. The long-run demand functions in comparison to short-run demand functions have performed better. Thus, there

is no reason to believe that people in developing countries like Nepal have shorter economic time horizon of decision making as against with developed countries.

10. The presence of empirically derived insignificant lag coefficient using Almon polynomial technique does not permit us to point out the importance of lagged or expected income. This estimation through Almon model, therefore, provides support to the conclusion that current income rather than lagged one is important as a scale variable in the demand for money.
11. There is no more distinction between OLS and 2SLS procedures in the estimation of the demand for money function under the simultaneous equations system. However, by making an evaluation of the estimated parameters and statistic, it can be said that the 2SLS performs better results on contrary to the findings from OLS procedure.

5.5 Concluding Remarks

From the foregoing discussion of empirical findings it is clear that income is the major determinant of the demand for money in Nepal. The impact of wealth on the demand for money is not established due to the unavailability of data and measurement problems.

After all, judged on the basis of sign and the required level of statistical significance of income, interest rate and price level, the simple linear specification seems to be more appropriate in the context of the Nepalese economy. Thus, it is obvious that mere simple models rather than complex specifications are more fruitful and justifiable in order to confirm the formulated hypotheses.

NOTES

1. See, Lewis and Breen's (1975) study based on the least developed countries such as, India, Pakistan, Ceylon, Costa-Rica, Portugal and United Arab Republic.
2. As pointed out by Courchene and Shapiro (1964), Gupta (1970), Clinton (1973), Kamath (1984), one of the popular tests for checking the structural stability in the money demand function is the Chow test. [For details, see Gujarati, 1978: 306].

3. The formula for computing Chow test is given as:

$$F = \frac{\frac{S}{K}}{\frac{S_4}{N_1 + N_2 - 2K}}$$

Where

$S_5 = S_1 - S_4$

$S_4 = S_2 + S_3$

K = No. of parameters estimated

S_1 = Residual sum of squares of pooled regression

S_1 & S_2 = Residual sum of squares of individual regression

4. In Mckinnon's words, "money is viewed as a conduit through which accumulation takes place rather than as a competing asset..The demand for money rises *pari passu* with the productivity of physical capital" (Mckinnon, 1973: 60). The Mckinnon's conduit effect occurs if the relationship between the investment/ income ratio and aggregate demand for money is positive [Charemza and Ghatak, 1990: 1160].

5. Durbin h statistic is computed by the expression

$$Dh = 1 - \frac{DW}{2}\sqrt{\frac{N}{1 - N(\text{var } \beta)}}$$

Where N is the total number of observations. Var β is the variance of the coefficient associated with lagged dependent variable, DW is the Durbin-Watson statistic, Dh is approximately normally distributed with unit variance so that the critical value for a level of significance of 5% is ±1.960 (Two tailed test) [Turnovsky and Wohar, 1984: 622].

6. To explain how the Almon scheme works, the logarithm of money demand function depending on the logarithm of income in the current year together with the three preceding years can be specified as

$$\ln M_t = \alpha + \beta_0 \ln Y_t + \beta_1 \ln Y_{t-1} + \beta_2 \ln Y_{t-2} + \beta_3 \ln Y_{t-3} + U_t \qquad ....(5.3.1)$$

$$\text{or } \ln M_t = \alpha + \sum_{i=0}^{3} B_i \ln Y_{t-1} + U_t \qquad ....(5.3.1)'$$

Further, βi can be approximated by the second-degree polynomial in the form

$$\beta i = a_0 + a_1 i + a_2 i^2 \qquad ....(5.3.2)$$

Substituting (5.3.2) into (5.3.1) and transforming the log of Y terms in the form of the constructed variables W_{0t}, W_{1t} and W_{2t}, we have,

$$\ln Mt = \alpha + a_0 W_{0t} + a_1 W_{1t} + a_2 W_{2t} + Ut \quad \text{....(5.3.3)}$$

Applying the OLS procedure in the transformed equation (5.3.3), we can estimate the following two regressions:

$$\ln M_{1t} = -4.44 + .77W_{0t} + .24W_{1t} - .01W_{2t} \quad \text{....(5.3.4)}$$

(t values) (1.56) (.24) (-.02) $R^2 = .997$

$$\ln M_{2t} = -6.04 + .71W_{0t} + .51W_{1t} - .23W_{2t} \quad \text{....(5.3.5)}$$

(t values) (.90) (.32) (-.22) $R^2 = .993$

Now, with the help of the estimated a's coefficients given in equation (5.3.4) and (5.3.5), we can get the original β's coefficient from the relation (5.3.2). Substituting all the β's in the demand function (5.3.1), the distributed lag models become :

$$\ln M_{1t} = -4.44 + .77\ln Y_t + 1.0\ln Y_{t-1} + 1.21\ln Y_{t-2} + 1.41\ln Y_{t-3} \quad \text{....(5.3.6)}$$

$$\ln M_{2t} = -6.04 + .71 \ln Y_t + 0.99 \ln Y_{t-1} + 0.81 \ln Y_{t-2} + .17 \ln Y_{t-3} \quad \text{....(5.3.7)}$$

The resulting lag pattern of both equations helps to conclude that weights have been increasing successively in the case of narrow money model. However, for broad money weights have declined from the second previous year providing the heaviest weight in the first previous year.

7. To determine the identification of equation the rank and order is employed for two equations.

$$M_d - \alpha_0 - \alpha_1 Y_t - \alpha_2 P_t - \alpha_3 r_t = U_t \quad \text{....(1)}$$

$$M_s - \beta_0 - \beta_1 Y_t - \beta_2 Y_{t-1} - \beta_3 GFD_t = V_t \quad \text{....(2)}$$

Given that M_t and Y_t are endogenous and P_t, r_t, Y_{t-1} and GFD_t are exogenous variables of both equations. Now, applying the order condition in the system, we have

Equation	M_t	1	Y_t	P_t	r_t	Y_{t-1}	GFD_t
1	1	$-\alpha_0$	$-\alpha_1$	$-\alpha_2$	$-\alpha_3$	0	0
2	1	$-\beta_0$	$-\beta_1$	0	0	$-\beta_2$	$-\beta_3$

Then,

Equation	*No. of predetermined or exogenous variables excluded from the model (K-k)*	*No. of endogenous variables included minus one (m- 1)*	*Identified*
1	2	1	over
2	2	1	over

Hence, each equation excludes two variables and it is over identified by the order condition. Let us recheck these equations with the rank condition for identification. We consider the first equation, which excludes M_s, Y_{t-1} and GFD_t variables. For this equation to be identified, there must be at least one non-zero determinant of order 3 ×3. To get the determinant, we first obtain the relevant matrix of the coefficients of excluded variables M_s, Y_{t-1} and GFD_t included in other equations. In the present case, there is one matrix, which is called matrix A.

$$\text{i.e., } [A] = \begin{bmatrix} 1 & 0 & 0 \\ 0 & -\beta_2 & 0 \\ 0 & 0 & -\beta_3 \end{bmatrix}_{3\times 3}$$

It can be seen that the determinant of the matrix A is non-zero. i.e. $|A| \neq 0$. Therefore, the rank of matrix A is (m-1) =3. Hence, the demand equation is over identified. In the same way, we can apply the rank condition in the supply function also. For the equation, we obtain the relevant matrix of excluded variable M_d, P_t and r_t as

$$[B] = \begin{bmatrix} 1 & 0 & 0 \\ 0 & -\alpha_2 & 0 \\ 0 & 0 & -\alpha_3 \end{bmatrix}_{3\times 3}$$

and such that the determinant $|B| > 0$. Therefore, the rank of matrix $[B] = 3$. Hence, the supply equation is over identified.

CHAPTER VI

MONEY DEMAND AND CURRENCY SUBSTITUTION IN NEPAL
A Case Study

6.1 Introduction 6.2 Exchange Rate System in Nepal 6.3 Status of Indian Currency in Nepal 6.4 Business Household Demand for Money in Nepal 6.5 Currency Substitution: Theory 6.5.1 Currency Substitution between NC and IC in Nepal 6.5.2 Empirical Findings 6.6 Concluding Remarks

6.1 Introduction

The purpose of this chapter is to explain and analyze the business households' demand for money and to find out the behavior of economic agents towards currency substitution. This chapter has been divided into five sections. The first section deals with the exchange rate system in historical prospective to understand the monetary economy of Nepal. The second section comprises of a discussion of methodology of data collection in order to show the present status of Indian currency in the Nepalese business transaction. The economic relationship of money demand with the relevant explanatory variables as transactional income, interest rate, employment and the proportion of Indian currency holding to the total transaction is discussed and analyzed empirically in the third section. In section four, currency substitution theory and its implication in the demand for money is derived in the form of log linear and constant elasticity of substitution (CES) model. The last section involves concluding remarks in which policy suggestions given by respondents are included.

6.2 Exchange Rate System in Nepal

In an open economy like ours, the internal and external forces are in principle, inextricably interwoven. Monetary flows though external trades are determinants of domestic monetary condition and are affected by disturbances and pressures within the domestic money market itself (Been stock, 1977:213).

No doubt, the open border of Nepal-India is a unique border, which creates an intimate relationship between the two countries. However, from the economic point of view, it has created some problems in Nepal, viz. price hike inflation, instability in exchange rate, smuggling, population growth or penetration from illegal immigrants and refugees and its adverse effect on limited job opportunities (Rajbahak, 1992:76). The physical configuration of the border between the two countries does not present any natural barrier. Due to this feature, many people from both countries residing in and nearby border areas cross the border without any restriction to fulfill their daily requirements. Under these circumstances, an appropriate (fixed/flexible) exchange rate between Nepalese currency (NC) and Indian Currency (IC) might prove to be a tool for economic growth where both volume of trade and balance of payments are adversely affected.

Considering the historical perspective of foreign exchange rate in Nepal, the exchange rate between the two currencies was fixed officially for the first time in and around 1876 at Rs. 128.12 NC for 100 IC (Shrestha, 1981:173) and that rate remained unchanged up to 1933. The government during this period used to purchase and sell IC at the official rate in order to check the upward and downward swings in foreign exchange rate. However, the stability thus obtained did not last long (Rawat, 1974:135).

After the abolition of Tejarath system[1] in 1937, Nepal Bank Limited was established to regulate the foreign exchange transaction and credit in the market. As a result, due to the prohibition of free exchange dealing in the market, IC's transaction received back door entry at the rate of about 140 to 150 NC for 100 IC (Rawat, ibid: 136). Immediately after the outbreak of the World War II (1939), the official rate of exchange became very ineffective as soon as the value of IC started falling drastically owing to the loss of confidence towards IC. Throughout the ward period (1939-1945), the value of NC appreciated considerably due to the inflation in India and reached Rs. 65 NC for 100 IC (Rajbahak, ibid: 118). In 1946, the rate of exchange between NC and IC went down to 71 NC: 100 IC on the average. After 1947, the exchange rate turned favourable to India because of the heavy imports in Nepal. Consequently, the rate of exchange went up as high as 185 NC: 100 IC in July 1956. In this way, fluctuations in the exchange rate were remaining unabated.

It was only from April 1960 onwards, HMG declared NC fully convertible into IC at official rate of 160 NC: 100 IC. The government gave authority to the NRB to fix the exchange rate within the range of 1% in order to solve the problem of exchange rate fluctuation. Thus, from the outset it is clear that Nepal was facing numerous problems in the process of improving her monetary economy. These problems were the substitution of NC in the preference of IC, unstable foreign exchange rate, circulation of NC in the limited areas and the outflow of capital from the country. To overcome these problems, a new Foreign Exchange Regulation Act (FERA) was passed in April 1962 and was brought into action from September 1963 (Rawat, ibid: 140). As a result, the rate of exchange remained stable and the confidence in NC began to restore.

The monetary relation of Nepal and India took a new turn when IC was devalued by 36.5% in 1966. Because of this situation, the production increased in India did not keep pace with the increase in the stock of money. Like in India, price rise in Nepal had been a great problem. In order to check the artificial rise in prices and thereby to control inflation, HMG followed a number of measures to maintain the NC status quo with other convertible currencies. In consequence of this, a new exchange rate of NC vis-à-vis IC was appreciated by 57.5% and fixed at 101 NC: 100 IC (NRB, 1995:58). Despite these, revaluation of

NC in comparison with IC did not produce any change in the monetary situation of Nepal.

Since then, until 1983 Nepal had to maintain fixed exchange rates against both IC and convertible currencies particularly, the US dollar. Whenever there was a deviation between Indian rupee and US dollar, a broken cross rate had created the exchange rates between IC-dollar and NC-dollar. So, to avoid the problem of cross rate difference between IC and dollar, Nepal had to make corresponding adjustment in NC's exchange rate. By this very fact, Nepal was being engaged in multiple currency practices during the decade of 1970s. When the country adopted a unified exchange rate abolishing the dual exchange rate system in 1985. NC was pegged to a basket to currencies inclusive of Indian currency too. Since 1986, there had been a continuous depreciation of NC against foreign currency so that NC would have been devalued against US dollar by 20.9% in July 1991. However, the exchange rate of NC against IC was revalued by 1.79% and reached at 160 NC: 100 IC on the same date.

Above all, regarding an appropriate exchange rate regime, the existing system of full convertibility of NC vis-à-vis IC at officially pegged exchange rate appeared anomalous and needed to be considered for its discontinuation. In consideration of this view, the sample survey was conducted by the researcher in 1996. However, no one respondent was found in favour of the flexible exchange rate against fixed exchange rate between NC and IC. Moreover, in the wake of the fixed exchange rate regime, the involvement of IC with other convertible currencies in the basket system in Nepal made a ground to expect that NC will have greater strength in the near future and the holding of IC is no more secured from the view point of speculative purposes.

6.3 Status of Indian Currency in Nepal

There is a considerable probability that in a relatively open economy, the domestic currency will be less desirable as a store of value due to its increased exchange rate variability (Kafka, 1978: 798 & Miles, 1978:428). In conformity with this view, an outlook of exchange rate between NC and IC discussed about helps to appreciate how IC has come to occupy special position in the Nepalese economy without any significant change in its status even today.

It is very difficult to exercise monetary control in Nepal over the circulation of IC because of geographical proximity, ease of accessibility, open border system and socio-economic and cultural linkages. In addition to this, holding of IC by the public has been allowed to be legal and the means of payments also have been IC for setting the transaction between Nepal and India. These are the main factors, which have made wide area of IC circulation in the Nepalese economy. Moreover, the close link of Nepal with India as a source of supply and dependence on trade and transit facilities through India for the third world countries has proved the special position of IC in Nepal.

It is also observed that business households in Nepal mainly hold two types of currency viz. NC and IC in their portfolio. Purchase of goods in the market would be backed by NC or IC. The price of Indian goods has always been determined on the basis of exchange rate of NC vis-à-vis IC. Therefore, ICs are held in preparation for buying goods while NCs are used for the convenience in business in the internal market. The reliable data, however, for IC circulating in Nepal are not available. It is for this reason that the present study was undertaken using the primary data from August 1995 to July 1996 to find out the position of IC (share of IC) in the business transactions in Nepal.

While collecting data from sample areas, the total number of 121 households questionnaires were distributed from eastern to far-western development regions of Nepal. Of the total questionnaires distributed in the five development regions, 54 (44.63%) from Parsa and Repandehi district of central and western development regions and 39 (32.23%) from Banke of mid-western and Kailali, Kanchanpur of far-western development regions respectively. On the basis of number of households obtained from the population census in 1991, these questionnaires were distributed proportionately in the above-mentioned districts from Mechi to Mahakali boarder areas. Out of the main 16 entry points between Nepal and India, 8 were purposively chosen while collecting the data during the survey period in 1996 (see, Appendix –G).

Table 6.3.1: Holding of Indian Currency in the Business Portfolio in Nepal, 1996.

Groups	*Business Shops*	*Total Annual Transaction (Rs. in lakh)*	*Holding of IC (Rs. in lakh)*	*Share of IC (%)*
1.	Food products/ groceries	674.46	117.91	17.48
2.	Clothing/Footwear	555.12	201.89	36.37
3.	Fancy stores/Foreign goods	985.68	628.17	63.73
4.	Medical halls/Optical shops	38.52	11.27	29.26
5.	Hardware/Construction materials	262.80	82.87	31.53
6.	Electrics/Electronic goods	307.80	140.76	45.73
7.	Hotels/Lodges	62.28	37.08	59.54
8.	Travel agencies/Banking business	576.00	208.26	36.16
9.	Miscellaneous	105.12	24.45	23.26
	Total	**3567.78**	**1452.66**	**40.72**

Source: Field Survey, 1996.

If one were to generalize the survey data presented in Table 6.3.1 as indicative of IC holdings in the business transactions of the country, the third group consisting of fancy stores/foreign goods could occupy the first position (59.54%) and the sixth group comprising electric/electronic goods secured the third position (45.73%). However, the first group including food products/groceries accounted for the last position (17.48%) in holding IC in the business transactions. Thus, from this study it can be concluded that IC had played a pivotal role (40.72%) in the overall business transactions.

As a matter of fact, if one looks at data presented in Table 6.3.1, he will have a clear picture of IC used as a long-term store of value as against NC. Further, it can also be justified from the study that the private money exchange counters have been opened for the convenience of businessmen and travelers in the border areas. These counters have gained 0.0025% net return form IC's transactions by paying the selling rate (0.0015%) of IC borrowed the NRB. During the bank holidays also, these are opened for making the profits from IC's transaction by taking short-term borrowings from the business households on the provision of the payment of IC at the selling rate. The business households in Nepal, therefore, do not exhaust IC in their business portfolio.

6.4 Business Household Demand for Money in Nepal

In an open and small economy, the import demand for business households can be met easily by the supply of products from the large economies of neighbouring countries. The excess demand generated through the monetary sector creates additional demand for goods and services. If the domestic supply sector is not responsive to the demand that could be met through imports only. Thus, an increase in import of goods or services without exports would result in trade deficit and adverse balance of payments.

Regarding the analysis of the household demand for money, a study made by Lane (1992: 827) in Poland concluded that household money holdings were in some case involuntary. Under the transactions motive, domestic currency (i.e. Zolty money) was needed for purchasing goods, while in the precautionary motive consumers had to show their money alertness in the shortage of goods. Thus, in Poland, holding of foreign currency was substantial alternative to domestic currency. In addition to this, a brief survey of eight cross-sectional studies of the demand of money based on US data (1945-60) was made by Peterson. Of these studies, those of Lydall (1958), Pesek (1963) and Nieuwenburg (1969) were found unique which concluded that wealth, but not income was a relevant determinant of the demand for money. However, his study based on US data (1960-62) indicated that the income was major determining factor compared to non-human wealth[2] (Peterson, 1974: 74-75).

C.R Coates also made effort in this regard by using quarterly time series data from 1961-II to 1963- IV of 103 US firms and derived a set of hypotheses from a transaction approach to the demand for money. He found in his study that the cash holdings of firms were interest elastic and the elasticity of money with respect to transactions was less than or equal to unity (Coates, 1976: 117).

Taking all these views into consideration, an attempt has been made in this section to find out the economic relationship of business household demand of money in Nepal. Also some relevant explanatory variables as transactional income, interest rate, employment in business and the proportion of IC holding to the total transactions have been selected in the demand function. In symbolic term, the estimating model may be specified as

$$M_d = \beta_0 + \beta_1 T_y + \beta_2 R_r + \beta_3 N_b + \beta_4 H_c + U \qquad ....(1)$$

Where M_d is the business household demand for money, T_y is the transactional income, R_r is the region-wise rate of interest, N_b is the employment in business, H_c is the holding of Indian Currency and U is the stochastic disturbance term.

The expected signs of the coefficients of all explanatory variables are:

$$\beta_1 > 0, \beta_2 < 0, \beta_3 > 0 \text{ and } \beta_4 > 0$$

It is a fact that very few studies on the household demand for money are found in the developing economies due to the unavailability of reliable data. No study has yet been made on the business household demand for money in Nepal so far.

6.4.1 Data Constraints

This study is based on primary data covering the sample period from August 1995 to July 1996. In the model (1) presented above, transactional income as an explanatory variable has been counted on the basis of daily turnover of the business households. While using the data about region-wise interest rates, a dummy variable has been used as a proxy for interest rate variable. It is because the rates of interest obtained from different regions are not uniform. For this purpose, the interest rates ranged from 10 to 18 per cent are denoted by dummy for 1. It is also known as official bank rate. Other rates beyond it are called unofficial spot (bazaar) rates and represented by dummy for 0.

In this context, it may be mentioned that the explanatory power of the regression model (1) may be increased by the addition of other socio-economic variables. However, it is neither possible to quantify nor easy to include all these variables in the model. So, for this case, a portmanteau variable U has been used in the above model which includes age of business households, family size, caste, religion, education, area of location and so forth. Furthermore, it is difficult to obtain the data for estimating the value of real estate, its share in business. Mortgages and other debts etc. In spite of these constraints of primary data, the researcher is confined to limit the regression model with the above-specified variables only.

6.4.2 Empirical Analysis

The results of different parameters used in estimating the various specifications of the demand for money models are presented in Table 6.4.2

Table 6.4.2: Regression Results
Business Household Demand for Money Model, 1996

Eq.	*Dep. Var.*	*Const.*	*Independent Variables* T_y	D_r	N_b	H_c	R^2 *(a)*	*SEE (b)*	*F (c)*	*DW (d)*
1	M_d	174.21	0.77	-0.09			0.592	784.8	85.5	1.43
			(13.08)***	(-1.47)						
2	M_d	-11.91	0.67	-0.10	0.21		0.625	754.9	65.1	0.35
			(10.29)***	(-1.80)*	(3.24)***					
3	M_d	-213.35	0.68	-0.11	0.22	0.09	0.634	749.5	50.2	0.35
			(10.30)***	(-1.88)*	(3.41)***	(1.64)*				

Note: Figures in parenthesis are 't' values * denotes 10% level of significance ** denotes 5% level of significance ***denotes 1% level of significance
a) R^2: The degree of explanation of the dependent variable
b) SEE: Standard error of estimate
c) F: F statistic for the joint significance of all coefficients
d) DW: Durbin-Watson statistic for the presence of autocorrelation

An examination of t-values associated with the various coefficients reveals that the transactional income (T_y) in all models (1,2 &3) is highly significant at 1% level. It means that income variable is more responsive in explaining variations in the household demand for money (M_d). Besides, the estimates of transactional income varied regularly from 0.67 to 0.77 in all models suggest that money is not considered as 'luxury' good in the business transactions. Likewise, the dummy variable (D_r) for the rate of interest is significant in all models (2 & 3) except in the first at 10% level of significance. The right sign (negative) of interest rate variable indicates that an increase in the administered rate of interest may be expected to reduce incentives to hold money by the business households.

Apart from this, the coefficient of employment (N) in models 2 and 3 is highly significant at 1% level. It shows that the business employment is more effective to determine the household demand for money. But, the coefficient of Indian currency holding (Hc) appears significant only at 10% level. This result implies that the proportion of IC holding has a weak long-run impact on the business household demand for money in Nepal.

On the basis of statistic, it is apparent that all regression models are highly significant at 1% level, as indicated by the size of F statistic. The percentage of variation explained by the regression R^2, in general, produces better results indicating the range from 0.592 to 0.634. However, the Durbin-Watson statistics are found very low with large SEE for all regressions. So, these statistic lie below the lower limit of critical value and support the hypothesis of strong positive autocorrelation. The reason may be omission of relevant socio-economic variables from the model, which were expected to be responsive to the business household demand for money. Thus, a summary of the results obtained from regression models presented above leads rather to tentative conclusions.

First, the transactional income and employment appear to be the most relevant determinants of the business household demand for money in Nepal. Second, the region-wise interest rate has a weak response to business money demand. Third, the performance of IC holdings from long run perspective is not robust in determining the household demand for money.

6.5 Currency Substitution: Theory

This section develops the theory of currency substitution and shows its economic implications in the demand function.

Currency substitution may be defined as a phenomenon in which foreign currency denominated money replaces either wholly or partly domestic money in serving as a store of value, medium of exchange and unit of account (Erian, 1988:86). The process of shifting towards the foreign currency in the preference of residents arises from the large growing economic and financial imbalances in the domestic economy. This type of liquidity preference for foreign currency has attracted a large amount of interest among researcher. So, several studies have been made on the process of currency substitution and its economic implications.

Basically, the currency substitution may be treated both from a macro and micro point of view. Within the macro economic tradition, currency substitution may be formulated in the model form by means of portfolio demand functions. But from the micro economic point of view, it may be tested applying some approaches towards modeling the demand for money. The micro based approach was followed by Cuddington (1983:111) in order to develop the theory and Vries (1988:512) found small and negative elasticity of currency substitution in the case study of Canada and the Netherlands Antilles.

One of the most potential sources of finding specification error in the demand for money function may be the currency substitution. It refers to that condition of economy in which the expected change in exchange rate affects the demand for money in opposite direction. Thus, individuals or residents of any country may satisfy their demand for money by holding balances in more than one currency (Kremers and Lane, 1990:781).

In an increasingly integrated open economy, demand for transaction balances becomes more significant. Thus, residents of one country may hold and use several foreign currencies in their transactions. The literature on the demand for money, therefore, implies that the individual demand for each of these currencies depends on the scale of transaction and the relative rate of returns from currency substitution (Daniel & Fried, 1983: 613).

In an economy subject to currency substitution, the capital

inflows might arise not only because of a global excess demand for money but also due to a portfolio shift among currency denominations. Keeping this view in mind, Rodriguez with Calvo (1977) focused on the demand side implications of a shift between domestic and foreign currency and with Guidotti (1992) presented a theoretical framework of currency substitution. In addition to this, a general survey of currency substitution issues was found in Calvo and Vagh's (1992) study. On the whole, these studies contributed to the analysis of demand for money and its effect on the economy derived form the portfolio shifts under currency substitution. Thus, Rodriguez (1993:417) gave emphasis on the area of currency substitution. He found that the capital inflows might arise a shift in the location of foreign currency holding and ultimately affect the economic performance of the country.

The practice of currency substitution may have a significant implication for monetary policy. Following this concept, Bordo and Choudhri (1982) argued that a properly specified money demand function provided evidence in favour of currency substitution between Canadian dollar and US dollar. But they failed to find the supportive evidence for measuring the currency substitution ratios. Taking these views into account, the present study has been designed to investigate the proper currency substitution ratio between NC an IC in Nepal. To this end, the primary data during the sample period from August 1995 to July 1996 have been used.

6.5.1 Currency Substitution between NC an IC in Nepal

It is a fact that foreigners do not hold a small developing country's currency and thus the holding of domestic currency is equal to the money supply determined by the monetary authority (Chen & Tsaur, 1983:177). Nepal being an open economy, the NC and IC are considered as the available assets in the business market. Since the country is small and underdeveloped, neighbouring countries do not hold her currency. The stock of domestic currency is exogenously determined while the foreign currency stock, particularly; IC is endogenously determined in the economy.

There are mainly two reasons behind the currency substitution in Nepal. First, if the exchange rate of NC vis-à-vis IC falls, the substitution is economically feasible. Second, if a decline in IC's rate is expected to be temporary, the economic agents may rush to substitute it for NC on the assumption that after a temporary decline in the exchange rate, the IC may increase beyond its previous level. Thus, NC is held as a substitute for IC. Moreover, if IC exists as a close substitute for NC, there will be a greater degree of substitutability between these two. For this purpose, the demand for money in the form of log linear and CES 'linearized' models has been used in order to show the effect of both currencies in the demand for money function and thereby to determine the degree of substitution.

Here, it is important to argue that the continuous process of currency substitution may contribute to widen the possibility of tax avoidance, reduce monetary control over domestic liquidity, initiate capital flight from the country and weaken the effectiveness of exchange rate policy. Besides, if a significant proportion of informal financial intermediaries lie outside the formal banking system, the measurement of currency substitution will not be appropriate. Keeping these possibilities into consideration, the present study has been taken with a view of measuring the appropriate magnitude of currency substitution for economic and financial policy management.

6.5.2 *Empirical Findings*

The basic assumption about currency substitution is that the ratio of domestic to foreign currency holding depends upon the expected difference of the rate of return on both assets. Following this assumption, two types of models cited above have been employed to determine the causal relationship between money demand and the ratio of domestic to foreign currency.

It is also rational to assume that IC is substituted for NC in the informal business market. Moreover, due to the appreciation of IC against NC, the residents would like to hold a large proportion of IC in their portfolio. In this situation, if NC replaces IC in the business management, the excess supply of money will be absorbed by the money market itself. Thus, to draw a concrete solution about the business demand for money and to articulate the share of IC in the business portfolio, the estimated loglinear model results are as follows:

$$\ln Md = 2.50 + 1.2 \ln NC - .87 \ln IC - .91 \ln NC/IC$$
$$(6.11)^{***} \quad (-4.30)^{***} \quad (-5.11)^{***}$$
$$N = 121,\ R^2 = .278,\ SEE = 1.04,\ F = 15.05,\ DW = 0.11$$

All coefficients in this model are found statistically significant at 1% level even though the coefficient of IC and the currency ratio (NC/IC) have negative sign. The value of elasticity in NC is highly significant but it is found significant with negative sign in case of IC. It indicates that the higher the proportion of IC in the business market lower will be the demand for liquid money by the business households. With regard to the negative sign of currency ratio, it can be expected that business households might have been engaged in currency substitution or in invoicing practices. So, the household demands for money is found to be declining as a result of increase in currency ratio. In spite of a low R^2, the F value is highly significant which shows the explanatory power of the loglinear model.

DW statistics is below the acceptance region implying significant positive serial correlation. Fro these results, it is clear that although the equation involving IC and currency ratio (NC/IC) have wrong signs, it would provide some insight into the currency substitution. To investigate this, the above loglinear model is re-estimated by adding the square of the currency ratio in the form of 'linearized' CES model[4] (Gujarati, 1978: 331).

In the absence of an explicit model of the currency substitution, an interpretation of the role of substitution parameter via the CES function is expected to remain effective. The main reasons behind using the CES model are as follows:

(*i*) The business household demand for money depends on the transactional income in terms of both NC and IC.

(*ii*) Substitution between NC and IC is possible in the sense that both currencies flow in a parallel way in the business market.

(*iii*) No body wants to reject the use of IC as a medium of exchange in the business transaction.

Incorporating these features, the regression in the form of 'linearized' CES model is estimated as

$$\ln M_d = 2.73 + .27 \ln NC + .10 \ln IC + .28 (\ln NC/IC)^2$$
$$(2.63)^{***} \quad (1.03) \quad (3.24)^{**}$$

N = 121 R2 = 0.19 SEE = 1.10 F = 9.15 DW = 0.30

In this model, all the slope coefficients except IC's coefficient are statistically significant at 1% level although the estimated R^2 is very low. The reason for low R^2 may be due to the omission of relevant variables or specification bias in the model. Besides, the poor performance of IC holdings to money demand may be the result of ėither business money holder being insensitive to the rate of return on IC. In regard to this, perhaps a more serious problem arises in measurement bias due to the pronounced tendency of respondents in understanding their IC holding in the business portfolio. DW statistic is also low suggesting the problem of autocorrelation in the regression model. The size of F statistic shows its large value, which is significant at 1% level. It reveals a meaningful explanatory power of the regression model. However, the fundamental purpose of using this model is to derive the different structural parameters from the original CES model, which may have wide economic implications. Thus, by applying the method of algebraic derivation, we can formulate the above-linearized model in the following non-linear form:[5]

$$M_d = 15.27 [.72 (NC)^{7.31} + .28 (IC)^{7.31}]^{.05}$$

Where, γ (efficiency parameter) = 15.27, δ (distribution parameter) = 0.72,

ρ (substitution parameter) = –7.31 and v (returns to scale parameter) = 0.37

In this model, the efficiency parameter is high (15.27) and satisfies the positive restriction. The distribution parameter shows the share of NC and IC in the CES model. From this, it can be concluded that NC covers 72% of its share in the total transactional income so that the share of IC turns to 28% in the CES model.

The next important conclusion is that the elasticity of substitution (ó = -.16) between NC and IC is negative and close to the lower bound of the imposed restriction. This implies that IC is a rather imperfect substitute for NC. The low elasticity of currency substitution may be due to the peg against the exchange rate of IC involving it in the 'currency basket system'. The return to scale parameter is less than one (í =.37) indicating the diseconomies of scale from currency holdings.

If one looks at studies made by Hynes (1967) in Chile and by Diz (1970) in Argentina, one has the impression that the economies of scale are existent in the economy (Laidler, 1977:148). According to them, broad money produces higher estimates of income (or wealth) elasticity of the demand for money than narrow one. However, in a study made by Edwards (1984:498), the demand for international reserves in LDCs faces strong diseconomies of scale. Despite these, the present study though cross sectional, has presented return to scale parameter of less than one. It implies that the diseconomy of scale in currency holding is operating in the business market. In short, the primary cross-sectional data in CES model shows the evidence that economies of scale in money holdings do not always remain important.

6.6 Concluding Remarks

On the basis of empirical results presented above, the following conclusions have been derived.

The study sheds light on the nature of the business households demand for money in Nepal. The empirical results are consistent with the view that the demand for liquid money is essentially a demand for transaction medium. The estimated coefficients of transactional income, interest rate, the size of employment and the proportion of currency holdings support this view in the household demand for money functions.

The apparent performance of loglinear demand for money model provides some evidence about the currency substitution between NC and IC. The theory currency substitution predicts the optimal currency mix depending upon the expected rate of return of foreign money and the habit of holding it. Several features obtained from the replication of loglinear model in the form of CES function are noteworthy.

All the coefficient estimates of the linearised CES model have the expected sign. The elasticity of the demand for money with respect to the transactional income in terms of NC and IC is not significantly different from unity. To sum up, the estimation of the conventional CES model yields result for the determination of currency substitution parameter, economies of scale and the elasticity of substitution, which have wide economic implications for the Nepalese monetary economy.

On the whole, from this study it may be concluded that the Indian currency had occupied 42.72% of its share in the overall business transaction in Nepal (6.3.1). Thus, in order to lessen the influence of IC in the Nepalese economy some policy suggestions given by respondents are mentioned below:

* The priority should be given to the Nepalese production and the more export-oriented industries should be established.
* The government for the industrial investment gives no incentive. Heavy import of foreign foods has proved the economy as 'price taker'. As a result, the business households have to be given priority for the substitution of domestic currency to the foreign currency.
* Unproductive items, like foreign brand liquor, which has created mass health hazard and misuse of financial resources, should be banned and strictly prohibited in the economy.
* Growing smuggling and rampant corruption, which has initiated currency substitution between NC and IC, should be controlled in harmony with the monetary and fiscal measures.
* Frequent devaluation of NC against IC is not favourable for the business management. Further, it promotes instability in the economy. Thus, it is advisable to follow the fixed exchange rate policy between NC and IC.
* There should be a provision for selling Nepalese products in the Indian market in order to make appreciation in the value of NC vis-à-vis IC.
* In respect of geo-economic situation of Nepal, the fiscal policy of the government on custom duties should be fair, broad based and transparent to collect more revenue from the business households.

NOTES

1. Tejarath is a government institution established by the Rana Ranoddip Singh to give credit facilities to the general public at 5% interest rate against the reserve of gold and silver.
2. Non-human wealth includes real estate, land purchasing, house construction, mortgages, and land contracts owned etc.
3. Informal financial intermediaries consist of business speculators, Sahukars, Dhikuri owners, Indigenous bankers and so on.
4. Arrow, Chenery, Minhas and Solow (1961) had fitted the regression model for 24 separate industries using international cross-sectional data (Nelson, 1965:326). The general form of their model, known as constant elasticity of substitution (CES) function (not necessarily equal to one) has been given in the following form:

   $$M_d = \gamma[\delta.NC^{-\rho} + (1-\delta)IC^{-\rho}]^{-\upsilon\rho}\, e^{u} \qquad (1)$$

   $\gamma > 0, 0 < \gamma\ 1, \rho > 1, \upsilon > 0$

   Where, M_d is the business household demand for money. NC is the Nepalese currency, IC is the Indian currency, U is the disturbance term, γ is the efficiency parameter, δ is the distribution parameter, ρ is the substitution parameter and υ is the return to scale parameter.

   The equation (1) is nonlinear in parameters. So as to make this function into linearized form, we can use a mathematical technique known as Taylor's series expansion. Thus, with the help of Taylor's series the above equation (1) may be derived as follows:

   $$\ln M_d = \alpha_0 + \alpha_1 \ln(NC) + \alpha_2 \ln(IC) + \alpha_3 \left[\ln\frac{NC}{IC}\right]^2 + U \qquad ....(2)$$

   Where $\alpha_0 = \ln\gamma$, $\alpha_1 = \upsilon\delta$, $\alpha_2 = \upsilon(1-\delta)$, $\alpha_3 = -\frac{1}{2}\rho\upsilon\delta(1-\delta)$
5. The structural parameters of the equation (1) may be obtained readily from the following relations:

   $$\gamma = \text{Anti log}\left(\hat{\alpha}_0\right) \qquad \hat{v} = \hat{\alpha}_1 + \hat{\alpha}_2$$

   $$\hat{\delta} = \frac{\hat{\alpha}_1}{\hat{\alpha}_1 + \hat{\alpha}_2} \qquad \hat{\rho} = \frac{-2\hat{\alpha}_3(\hat{\alpha}_1 + \hat{\alpha}_2)}{\hat{\alpha}_1\hat{\alpha}_2}$$

   and the elasticity of substitution $\hat{\sigma} = \frac{1}{1+\hat{\sigma}}$

Chapter VII

MONETARY PLANNING AND POLICY IN NEPAL

7.1 Introduction 7.2 Monetary Planning: An Appraisal 7.3 Monetary Development under the Different Economic Plans 7.4 Monetary Control Instruments 7.5 Money Supply Analysis 7.6 Money Demand Implications 7.7 Monetary Policy and its Impact on Economic Activity 7.8 Concluding Remarks

7.1 Introduction

To begin with monetary planning, it would be better quote Lewis' saying:

> *"Making a plan is an exercise of implementation while implementation is a struggle with reality".*

From this statement it is clear that planning is an integral part of the economic development. Planning in general signifies a procedure in order to achieve the pre-specified objectives. The need for planning arises whenever some rational idea is required to allocate scarce resources among different competing uses for achieving maximum output and employment and to ensure balanced growth in the economy.

Monetary planning in strict sense of the word is the controlled changes in the stock of money with a view of achieving the well-defined social objectives (Gupta, 1995). From this definition it follows that monetary planning is the planning about the stock of money. Thus, monetary planning requires a thorough understanding of the working of monetary system and monetary control instruments.

All planning must be purposive. By the same token, monetary planning may also be associated with the attainment of some specific objectives as higher level of output, high employment, price stability, income equality and satisfactory balance of payments. It is well known that the amount of money demanded by the public at he maximum feasible output would be equal to the money supply. Thus, the equality between demand and supply would establish equilibrium in the money market.

Apart from this, the objective of price stability may be best served by planning. Furthermore the growth rate in money supply would be equal to the expected rate of growth in money demand at the stable price level. Monetary planning in this sense is a mechanism of allocation of money supply in order to obtain the full capacity output with price stability in the economy.

7.2 Monetary Planning: An Appraisal

It has been argued that in a non-monetized capital scarce country like Nepal, inflation is considered as an important factor of accentuating the inequality of income and wealth in the society. Moreover, an increase in money stock without raising output may be an important source of persistent inflation. Thus, in these circumstances, the objectives of monetary planning should be directed to encourage savings by expanding commercial bank branches and establishing cooperative institutions especially in rural areas, and to increase employment opportunities to reduce inequalities in the distribution of income and wealth.

While considering the objectives of monetary planning in Nepal, it seems better to concentrate on the attainment of the three fundamental objectives as the full utilization of economic resources - land, labour, capital and raw materials, price stability and the progressive growth in the living standard of the general public. As regards these objectives, Bowles and Whynes (1979) were of the view that an economic programme stimulating employment, stability and growth would be welcomed in any corner of the world.

It is believed that the objective of price stability may be best policy objective for a healthy balance of payments. Keeping a relatively stable domestic price level may encourage a source of foreign exchange receipts in terms of remittances from abroad on capital account of the balance of payments. Similarly, on trade account of the balance of payments, exports of the country would have a better chance of promotion if the domestic price level remains stable. Hence, from the viewpoint of the foreign trade, the policy of domestic price stability may be the best policy to maintain external balance in the country. Nevertheless, a source of inflation created by the continuous deficit financing of the government causes real value depreciation of all monetary assets and reduces their real rate of return. The objective of price stability in such situation seems reasonable to generate confidence about the purchasing power of all monetary assets[1]. As a result, the demand for these assets in real term would grow faster in the regime of price stability.

Taking all these issues into consideration, it may be said that the objective of price stability along with the maximum feasible output is the best component of monetary planning in Nepal. Moreover, it should be carefully watched and the money supply in the economy should be controlled because of the fact that monetary planning is based on appropriate changes in the stock of money. Finally, one more point should be noted here that fulfilling the basic needs of the people through monetary planning would be more possible rather than to make a change in the distribution of income and wealth.

7.3 Monetary Development Under the Different Economic Plans

Needless to say that for the purpose of monetary planning one should have a detailed knowledge about the relationship among monetary instruments and ultimate goals of monetary policy. In this context, once a particular plan has been envisaged and implemented, it is essential to take a postmortem of the previous plans in order to highlight the false assumptions, incorrect specifications of monetary targets, instruments and so forth. Thus, with these views, a review has been made about the monetary development in Nepal during the different plan periods.

Planning as argued by Sharma (1968) in all under developed economies has been adopted as an instrument to raise the production and thereby to raise the living standard of the people. In this connection, Nepal switched to planning in 1956 and the monetary policies of the country have been constantly geared to the needs of economy. From the planning scenario, it seems clear that the first five-year plan (1956-61) was started in September 1956. A series of the development plans since then were implemented for the fulfillment of different objectives envisaged in various plans (Pant, 1982: 142).

As against with the working of the first plan, the second plan (1962-65) was released as a preparatory plan to create the basic preconditions for nationwide economic programmes. However, the plan could not produce any marked improvement on economic condition.

On the completion of the second plan, the third plan (1965-70) was launched with a strategy of making investment not only massive in size but also more productive and growth oriented. While considering the planning on monetary field, few of the financial institutions were lending their funds usually to the large farmers than smaller ones. So, the large farmers during the third plan were the primary beneficiaries of the public credit programmes (Reejal, 1986:53).

The fourth plan (1970-75) was launched for making effective use of prior objectives enlisted in the third plan associated with the output maximization, and the long-term sustainable economic growth. In 1974 the Nepal Rastra Bank (NRB) as a central bank issued directives to commercial banks to invest 5% of their deposit liabilities as a supervised loan in small sectors[2] with a view to achieve a balanced growth in the economy. However, due to the lack of public awareness, that programme had not reached to the target groups.

Under the fifth plan period (1975-80), priority had been given to fulfill the objective of regional balanced development in the economy. In order to cope with this objective, the NRB tried to introduce Intensive Banking Development Programme on regional basis. Priority Sector Coordination Committee had been formed for the purpose of proper utilization of granting loans and for better coordination among concerned agencies. However, these programmes on the whole were found to be costlier in the form of administrative and other opportunity costs. A restriction was imposed by the NRB in 1975 on the lending of commercial banks and made compulsory fro them to invest at least 5% of their deposit liabilities on the priority basis. In addition, some adjustment had been made in interest rate structure to increase productive investment and thereby to make of favorable balance of payments. However, investment on the priority sectors was remained below the target for almost all the years.

Since the beginning of the sixth plan period (1980-85) onwards, there had been created excess liquidity in the economy due to a large increase in money supply. As a result, the rate of consumption increased while the rate of savings declined each year. In the document of the sixth plan, a reference was made for controlling credit channel in the unproductive sector with a view a keeping money supply within the required limits. In the light of this policy the NRB set up a credit planning[3] cell to strengthen to monetary control and to monitor the credit expansion (Paudel, 1992: 56).

During the seventh plan period (1985-90), there was a great pressure on the price level. The internal causes for the high rate of price increase was mainly due to the devaluation of Nepalese currency against foreign currencies (by 14.7%) as well as the high rate of increase in money supply. Moreover, a rise in prices abroad particularly in India put a great pressure on the domestic price level. In August 1989, the NRB liberalized the bank interest rates and allowed full autonomy to the commercial banks in this respect. This policy of interest rate was expected to reduce the disparity between deposit rates and lending rates of commercial banks. Consequently, the NRB raised the bank rate for the commercial banks to adopt tight monetary policy. The operation of this rate could not control the money supply expansion to the desired extent.

It was stated in the eighth plan (1992-97) that the

expansionary policy adopted in the past plans had created excessive liquidity, thereby increased money supply, and price level and trade deficit in the economy. Thus, in this connection the eighth plan had given special emphasis on better management of public expenditure, raising revenue through appropriate monetary and fiscal policies and maintaining the growth rate of money supply within the stipulated limit.

During the ninth plan (1997-2002) period, a remarkable change was brought in the area of financial development. Financial position of final companies had substantially improved. As a result, the pace of monetization was also found quite impressive (Sharma, 1989: 32). However, this process was mainly confined to some commercial centers and urban areas. Merely, little practices were done in extending banking services and monetary transaction in rural areas.

After empowering full liberty to commercial banks to adjust interest rates, NRB issued directives to all commercial banks to continue the spread interest rate regime within 5% of weighted difference in the deposit and credit portfolio with effective from 1998 (Economic Survey, 1998/99: 110). Some arrangements from the commercial banks had been enforced for the credit expansion to the deprived community. In this regard, NRB had given permission to established Rural Micro Finance Development Centre under the provision of Development Bank Act 1995. With the objective of making credit available without collateral to the people in rural areas. Village Development Bank had been established in all five-development regions. In order to supply financial resources at a lower rate of interest in priority sectors, the rate of refinancing (or the bank rate) had been reduced to 7.5% from the existing rate of 9.0% effective from April 13, 2000 (Eco. Survey, 1999/2000: 123).

All these hold that monetary planning alone is insufficient in bringing about notable changes in economic structure conductive sustainable economic growth. Lastly in the context of monetary development it is noteworthy that most of the development expenditure in various plans has to be financed by taking foreign loans and grants. This has increased the net foreign assets and money supply in the economy. Also the high rate of increase in the government borrowings and private sectors loans from the banking agencies has helped to further monetary expansion. Thus, in such situation it has become a challenging job for maintaining internal and external stability in the economy by controlling money supply expansion in harmony with the development of real sector. It is, therefore, incumbent upon concerned authorities to watch carefully in the implementation of the flexible monetary policy. For this purpose, monetary policy as a resource mobilizing instruments should directed towards encouraging the people to say more through the creation of attractive environment among banks and financial institutions. The entrepreneurs should be motivated to mobilize the existing resources into productive and employment oriented channels. It is in this perspective that monetary planning with flexible monetary policy is a necessary step to create new financial bases, consolidate the existing ones and initiate healthy competition among banks and financial institutions in the economy.

To sum up, a notable feature of the Nepalese money market is its preliminary stage that has prevented monetary development with stability. Furthermore, the money market even after having traversed through a long stretch of more than four decades of planned economic development still remained in the stage of its foot in the door. Thus, in such circumstances, it has become obligatory to appropriate instrument in order to introduce the dynamism in the money market.

7.4 Monetary Control Instruments

It is generally agreed that after the introduction of Credit Control Regulation Act in 1966, the NRB tried to impose some quantitative and qualitative instruments, which were helpful in achieving short run monetary stability in the economy. Of these various instruments, the two quantitative instruments such as, refinancing of commercial banks and open market operations directly affect the stock of reserve money and they are most potent in varying the supply of money and credit. Similarly, the other two techniques as reserve requirements and interest rate regulations work on the component of money multiplier. However, the qualitative tool as moral suasion can affect the stock of reserve money or the multiplier or both (Aghevli et al, 1979: 796).

The impact of the product of reserve money and multiplier on money supply will be derived under the money supply analysis in section 7.5. In this section, the characteristics of various instruments and their use in the Nepalese money market have been discussed in the following way:

(i) Refinancing of Commercial Banks

Refinancing of commercial banks has the basic advantage of affecting the stock of money by directly affecting bank reserve positions. The refinancing[4] cannot be initiated when the central bank desires to reduce the growth of money and credit in the economy. As pointed out by Aghevli et al (1979), refinancing of commercial banks in Nepal was very large (20.14%) in 1975. Since then it has become very small (.07%) in 1992 (NRB, 1996: 13). Such types of refinancing facilities in the recent time period have been withdrawn and those securities having not more than 45 days of maturity have been made eligible for the access of refinancing at the NRB.

(ii) Open Market Operations

As an instrument of monetary control, the purposes of open market operations[5] are associated with the restriction of bank reserves and thus affecting their power to expand credit and providing a regular market for government securities (Sethi, 1992:470). In the context of Nepal, the efficacy of open market operation as a monetary tool is particularly limited due to the existence of large unorganized money market on the one hand and the lack of well developed financial market on the other. Besides, the commercial banks are generally used to maintain excess cash reserves, which constitute a serious limiting factor in the successful operation of open market policy. While considering this operation in the study period (1965-99), the NRB was found purchasing more treasury bills and government bonds and thereby making a useful addition to the inflationary pressure in the economy. Thus, in this regard, it seems advisable to follow Gupta's View (1995:116) that if an active Treasury bill market were cultivated in the economy, the excessive dependence of the government on the central bank for fulfilling the needs of the short-term funds would be reduced. Furthermore, it would curtail the quantum of excessive deficit financing and thereby reduce the excess supply of high-powered money and bank reserves also.

Thus, the development of Treasury bill market would largely mean a diversion of funds from bank deposits to treasury bills with a view of accelerating the efforts of banking at deposit mobilization. Besides, the growth of public demand for treasury bills would mean to bring down a part of the pressure on the NRB and the market of government securities.

(iii) Variable Reserve Requirements

The method of changing reserve requirements is more practical in underdeveloped countries where the indirect instrument like open market operations can have little use owing to the lack of suitable securities to deal by the central bank. This method was introduced by the NRB in 1966 in which it was given directives to the commercial banks to maintain at least 8 % of their deposit liabilities as reserves in the NRB (Reejal, ibid: 43). After that it has been continued till now even if the ratio has changed several times.

In respect of this instrument, the ratio of statutory reserve requirement was brought in 1981 whereby a distinction was made between the required holding of cash (4%) in vault and the cash (5 %) with the NRB for the purpose of minimum reserve requirements (Sharma, 1987:135). Since then, the NRB till recently has imposed the ratio of 34% statutory reserves to the total deposits of commercial banks. The aggregate requirement of statutory reserves comprises of 12% cash reserves including 4 % cash in vault and 22% investment in the form of government securities and the NRB bonds (Thapa, 1993[b] : 87). However, some advocates have argued that the instrument has not become a perfect one for controlling money supply and credit due to its own leakages just as other control measures have.

(iv) Interest Rat Regulations

As far as the financial system is responsive to interest rates, the interest rate regulation influences economic aggregates through the interaction of demand for and the supply of money and bank credit (Aghevli et al, ibid: 802). In this regard, the NRB had changed interest rate upwards by regulation in 1975. As a result, large capital inflows played a major part in the moderation of deposit interest rates in 1976 and 1977. Nevertheless, it is the real fact that the NRB could no longer administer and reduce the interest rate directly. Thus, in view of this situation, the NRB in 1986 gave autonomy to all commercial banks to set their deposit rates according to their competition and development (NRB, 1997:66). Since then interest rates have been determined regularly by the operation of market forces.

(v) Exchange Rate Stabilization

At present, a country opting for floating exchange rate has an option of letting the currency float independently or float in a group. Similarly, a country choosing for pegged currency has to decide between pegging in terms of a single major foreign currency or of a composite or 'basket' of foreign currencies. Accordingly, the Nepalese monetary authority has done in the case of IC including it in the basket of foreign currencies. This system was virtually started in Nepal since 1983 in order to manage the exchange rate under the currency basket system and to make a support for the reduction in unfavourable balance of payments[6](Adhikari, 1997: 12). However, the advocates of the free floating exchange rate have argued that it is closer to the fixed exchange rate due to the fact that Nepalese currency has been made fully convertible to all transactions in the current account since 1993 onwards (Pant, 1993: 36). On the line of financial liberalization policy, the individuals have been given a privilege of the opening deposit accounts in terms of foreign currencies. Furthermore, in view of the persistent trade deficit particularly with India, the policy of maintaining full convertibility between NC and IC under the managed floating exchange system has been followed regularly. Finally, it can be argued that the present exchange rate system can absorb the external shocks to some extent. However, it cannot insulate the monetary sector from the external shocks totally. Considering this fact, it would be a challenging task for the NRB to consider the prudent monetary policy so that the continued growth in money supply may be controlled.

Thus, from the above discussion of monetary instruments, it may be inferred that for an open economy operating under fixed exchange rate system, the interest rate regulations would be primary instruments of monetary control. But, in the Nepalese context, interest rate adjustment is one step behind the changes in the rate of inflation. The setting of interest rates, therefore, in Nepal requires the rate, which should be kept relative to the rate of inflation. In this perspective, following Mathieson (1975: 89) and Obstfled (1982: 45), it can be argued that the required reserve ratio would become an effective instrument when the economy is open and the foreign trade as well as capital flows is allowed to exert their influence on the economy. Thus, if monetary policy is to influence economic activity in an open economy, the monetary authorities must be careful in selection of monetary instruments.

In recent years, floating exchange rates have been recommended on the ground that they provide the authorities with direct control over the money supply. However, a fixed exchange rate system could provide an additional power to policy makers to use in resisting political and economic pressures for monetary expansion. Indeed, a freely floating exchange rate system may not be suitable for most of the developing countries like Nepal. It is, therefore, advisable to continue fixing the rate to single currency or a basket of major currencies for controlling money supply with an appropriate monetary policy.

7.5 Money Supply Analysis

Money supply in the simple sense may be expressed as highly stable increasing function of the reserve money or high-powered money[7]. On the analytical front, it can be interpreted as the product of money multiplier[8] and high-powered money.

The factors governing high-powered money are largely policy-controlled variables. However, the factors influencing money multiplier are chiefly dependent on the behavioural choices of the public and banks. The knowledge about this factor, therefore, embodied in money supply equation is empirically meaningful (chapter-II) and highly useful for the purpose of monetary planning.

As argued by Reejal (1986), it is almost impossible for any country to control money supply absolutely. Nevertheless, the NRB along with the Ministry of Finance may have an influence over the supply of money via the method of controlling reserve money. For this purpose, monetary policy would become a potent vehicle that can promote savings and investment by maintaining price stability and adjusting the adverse balance of payments through changes in foreign exchange rate.

It is apparent from the section 4.1 of chapter- IV that there has been a secular rise in money supply and its increment remained over and above the rate of growth in GDP. If this situation persists for a long time, it would create a wide resource gap, deficit financing and ultimately monetary disquilibrium in the economy. Thus, with a view to show and analyze the

Table 7.5.1: Growth Rate of Money Supply in Nepal (1990-1999)

Year	*Narrow Money* (M_1)	*Broad Money* (M_2)	*Reserve Money* (M_r)	*Multiplier* m_1	m_2
1991	14.49	19.64	20.55	0.97	2.25
1992	19.49	20.86	12.37	1.03	2.42
1993	22.49	27.95	29.59	0.98	2.39
1994	19.63	19.64	16.21	1.00	2.46
1995	15.70	16.06	15.07	1.01	2.48
1996	10.65	14.41	8.27	1.03	2.62
1997	5.38	11.95	15.93	0.93	2.53
1998	17.43	21.93	12.11	0.98	2.75
1999	13.06	20.83	13.54	0.98	2.93
Total Average	**15.37**	**19.25**	**15.96**	**0.99**	**2.54**

Source: Appendix-D

influence of monetary variables on money supply, some basic statistic describing the recent behaviour of the main monetary aggregates have been presented in Table 7.5.1.

Table 7.5.1 depicts the growth rates of the three monetary aggregates (M_1, M_2 and M_r) and the multiplier of both narrow and broad money particularly from the period of restoration of multiparty democratic system in Nepal. During the sample period (1990-99), broad money (M_2) grew faster than narrow (M_1) and reserve money (M_r) in each year except in 1991, 1993 & 1997 for reserve money. This growth rate of monetary aggregates indicates that the time and saving deposits (in terms of M_2) have increased more rapidly than currency and demand deposits (in terms of M_1) in the economy. Taking into account the average rate of growth of money supply, it becomes clear that in case of broad money it is greater (by 25.24%) than that of narrow money. The other important factor of increasing money supply is the money multiplier. It shows the higher magnitude of broad money multiplier continued in each year in comparison to the narrow one.

Thus, from this analysis it becomes apparent that the traditional instruments of monetary control are still working in controlling money supply in Nepal through the changes either in the stock of reserve money or in money multiplier. Nevertheless, money control measures may be limited in most developing countries on account of the special relationship between the central bank and the government. Considering this fact, it is of the utmost importance to say that without the full and active co-operation of the government no plan of monetary control for stability can ever be successful. Thus, in such a situation, one of the major instruments for successful monetary control is the restraint of deficit financing by the government with a view to maintain monetary stability in the economy. Therefore, Money supply analysis, in brief, implies that the key to the control of money supply is the control of high-powered money and the successful control of high-powered money would ultimately control the government deficit.

7.6 Money Demand Implications

With regard to the implementation of target oriented monetary policy, it is generally contended that monetary authorities should have to decide on economic objectives and then choose a value for monetary aggregates consistent with the ultimate targets. The value opted for monetary targets depend upon the preferences of monetary authorities subject to the economic and institutional constraints. Moreover, in the line of the derivation of target value, the demand for money function is considered as a cornerstone and has been explained theoretically and empirically in chapters III, V and VI respectively. The tentative conclusions derived from the empirical demand functions have been reviewed briefly in this section for the judgment of suitable monetary policy.

It has been pointed out that a stable demand for money function is necessary to show the effective implementation of monetary policy in the economy (Khatiwada, 1997: 34). If the demand for money is predictable, the supply of money can be adopted suitably to ensure equilibrium in the money market. But, in fact, money supply cannot be maintained at the desired level due to its expansionary effect on net foreign assets and the government borrowings from the central bank. At this juncture, the NRB as a central bank should be in a position to restrain credit expansion in order to control the money supply. Moreover, if the demand function is stable and predictable, the monetary policy can be an effective tool for economic stabilization.

From the estimated parameters of the demand for money functions from the preceding chapters, the income variable is found to be a major determinant of the demand for money. The high income elasticity coefficient of the narrow money in comparison to broad money justifies the characteristics of non-monetized economy. The coefficient of interest rate in both narrow and broad definitions of money does not show its significant influence. The rate of inflation represents the opportunity cost variable than interest rate in the demand for money function. The inflationary target is set at a higher level due to openness of the country, which has led to currency substitution practices in the economy. The significant coefficient of lagged money stock for both definitions of money implies a very small proportion of the desired money stock released in a year. From this, it appears that money market in Nepal has taken a longer time to attain equilibrium. The McKinnon type of demand for money function may be fitted in the Nepalese context. It supports the hypothesis that the physical capital and real money balances are not substitutes but they are complementary in public portfolio.

Needless to say, the practice of currency substitution has created instability in the money market. Further, with a view of lessening the excessive influence of IC in the economy, the objective of monetary policy should be oriented to maintain exchange rate stability through managed floating exchange rate system. Thus, it seems worthwhile to follow Swamy and Tavlas (1989) that the demand for money in an open economy framework, has the implication for exchange rate behaviour and therefore for the transmission mechanism of monetary policy. In brief, from the money demand analysis it can be inferred that the monetary policy should be implemented through the exchange rate stabilization rather than other monetary instruments.

7.7 Monetary Policy and its Impact on Economic Activity

Monetary policy is regarded as an indispensable tool for monetary management. It is a summary of policies implemented by the government or monetary authority of the country in relation to money supply, exchange rate, price level, credit flow and the interest rates on various deposits and loans. It plays a dominant role in pursuit of achieving the monetary targets related to the maximum level of output, higher employment, stable price level and external balance in the economy.

The conduct of monetary policy is a complex matter. There is a divergence of views about the effectiveness of monetary policy and the channel through which it should primarily aim to operate. Thus, Sayers (1960) was of the opinion that the value of money is dependent on its quantity and therefore some control on the supply of money is essential for monetary policy.

Hence, it follows that the quantity of money is the basic indicator of monetary policy.

There exists a considerable debate among economists on the selection of appropriate indicators of monetary policy. As proposed by Willms (1971) and Laufer (1977) in the context of Germany, the money stock as an indicator of monetary policy is affected not only by the movement in the monetary base[9] and the money multiplier but also influenced by the bank and non-bank public behaviour. Thus monetary indicators are the monetary base, narrow and broad money stocks, bank credit and bank liquidity.[10] Out of these, bank liquidity has been found servicing for a long time in German economy as an official indicator of monetary policy. The reason is that a reduction in liquidity ratio can lead to an increase in interest rate and thereby lessens the credit expansion. Thus, a bank liquidity can be interpreted as a restrictive indicator. Nevertheless, an introduction to the floating exchange rate is a restrictive indicator as it can act against inflation.

For underdeveloped countries like Nepal, it is a Herculean task to identify an indicator that is much dependable on monetary policy. To this end, the rate of interest may be taken as an indicator in the case where the central bank plays a crucial role in pegging the rate of interest. However, in the context of free, open and liberalized market economy, interest rate is considered as a poor indicator because of the fact that the attempts made by monetary authority to control interest rate would create instability in money supply (Mitchel, et al, 1974: 273). From this it is obvious that the rate of interest generally fails to serve as an indicator of monetary policy. Furthermore, as argued by Bain (1971) and Sharma (1987), the external sector open economy has a dominant role in the sense that eve the amount of reserve money is not under the control monetary authority. Thus, in such circumstances, the domestic credit supply by the banking system may alone be chosen as an indicator of monetary policy.

It is true that the role of monetary policy in a developing economy is bound to be different from that of developed economy on account of the nature of economic problems. The monetary policy as a tool for monetary planning in developing economies is to be utilized for achieving the growth with stability. This objective implies the controlled expansion of money and credit and provides a special role of monetary policy in monetary management.

Regarding the control of money supply, a question arises that whether the control of reserve money may be sufficient to control money supply. The answer to this may be the foreign sector, which remained as a factor of producing volatile effect in the reserve money so that the money supply determined by the influence of the foreign sector. Thus, the role of monetary policy in the Nepalese economy seemed to be weaker domestically in controlling money supply. Besides, the NRB as a central bank is obliged to cater the fiscal needs of the government. The continuous increase in budget deficit of the government has led to the situation in which the scope of national savings has deteriorated, the problem of loan service become worse and the financial resources for the private sector become scarce. Moreover, it has created some distortions like the erosion of people's purchasing power due to declining in internal and external value of the Nepalese currency, capital flight and the distraction of foreign investment. The growing deficit, therefore, has created many problems for controlling money supply with the help of monetary policy only.

Now-a-days, there has been an increasing interest in the relative efficacy of monetary and fiscal policy as a vehicle for achieving economic growth with stability. In this regard, Waud (1974) concluded from the empirical findings that influences of both monetary and fiscal policies were significant and equally important. In the same way, Upadhyaya (1991), Kaur (1995) and Owoye et al (1995) presented empirical evidences on the relative importance of monetary and fiscal policies in economic stabilization of developing countries[11]. On the basis of empirical findings, they concluded that the monetary policy influences were relatively stronger than fiscal policy influences.

Despite this, some economists are of the opinion that the balance of payments is a monetary phenomenon. It is considered as a source of disequilibrium in the money market. The logic behind this is that if the domestic goods were not substantially produced within the country, the import of goods from abroad would create the deficiency in foreign exchange reserves. Consequently, there appears a wide deficit in trade balances in the economy. Thus, in such a situation, monetary policy as an effective instrument can promote savings and investment by maintaining price stability and adjusting the adverse balance of payments through foreign exchange rates.

Basically, in underdeveloped countries, monetary policy may not be much effective due to the lack of awareness of the people regarding financial institutions and also due to the existence of an unorganized money market, the weak linkage between interest rate, investment and output and the limited array of financial assets (Paul, 1992: 310). Considering these constraints in the context of Nepal, it may be argued that the monetary policy should aim at facilitating the flow of bank credit in various sectors, providing encouragement to the deprived sections of the community, curbing the inflationary pressures in the economy by restraining undue expansion of bank credit for unproductive purposes, and ensuring controlled expansion in money supply. The monetary policy may be considered less effective because of the following limitations:

Firstly, a large part of the money stock is held in the form of cash due to the preference of people for fulfilling their transaction demand and the lack of banking habits among savers.

Secondly, the Nepalese money market is dichotomized by organized and unorganized market. The monetary authority has regulated the organized market. However, the substantial unorganized money market is beyond the control of monetary authority.

Thirdly, there is a wide disparity of interest rates prevailing in the different sectors and these rates do not respond to the banking rate.

Fourthly, the expenditure on development schemes has increased the inflow of foreign capital on one hand and the continuous deficit in annual budget on the other resulting into a pressure on price level and current account of the balance of payments. Furthermore, the excess supply of money on account of the inelastic supply of output has been adjusted to an inflow of goods and services from abroad and thereby has caused the loss of trade and adverse balance of payments.

Lastly, an excessive time lag is found between the application of monetary measures and the effect.

Regardless of these limitations, monetary policy has to play a positive role in facilitating the attainment of growth with stability. So its role in the Nepalese economy may be found in economic stabilization rather than in economic growth. In this connection, the empirical analysis made in chapter V is evidence that the demand for money with respect to income and interest rate is less elastic. It justifies the application of monetary policy as effective in restoring economic stability. Furthermore, in the context of economic stabilization, money supply analysis is equally important. On the money supply front, Pant (1970: 103) has argued the coordination of fiscal and monetary tools in such a way that money supply may not expand beyond limits. Nevertheless, Adhikari (1977) has suggested that monetary authorities should try to maintain a balance between demand for and supply of money for ensuring economic stability.

Thus, it may be concluded that monetary policy in Nepal has been oriented towards controlling the inflationary pressures in the economy. It is true that under the inflationary pressures, when easy monetary policy is pursued by the NRB, rising prices will hindrance the effect of monetary policy. Thus, monetary policy as a weapon of short-term stabilization has been relatively ineffective. However, it cannot be denied that the monetary policy together with fiscal policy would have been more effective for the purpose of the long-term economic stabilization.

7.8 Concluding Remarks

It is obvious from the foregoing discussion that the Nepalese money market is influenced by the high degree of openness to India and the existence of a large non-monetized sector in the economy. The pace of monetary development even after crossing the long range several economic plan periods has still remained in the embryonic stage. The maintenance of price stability as an objective of monetary planning would employ a rate of monetary expansion much greater than the rate of growth in real income or output. Besides, the failure of Nepalese economy to raise the productivity is strongly supported by the fact that the real sector has remained unable to mop up the excess liquidity held by the commercial banks. The implications of the demand for money functions manifest that the money has a decisive role in formulating a suitable monetary policy and to find out the effect of monetary variables in the real and external sectors of the economy. Monetary authorities cannot directly control the demand for money. However, the supply of money can be limited under the grip of monetary authorities. Thus, the equilibrium in the money market may be maintained by suitably adjusting the supply of money to the demand.

In the context of Nepal, the financial intermediaries established so far have not been activated to encourage savings in non-monetized rural areas. The existing branches too have failed to deliver the banking services to the rural people. As a result, the large disparities between interest rates of banking institutions and unorganized rural market have created dual credit system and there by have reduced the efficacy of monetary policy. On the basis of such issues, it may be concluded that the instrument of exchange rate stabilization through managed floating exchange rate system and the target oriented monetary policy are better suited to the circumstances of the Nepalese economy. Moreover, the scope of monetary policy can be limited unless it is accompanied by the fiscal policy. Monetary policy should, therefore, serve to control inflationary pressures. More specifically, the effectiveness of monetary policy on the one hand lies in controlling money supply expansion by the monetary system and discouraging deficit financing by the government on the other.

On the whole, the stability of the demand for money function together with a capacity of monetary authority to influence the supply of money would seem to be a necessary condition for the successful implementation of monetary policy in Nepal.

NOTES

1. All monetary assets comprise of narrow money, broad money, bonds and securities, life insurance and so on.
2. Small sectors represented agriculture, small-scale industries and services during the fourth plan period.
3. Monetary planning should not be confused with credit planning. Since money is not credit, it is an asset of the holding of public and credit is the liability of the borrowing of public. Thus, credit planning refers to the synchronization of credit creating capacity of the banking system and the rate of capacity utilization of an economy (Ghosh, 1971: 8).
4. The amount of refinancing can be measured in terms of proportion of the borrowings from the NRB to the liabilities of commercial banks.
5. Open market operations consist of deliberate and direct sale and purchase of all government securities by the central bank on its own account.
6. For details, see Adhikari, D. (1997) "Monetary Policy, Instruments, and their Implications in Nepal", *Rajaswa*, Nepali Publication, Vol. 1(17), HMG/Ministry of Finance, Revenue Administration Training Centre, Lalitpur, April-May, 7-13.
7. High-powered money in empirical sense includes currency held by the public, cash reserves of banks and the other deposits of the central bank. Here, the other deposits constitute the deposits held by the government, banks and other quasi government institutions like NIDC, Employees Provident Fund, Insurance Companies etc.
8. Money multiplier in the simplest form is the ratio of money supply to the high-powered or reserve money. i.e., $m = M_s/M_r$.
9. Monetary base from the sources side is the amount of high-powered money in the economy adjusted for legal reserves and borrowings of commercial banks through discounts and advances.
10. Bank liquidity refers to the free liquid reserves in the hands of banks.
11. Upadhyaya, K.P. (1991) examined this issue especially for Pakistan and three other South Asian Countries- India, Nepal and Srilanka. Kaur, G. (1995) evaluated the working of fiscal and monetary policy in India from 1961-91 and tested their

effectiveness empirically, and Owoye et al (1995) conducted the studies for eight Asian Countries consisting of India, Nepal, Pakistan, Srilanka, Malaysia, Philippines, Singapore and Thailand.

Chapter VIII

SUMMARY OF FINDINGS AND SUGGESTIONS

8.1 Summary of Findings

The following summary brings together the concluding remarks of the previous chapters in order to draw the broad outline of the findings of this study.

The monetary system of Nepal exhibits its preliminary stage in the pace of monetization. As the economy develops the more money with a large number of banking and financial institutions is needed for the process of monetization.

Money supply is considered as a policy determined variable in the supply function. In this regard, money supply functions involving positive monetary feedback ($h_1 = 0.15$ & $h_2 = 0.40$) coefficients tend to increase the strength of economic fluctuations. Moreover, the successive increase in overdraft arrangements to the government has become the main reason for monetary expansion. Money and capital markets in Nepal are set up a dichotomy between organized and unorganized sectors of the economy. Besides, the existence of large unorganized sector is one of the principal causes of underdeveloped money and capital markets. Furthermore, the small amount of savings, puny inducement to investment, social insecurity and political instability has become the major factors for low capital formation. Thus, the significant role of the NRB lies in its developmental function for well managing the monetary system in Nepal.

All the theoretical models discussed in the present study have sketched out the development of the demand for money functions by treating money supply as exogenous variable. The classical approach (Marshall-Pigou) indicates the transaction demand for money as a constant function of the level of income. The predictions from Keynes' transactions and precautionary motives are similar to the classical quantity theory. However, the speculative demand for money introduces uncertainty about the future rate of interest. The inventory (Tobin) model seems inappropriate than Baumol's square root relationship. Towards making the restatement of the quantity theory of money, Friedman has empirically determined the demand for money depending upon a set of interest rates. But, he could not find the significant response of interest rate on the demand for money. Keynes-Friedman model and Meltzer's model also provide a correct explanation to the demand for money. Considering these different approaches of the demand for money functions, it can be concluded that the implication of quantity theory approach seems better than the Keynesian approach in the context of Nepal.

The overview of the Nepalese monetary economy (1965-1999) exhibits the large part of non-monetized sector, consisting of 69.1% currency in the total money stock held by the public. Besides, the slow growth in national income, the presence of inflationary spiral, import oriented trade and the continuous negative trend in trade account balances have created a hindrance to the process of monetary management.

Numerous factors, which determine the demand for money, are categorized under the major determinants. The income in terms of GDP, the interest rate on fixed deposits, the price level in consumer price index, the exchange rate and the balance of payments have emerged as the major determinants. Also the factors affecting the demand for money like inflation, population, budget deficits and the rate of monetization may be considered as other determinants. This analysis has helped us to find the income as the pivotal element to determine the demand for money.

The empirical analysis of simple linear models indicates that the narrow definition of money is appropriate in the context of Nepalese economy. The stronger prediction made by income, interest rate and price level in the narrow money demand function shows its superiority over the broad definition of money demand. The significant relationship of income with the demand for money implies that income may be opted as an efficient tool for economic stabilization. The inclusion of interest bearing assets and the rate monetization provide statistically good fit in all equations. The association between the balance of payments and the demand for reserve money has been analyzed by applying monetary approach to the balance of payments.

The income elasticity coefficients in loglinear models lie within the range of 0.53 to 0.82 (Table 4.0). It suggests that money is not a luxury good in Nepal. The elasticity of interest rate is found to be insignificant with the expected sign. From this result, we can deduce that interest rate has not been significant in determining the demand for money. The price level in simple linear model exposes its negative sign, while in loglinear model it is positive. This contradictory finding implies the presence of price instability in the economy.

Under the single equation system, McKinnon's hypothesis performs better than the other conventional semi-loglinear models. This statement holds good in the sense that money and physical assets in Nepal are more complementary than substitutes. The adjustment coefficient in autoregressive distributed lag model is estimated to be 16% for narrowly defined money demand and 8% for broad demand functions (Table 5.1). This justifies the argument that there is quite slow annual arrangement with the actual and desired money balances in the economy. To measure the short-run behaviour of the demand function, the partial adjustment model seems more appropriate than the price expectation model. By comparing the income elasticity in partial adjustment model, it may be inferred that the Nepalese people prefer narrow money balances both in short-run as well as in long- run periods.

The use of Almon (second degree) polynomial lag model

does not permit us to decide whether the partial adjustment or adaptive expectation phenomenon is correct and applicable for the estimation of the demand for money function. However, the computed value of expected income through this model gives adequate support to the argument that current income is more useful than preceding income.

The possibility of simultaneity between money demand and money supply equations is also explored to find out the response of income, interest rate and government fiscal deficit. To analyze this, two stage least square (2SLS) technique has been employed on the assumption of equality between demand and supply functions. Regarding the measurement of the bias, the prediction of demand function under the simultaneous equations system, symbolizes a positive bias in interest rate. There is not much difference between the results of OLS and 2SLS procedures; however, the latter one appears slightly impressive. To sum up, from the empirical analysis on the basis of the signs and the statistic of some basic variables, the simple linear model comes out to be the best in the Nepalese context.

According to the survey report (1996), the Indian currency (IC) has occupied 40.72% of its share in the overall business transactions in Nepal (Table 6.2.1). The main reason for holding IC is to make a means of payments for setting the trade between India and Nepal. Besides, the currency exchange between NC and IC has been followed to be legal in the market so that IC has played a crucial role in the business dealings from the very beginning.

In the computation of business household demand for money function, the transactional income and employment turn out to be the most relevant determinants. The performance of region-wise interest rate and IC holdings is found less important in the demand equation. The linear constant elasticity of substitution (CES) model provides some evidence about the currency substitution. The nonlinear form of CES model presents the consistent estimates of currency substitution ratio, economies of scale and the elasticity of substitution. The return to scale parameter of less than one ($\tilde{o}$ =0.37) shows the indication of diseconomies of scale operating in the business market. This result manifest that economies of scale in money holdings do not always remain valid in the trade community.

Monetary planning is based on appropriate changes in the stock of money. For this purpose, the demand for money should be stable. The supply of money should be carefully observed and controlled by the monetary authority. In view of this, the money market in Nepal having a long experience of more than four decades (1956-2001) of planned economic development has still remained in the initial stage.

With regard to the effective implementation of monetary policy, the financial intermediaries have not been activated to increase savings in non-monetized rural areas. The interest rate has generally failed to serve as an indicator of monetary policy. Furthermore, the large inequality between interest rates of financial institutions and unorganized rural markets has created dual credit system. Thus, in such circumstances, the target oriented monetary policy and the instrument of exchange rate stabilization may be more effective for the development of non-monetized economy.

8.2. Suggestions

From the foregoing discussion, there appears the importance of the supply and demand for money for the need of monetary management, planning and policy for economic development. In this respect, some suggestions may be given as:

The supply of money in Nepal should expand with the growth rate of GDP of the country. Irregular variation in money supply should be minimized in order to make zero or negative monetary feedback coefficient of the money supply function.

Few measures carried out by monetary authority, viz. the variation in reserve requirements, interest rate liberalization, managed floating exchange rate or currency basket system may be suggested to restrain the destabilizing factors of the demand for money.

To raise the slow speed of income (or GDP) compared to population growth, monetary policy in Nepal should be directed towards the regulation of credit to the productive sectors only.

Under the monitoring process of money supply, the NRB

as a central bank should evaluate the money control measures for reducing the higher rate of inflation. The monetary authorities should develop a plan to tap idle resources from the non-monetized areas with a view to mobilize them in the priority sectors.

The steps towards deregulation of interest rates may be preferable for creating competitive financial environment. However, the low interest rate policy may not be effective to encourage investment in the Nepalese context.

The increasing tendency of currency substitution for illegal trades should be discouraged by regulating fiscal administration effectively. In respect of geo-economic condition of Nepal, frequent changes in NC vis-à-vis IC are not favourable for the business management. Thus, it is reasonable to follow the fixed exchange rate policy between NC and IC.

On the lines of formulating target oriented monetary policy, monetary planning should be utilized for achieving maximum output and price stability in the economy. Monetary policy as an instrument of short-term stabilization may be ineffective. Therefore, the combination of monetary and fiscal policy would be more potent for the purpose of economic stability.

APPENDICES

Appendix-A

(Rs. in Million)

*Year**	*Nominal Gross Domestic Product*	*Annual Growth (%)*	*Real Gross Domestic Product (1975 =100)*	*Annual Growth (%)*
1965	5602	-	13328	-
1966	6909	23.33	14266	7.04
1967	6411	-7.21	14042	-1.57
1968	7173	11.89	14137	0.67
1969	7985	11.32	14768	4.46
1970	8768	9.80	15148	2.57
1971	8938	1.94	14967	-1.19
1972	10369	16.01	15434	3.12
1973	9969	-3.86	15360	-0.48
1974	12808	28.48	16333	6.34
1975	16571	29.38	16571	1.46
1976	17394	4.97	17300	4.39
1977	17280	-0.66	17822	3.02
1978	19732	14.49	18607	4.40
1979	22215	12.58	19048	2.37
1980	23351	5.11	18606	-2.32
1981	27307	16.94	20158	8.34
1982	30988	13.48	20920	3.78
1983	33761	8.95	20297	-2.98
1984	39390	16.67	22262	9.68
1985	44441	12.82	23636	6.17
1986	53215	19.74	24677	4.40
1987	61140	14.89	25076	1.62
1988	73170	19.68	26824	6.97
1989	85830	17.30	28306	5.52
1990	99702	16.16	29729	5.03
1991	116128	16.47	31481	5.89
1992	144931	24.80	32713	3.91
1993	165262	14.03	33637	2.82
1994	191540	15.90	36283	7.87
1995	209974	9.59	38126	5.08
1996	239388	14.01	40300	5.70
1997	269570	12.61	42223	4.77
1998	289798	7.50	43675	3.44
1999	330018	13.88	45636	4.49

Source : Economic Survey, HMG/N (Various Issues).
*Fiscal Year 1964/65 is equivalent to 1965 and so on.

APPENDIX - B

(Rs. in Million)

Year	Gross Domestic Savings (GDS)	Annual Growth (%)	Gross Domestic Investment (GDI)	Annual Growth (%)	Savings Gap	Annual Growth (%)
1975	1662	—	2402	—	740	—
1976	2040	22.74	2632	9.58	592	–20.0
1977	2332	14.3 1	2768	5.17	436	–26.4
1978	2540	8.92	3507	26.70	967	121.8
1979	2585	1.77	3514	0.20	929	–3.9
1980	2591	0.23	4270	21.51	1679	80.7
1981	2974	14.78	4808	12.60	1834	9.2
1982	3088	3.50	5314	10.52	2236	21.9
1983	2887	–6.51	6628	24.73	3741	67.3
1984	3886	34.60	7351	10.91	3465	–7.4
1985	6239	60.55	10184	38.54	3945	13.9
1986	5887	–5.64	10599	4.08	4712	19.4
1987	7321	24.36	12898	21.69	5577	18.4
1988	7604	3.87	15237	18.13	7633	36.9
1989	10150	33.48	19415	27.42	9265	21.4
1990	8143	–19.77	19076	–1.75	10933	18.0
1991	11515	41.41	25074	31.44	13559	24.0
1992	16207	40.75	31619	26.10	15412	13.7
1993	23172	42.98	39653	25.41	16481	6.9
1994	29220	26.10	44644	12.59	15424	–6.4
1995	32465	11.11	55231	23.71	22766	47.60
1996	34426	6.04	68017	23.15	33591	47.55
1997	39162	13.76	71084	4.51	31922	–4.97
1998	41438	5.81	74728	5.13	33290	4.29
1999	46563	12.37	70061	-6.25	23498	–29.41

Source : Economic Survey, HMG/N, Fiscal Year, 2000/01.

APPENDIX -C

Year	*Consumer Price Index*⁺*(1984=100)*	*Annual Rate of Inflation (%)*
1974	43.8	—
1975	51.1	16.7
1976	50.8	-0.6
1977	52.1	2.6
1978	58.0	11.3
1979	60.0	3.5
1980	65.8	9.7
1981	74.6	13.4
1982	82.4	10.5
1983	94.1	14.2
1984	100.0	6.3
1985	104.1	4.1
1986	120.6	15.9
1987	136.6	13.3
1988	151.7	11.1
1989	164.0	8.1
1990	179.9	9.7
1991	197.5	9.8
1992	239.2	21.1
1993	260.3	8.8
1994	283.7	9.0
1995	305.4	7.6
1996	330.2	8.1
1997	355.9	7.8
1998	370.0	4.0
1999	417.1	12.7

Source : NRB, Quarterly Economic Bulletin, Vol. 33 (3&4) Mid-April to Mid-July, 1999, P. 40

APPENDIX D

(Rs. in Million)

Year Mid-July	*Narrow Money (M_1)*	*Annual Growth (%)*	*Broad Money (M_2)*	*Annual Growth (%)*	*Reserve Money (M_r)*	*Annual Growth (%)*
1965	446.3	—	489.7	—	382.6	—
1966	521.5	16.8	570.7	16.5	462.5	20.9
1967	568.3	9.0	641.4	12.4	487.6	5.4
1968	618.8	8.9	721.7	12.5	552.5	13.3
1969	700.4	13.2	857.2	18.8	638.3	15.5
1970	763.3	9.0	975.3	13.8	707.2	10.8
1971	793.4	3.9	1072.1	9.9	700.3	–1.0
1972	857.7	8.1	1261.8	17.7	740.4	5.7
1973	1015.8	18.4	1529.2	21.2	885.6	19.6
1974	1281.1	26.1	1911.0	25.0	1117.2	26.1
1975	1337.7	4.4	2064.4	8.0	1178.9	5.5
1976	1452.5	8.6	2524.0	22.3	1278.5	8.4
1977	1852.9	27.6	3223.0	27.7	1594.8	24.7
1978	2060.6	11.2	3772.1	17.0	1849.7	16.0
1979	2504.9	21.6	4511.4	19.6	2117.3	14.5
1980	2830.4	13.0	5285.3	17.2	2468.6	16.6
1981	3207.8	13.3	6307.7	19.3	2706.2	9.6
1982	3611.5	12.6	7458.0	18.2	3375.6	24.7
1983	4348.9	20.4	9222.4	23.7	4012.6	18.9
1984	4931.5	13.4	10455.2	13.4	4624.1	15.2
1985	5480.0	11.1	12296.6	17.6	5177.3	12.0
1986	7029.3	28.3	15159.0	23.3	6857.3	32.4
1987	8120.2	15.5	17498.2	15.4	7600.0	10.8
1988	9596.6	18.2	21422.6	22.4	8995.9	18.4
1989	11775.4	22.7	26605.1	24.2	11336.8	26.0
1990	14223.0	20.8	31552.4	18.6	13924.8	22.8
1991	16283.6	14.5	37712.5	19.6	16786.0	20.5
1992	19457.7	19.5	45580.5	20.9	18863.1	12.4
1993	23833.0	22.5	58322.5	27.9	24443.8	29.6
1994	28510.4	19.6	69777.1	19.6	28405.7	16.2
1995	32985.4	15.7	80984.7	16.1	32686.3	15.1
1996	36498.0	10.6	92652.2	14.4	35390.0	8.3
1997	38460.3	5.4	103720.6	11.9	41027.3	15.9
1998	45163.8	17.4	126462.6	21.9	45995.5	12.1
1999	51062.4	13.1	152800.1	20.8	52225.3	13.5

Source : NRB, Quarterly Economic Bulletin (Various Issues).

APPENDIX - E
Annual Data used for Estmation of Models

Year	Π_t (%)	Y_t^+	Y_{pt} (1974/75)$^+$ price	YAG^+	$YNAG^+$	$M_1=(C+DD+OD)^+$	$M_2=(M_1+TD)^+$	M_r^+
1	2	3	4	5	6	7	8	9
1965	10.8	5602	13328	3654	1948	446.3	489.7	382.6
1966	8.9	6909	14266	4794	2115	521.5	570.7	462.5
1967	-18.2	6411	14042	4292	2119	568.3	641.4	487.6
1968	19.5	7173	14137	4883	2290	618.8	727.1	552.5
1969	8.0	7985	14768	5357	2628	700.4	857.2	638.3
1970	-2.1	8768	15148	5922	2846	763.3	975.3	707.2
1971	7.2	8938	14967	6034	2904	793.4	1072.1	700.3
1972	10.1	10369	15434	7106	3263	857.7	1261.8	740.4
1973	13.1	9969	15360	6578	3391	1015.8	1529.2	885.6
1974	18.1	12808	16333	8851	3957	1281.1	1911.0	1117.2
1975	16.7	16571	16571	11550	5021	1337.7	2064.4	1178.9
1976	-0.6	17394	17300	11611	5783	1452.5	2524.0	1278.5
1977	2.6	17280	17822	10506	6774	1852.9	3223.0	1594.8
1978	11.3	19732	18607	11752	7980	2060.6	3772.1	1849.7
1979	3.5	22215	19048	13522	8693	2504.9	4511.4	2117.3
1980	9.7	23351	18606	13683	9668	2830.4	5285.3	2468.6
1981	13.4	27307	20158	15679	11628	3207.8	6307.7	2706.2
1982	10.5	30988	20920	17903	13085	3611.5	7458.0	3375.6
1983	14.2	33761	20297	19282	14479	4348.9	9222.4	4012.6

1984	6.3	39390	22262	22771	16619	4931.5	10455.2	4624.1
1985	4.1	44441	23636	22761	21680	5480.0	12296.6	5177.3
1986	15.9	53215	24677	27136	26079	7029.3	15159.0	6587.3
1987	13.3	61140	25076	30623	30517	8120.2	17498.2	7600.0
1988	11.1	73170	26824	36755	36415	9596.6	21422.6	8995.9
1989	8.1	85830	28306	42572	43258	11775.4	26605.1	11336.8
1990	9.7	99702	29729	50470	49232	14223.0	31552.4	13924.8
1991	9.8	116128	31481	55368	60760	16283.6	37712.5	16786.0
1992	21.1	144931	32713	65156	79775	19457.7	45580.5	18863.1
1993	8.8	165262	33637	70090	95172	23833.0	58322.5	24443.8
1994	9.0	191540	36283	80589	110951	28510.4	69777.1	28405.7

Year	CPI* (1984 = 100)	IA(SD+ID)+	r_t(%)	Lr (%)	NCB#	POP@	FER+	EXNI	IFA+(G+L)	GRs+	GFD+
1965	24.7	43.4	3.5	6.0	32	10.10	431.3	1.60	146.9	23.2	157.5
1966	26.9	49.2	6.0	6.0	43	10.27	363.2	1.01	178.6	25.0	211.5
1967	22.0	63.7	6.0	9.0	56	10.56	282.1	1.01	145.9	25.0	182.1
1968	26.3	99.5	6.0	9.0	61	10.82	624.6	1.35	158.9	93.8	136.0
1969	28.4	147.2	6.0	9.0	72	11.01	805.3	1.35	185.9	82.6	124.2
1970	27.8	196.8	6.0	9.0	80	11.32	924.4	1.35	251.3	82.4	219.8
1971	29.8	262.3	7.5	10.0	86	11.55	1032.9	1.35	303.2	49.6	309.8
1972	32.8	383.6	7.5	13.0	92	11.87	1119.9	1.39	281.0	52.1	336.3
1973	37.1	458.9	7.5	13.0	103	12.20	1288.7	1.39	227.6	57.7	367.0
1974	43.8	570.1	7.5	13.0	118	12.52	1368.1	1.39	310.5	57.7	459.9
1975	51.1	690.1	9.5	15.0	129	12.83	1173.2	1.39	386.7	68.4	505.3
1976	50.8	1005.4	15.0	18.0	173	13.17	1498.2	1.39	505.6	69.8	797.7
1977	52.1	1330.0	14.0	17.0	216	13.53	1809.3	1.39	556.9	73.4	1007.5
1978	58.0	1711.7	12.0	16.0	231	13.88	1673.0	1.45	848.4	74.7	1092.9
1979	60.0	1932.2	12.0	16.0	231	14.25	2139.1	1.45	989.4	76.0	1208.6
1980	65.8	2386.1	12.0	16.0	241	14.63	2223.3	1.45	1340.5	76.0	1590.7
1981	74.6	2945.0	12.0	16.0	263	15.02	2335.9	1.45	1562.2	83.7	1673.1
1982	82.4	3667.2	12.0	16.0	284	15.34	3060.9	1.45	1723.2	92.0	2681.8
1983	94.1	4486.6	12.5	17.0	357	15.66	2349.7	1.45	2075.9	104.1	4137.6
1984	100.0	5246.2	12.5	17.0	381	15.99	2006.2	1.45	2547.5	112.4	4028.0
1985	104.1	6469.9	12.5	17.0	393	16.32	1346.4	1.45	2676.4	134.8	4478.2
1986	120.6	7888.2	12.5	17.0	409	16.67	2128.6	1.68	3491.5	139.2	5153.0
1987	136.6	9058.4	12.5	18.0	425	17.02	2795.8	1.68	3314.4	140.4	5538.1

1988	151.7	11375.2	12.5	18.0	425	17.37	5594.1	1.68	5088.5	152.6	6754.6
1989	164.0	14366.5	12.5	18.0	437	17.74	6837.1	1.68	5666.9	178.7	10228.1
1990	179.9	16979.7	12.0	18.0	439	18.11	8979.4	1.68	6427.1	187.7	10381.8
1991	197.5	21054.1	12.0	18.0	441	18.49	15390.0	1.65	5990.0	275.5	12819.9
1992	239.2	25961.3	12.5	17.0	440	18.88	20182.2	1.65	7800.4	274.8	12905.5
1993	260.3	34338.0	12.0	15.0	434	19.27	28647.9	1.60	9235.6	316.1	15749.3
1994	283.7	40819.4	9.0	13.5	438	19.65	35261.3	1.60	11557.2	316.8	14016.6

\+ Rs in million, * Index, % in Percent, # Number, @ in million.

Sources : 1. Nepal Rastra Bank, Quarterly Economic Bulletin (Various Issues)
2. Economic Survey, HMG/N (Various Issues)
3. Population Projection for Nepal, CBS, (1994)
4. International Financial Statistics (Various Issues)

Year	M_1/P	M_2/P	A/L (%)	M_1/POP^+	M_2/POP^+	M_r/POP^+	CGN^+	GRs/FER (%)
1965	18.07	19.82	34.21	44.19	48.48	37.88	-51.7	5.38
1966	19.39	21.21	16.64	50.78	55.57	45.03	-24.2	6.88
1967	25.83	29.15	31.76	53.82	60.74	46.17	5.8	8.86
1968	23.53	27.65	32.50	57.20	67.20	51.06	-88.9	15.02
1969	24.66	30.18	48.87	63.61	77.86	57.97	-201.6	10.26
1970	27.46	35.08	43.34	67.43	86.16	62.47	-201.2	8.91
1971	26.62	35.98	42.79	68.69	92.82	60.63	-145.3	4.80
1972	26.15	38.47	40.96	72.26	106.30	62.37	-80.3	4.65
1973	27.38	41.22	39.24	83.26	125.34	72.59	42.2	4.48
1974	29.25	43.63	31.03	102.32	152.63	89.23	139.9	4.22
1975	26.18	40.40	32.27	104.26	160.90	91.89	285.7	5.83
1976	28.59	49.68	44.06	110.29	191.65	97.08	479.8	4.66
1977	35.56	61.86	39.19	136.95	238.21	117.87	749.8	4.06
1978	35.53	65.04	38.09	148.46	271.76	133.26	965.5	4.46
1979	41.75	75.19	39.20	175.78	316.59	148.58	1129.3	3.55
1980	43.01	80.32	34.18	193.46	361.26	168.73	1258.3	3.42
1981	43.00	84.55	37.37	213.57	419.95	180.17	1262.7	3.58
1982	43.83	90.51	34.21	235.43	486.18	220.05	2061.5	3.00
1983	46.21	98.01	35.38	277.71	588.91	256.23	4089.6	4.43
1984	49.31	104.55	34.58	308.41	653.86	289.19	5028.7	5.60
1985	52.64	118.12	32.40	335.78	753.47	317.24	6492.1	10.01
1986	58.29	125.70	32.19	421.67	909.36	395.16	7495.7	6.54
1987	59.44	128.10	32.10	477.10	1028.10	446.53	8712.3	5.02

1988	63.26	141.22	30.44	552.48	1233.31	517.90	9259.0	2.73
1989	71.80	162.23	25.17	663.78	1499.72	639.05	12345.1	2.61
1990	79.06	175.39	31.24	785.37	1742.26	768.90	13940.2	2.09
1991	82.45	190.95	34.67	880.67	2039.62	907.84	16821.4	1.79
1992	81.34	190.55	35.16	1030.60	2414.22	999.10	19001.6	1.36
1993	91.56	224.06	41.78	1236.79	3026.59	1268.49	23446.2	1.10
1994	100.49	245.95	43.44	1449.43	3547.39	1444.11	23482.0	0.90

+ Rs in million, * Index, % in Percent, # Number, @ in million.

Sources : 1. Nepal Rastra Bank, Quarterly Economic Bulletin (Various Issues)
2. Economic Survey, HMG/N (Various Issues)
3. Population Projection for Nepal, CBS, (1994)
4. International Financial Statistics (Various Issues)

Year	Y_t/POP^+	Y_{pt}/POP^+	YAG/Y_t (%)	$YNAG/Y_t$ (%)	$r_t - \Pi_t$ (%)	I_t/Y_t (%)	BOP^+
1965	554.65	1319.60	65.23	34.77	–7.3	N.A	N.A
1966	672.74	1389.09	69.39	30.61	–2.9	N.A	N.A
1967	607.10	1329.73	66.95	33.05	+24.2	N.A	N.A
1968	662.94	1306.56	68.07	31.93	–13.5	N.A	N.A
1969	725.25	1341.33	67.09	32.91	–2.0	N.A	N.A
1970	774.56	1338.16	67.54	32.46	+8.1	N.A	N.A
1971	773.85	1295.84	67.51	32.49	+0.3	N.A.	N.A
1972	873.55	1300.25	68.53	31.47	–2.6	N.A	N.A
1973	817.13	1259.02	65.98	34.02	–5.6	N.A.	N.A
1974	1023.00	1304.55	69.10	30.90	–10.5	N.A	N.A
1975	1291.58	1291.58	69.70	30.30	–9.2	14.49	–418.9
1976	1320.73	1313.59	66.75	33.25	+15.6	15.13	358.2
1977	1277.16	1317.22	60.80	39.20	+11.4	16.02	310.8
1978	1421.61	1340.56	59.56	40.44	+0.7	17.77	10.8
1979	1558.95	1336.70	60.87	39.13	+8.6	15.82	583.4
1980	1596.10	1271.77	58.60	41.40	+2.3	18.29	26.4
1981	1818.04	1342.08	57.42	42.58	–1.4	17.61	194.1
1982	2020.08	1363.75	57.77	42.23	+1.6	17.15	501.5
1983	2155.87	1296.10	57.11	42.89	–1.7	19.63	–675.0
1984	2463.41	1392.24	57.81	42.19	+6.2	18.66	–126.0
1985	2723.10	1448.28	51.22	48.78	+8.4	21.86	–866.0
1986	3192.26	1480.32	50.99	49.01	–3.3	19.02	563.0
1987	3592.24	1473.32	50.09	49.91	–0.8	20.20	376.5

1988	4129.53	1544.27	50.23	49.77	+1.5	19.81	2273.0
1989	4838.22	1595.60	49.60	50.40	+4.4	21.75	75.9
1990	5505.36	1641.58	50.62	49.38	+2.3	18.44	2649.6
1991	6280.58	1702.59	47.68	52.32	+2.2	20.83	4132.2
1992	7676.43	1732.68	44.96	55.04	-8.6	22.43	3394.4
1993	8576.13	1745.56	42.41	57.59	+3.2	23.14	7473.7
1994	9737.67	1844.48	42.07	57.93	0.0	22.41	6632.0

+ Rs in million, * Index, % in Percent, # Number, @ in million.

Sources :
1. Nepal Rastra Bank, Quarterly Economic Bulletin (Various Issues)
2. Economic Survey, HMG/N (Various Issues)
3. Population Projection for Nepal, CBS, (1994)
4. International Financial Statistics (Various Issues)

APPENDIX -F :
Cross-Sectional Data Used for Estimation, 1996

M_d^+	T_y^+	$N_b^\#$	$R_r(\%)$	$H_c(\%)$	NC^+	IC^+	NC/IC	D_r
1.0	54.0	6	18.0	18.0	44.3	9.7	4.57	1.0
2.5	25.2	3	18.0	15.7	21.2	4.0	5.30	1.0
2.5	54.0	4	18.0	67.0	17.8	36.2	0.49	1.0
4.0	36.0	2	18.0	22.0	28.1	7.9	3.56	1.0
5.0	18.0	1	24.0	10.0	14.0	4.0	3.50	0.0
5.0	18.0	2	36.0	22.0	5.4	12.6	0.43	0.0
5.0	18.0	1	18.0	70.0	16.2	1.8	9.00	1.0
5.0	27.0	2	24.0	33.3	18.0	9.0	2.00	0.0
5.0	36.0	3	18.0	20.0	28.8	7.2	4.00	1.0
5.0	61.2	3	18.0	30.0	42.8	18.4	2.33	1.0
5.0	72.0	3	18.0	40.0	18.0	54.0	0.33	1.0
5.0	72.0	1	36.0	30.0	43.2	28.8	1.50	0.0
5.0	72.0	3	36.0	25.0	50.4	21.6	2.33	0.0
5.0	72.0	2	18.0	75.0	54.0	18.0	3.00	1.0
5.0	72.0	1	24.0	60.0	28.8	43.2	0.67	0.0
5.0	144.0	3	36.0	55.0	64.8	79.2	0.82	0.0
5.0	360.0	5	24.0	20.0	288.0	72.0	4.00	0.0
6.0	90.0	2	18.0	26.0	66.6	23.4	2.85	1.0
7.8	18.0	6	18.0	20.0	14.4	3.6	4.00	1.0
10.0	36.0	1	24.0	20.0	30.6	5.4	5.67	0.0
10.0	36.0	1	18.0	15.0	28.8	7.2	4.00	1.0
10.0	57.6	4	36.0	18.7	14.4	43.2	0.33	0.0
10.0	57.6	3	18.0	75.0	46.8	10.8	4.33	1.0
10.0	63.0	2	17.5	40.0	38.5	24.5	1.57	1.0
10.0	72.0	6	24.0	25.0	54.0	18.0	3.00	0.0
10.0	108.0	3	24.0	56.7	46.8	61.2	0.76	0.0
10.0	108.0	2	24.0	66.7	36.0	72.0	0.50	0.0
10.0	144.0	7	16.0	48.7	111.6	32.4	3.44	1.0
10.0	144.0	3	24.0	22.5	73.8	70.2	1.05	0.0
10.0	162.0	4	18.0	44.4	90.0	72.0	1.25	1.0
10.0	252.0	4	18.0	16.0	211.7	40.3	5.25	1.0
10.0	360.0	7	18.0	60.0	144.0	216.0	0.67	1.0
11.0	36.0	1	18.0	25.0	27.0	9.0	3.00	1.0
11.0	36.0	1	30.0	20.0	28.8	7.2	4.00	0.0
11.0	36.0	6	18.0	22.0	28.1	7.9	3.56	1.0
12.3	43.2	1	36.0	25.0	32.4	10.8	3.00	0.0

M_d^+	T_y^+	$N_b^\#$	$R_r(\%)$	$H_c(\%)$	NC^+	IC^+	NC/IC	D_r
12.4	43.2	8	18.0	30.0	30.2	13.0	2.32	1.0
13.0	46.8	2	24.0	60.0	18.7	28.1	0.66	0.0
14.3	54.0	2	24.0	20.0	43.2	10.8	4.00	0.0
14.3	54.0	2	18.0	26.0	39.6	14.4	2.75	1.0
15.0	43.2	6	30.0	25.0	32.4	10.8	3.00	0.0
15.0	180.0	2	36.0	25.0	135.0	45.0	3.00	0.0
15.6	61.2	3	24.0	29.4	43.2	18.0	2.40	0.0
16.3	64.8	1	24.0	35.0	42.1	22.7	1.85	0.0
17.6	72.0	3	18.0	25.0	57.6	14.4	4.00	1.0
17.6	72.0	2	36.0	20.0	61.2	10.8	5.67	0.0
17.6	72.0	1	24.0	25.0	14.4	57.6	0.25	0.0
17.6	72.0	3	18.0	20.0	54.0	18.0	3.00	1.0
17.6	72.0	2	24.0	15.0	57.6	14.4	4.00	0.0
17.6	72.0	1	30.0	80.0	54.0	18.0	3.00	0.0
17.6	72.0	2	18.0	55.0	32.4	39.6	0.81	1.0
17.6	72.0	7	18.0	5.0	68.4	3.6	19.00	1.0
18.2	75.6	5	18.0	47.6	39.6	36.0	1.10	1.0
20.0	54.0	3	14.5	22.7	41.8	12.2	3.43	1.0
20.0	108.0	5	24.0	53.3	75.6	32.4	2.33	0.0
20.0	108.0	3	24.0	30.0	50.4	57.6	0.87	0.0
20.0	144.0	3	24.0	75.0	36.0	108.0	0.33	0.0
20.0	360.0	5	18.0	10.0	306.0	54.0	5.67	1.0
20.0	360.0	5	18.0	15.0	324.0	36.0	9.00	1.0
20.0	1080.0	4	18.0	80.0	216.0	864.0	0.25	1.0
20.0	1800.0	4	18.0	24.0	1368.0	432.0	3.17	1.0
24.1	108.0	1	24.0	75.0	64.8	43.2	1.50	0.0
24.1	108.0	2	16.0	51.6	81.0	27.0	3.00	1.0
24.1	108.0	6	24.0	25.0	27.0	81.0	0.33	0.0
24.1	108.0	2	18.0	40.0	52.2	55.8	0.93	1.0
25.0	360.0	3	36.0	30.0	252.0	108.0	2.33	0.0
27.4	126.0	14	16.0	71.4	36.0	90.0	0.40	1.0
27.4	126.0	3	18.0	80.0	25.2	100.8	0.25	1.0
30.0	54.0	3	48.0	50.0	27.0	27.0	1.00	0.0
30.0	54.0	6	16.0	75.0	13.5	40.5	0.33	1.0
30.0	72.0	1	24.0	60.0	28.8	43.2	0.67	0.0
30.0	90.0	8	18.0	52.0	43.2	46.8	0.92	1.0
30.0	99.0	1	16.0	24.0	75.2	23.8	3.16	1.0
30.0	108.0	4	18.0	24.2	81.0	27.0	3.00	1.0
30.7	144.0	4	12.0	45.0	79.2	64.8	1.22	1.0
30.7	144.0	6	16.5	22.5	111.6	32.4	3.44	1.0

M_d^+	T_y^+	$N_b^\#$	$R_r(\%)$	$H_c(\%)$	NC^+	IC^+	NC/IC	D_r
30.7	144.0	2	24.0	40.0	86.4	57.6	1.50	0.0
34.0	162.0	2	24.0	40.0	97.2	64.8	1.50	0.0
35.0	144.0	5	17.0	75.0	36.0	10.80	0.33	1.0
35.0	144.0	2	24.0	20.0	115.2	28.8	4.00	0.0
37.2	180.0	1	18.0	75.0	45.0	135.0	0.33	1.0
37.2	180.0	4	18.0	55.0	91.8	88.2	1.04	1.0
37.2	180.0	1	24.0	24.0	72.0	108.0	0.67	0.0
37.2	180.0	5	24.0	80.0	81.0	99.0	0.82	0.0
37.2	180.0	8	18.0	40.0	136.8	43.2	3.17	1.0
37.2	180.0	4	24.0	75.0	108.0	72.0	1.50	0.0
37.2	180.0	3	18.0	49.0	45.0	135.0	0.33	1.0
37.2	180.0	4	18.0	60.0	36.0	144.0	0.25	1.0
37.2	180.0	10	18.0	10.0	162.0	18.0	9.00	1.0
37.2	180.0	3	18.0	90.0	18.0	162.0	0.11	1.0
40.0	61.2	1	36.0	6.0	57.5	3.7	15.54	0.0
40.0	360.0	6	18.0	10.0	324.0	36.0	9.00	1.0
43.8	216.0	1	24.0	48.0	112.3	103.7	1.08	0.0
50.0	54.0	5	24.0	22.0	42.1	11.9	3.54	0.0
50.0	108.0	3	18.0	54.0	49.7	58.3	0.85	1.0
50.0	360.0	3	24.0	70.0	108.0	252.0	0.43	0.0
56.9	288.0	5	24.0	56.2	250.6	37.4	6.70	0.0
56.9	288.0	3	18.0	13.0	126.0	162.0	0.78	1.0
69.9	360.0	8	18.0	48.0	187.2	172.8	1.08	1.0
69.9	360.0	17	24.0	75.0	90.0	270.0	0.33	0.0
100.0	180.0	3	24.0	52.0	86.4	93.6	0.92	0.0
100.0	360.0	11	24.0	75.0	90.0	270.0	0.33	0.0
100.0	360.0	11	18.0	52.0	172.8	187.2	0.92	1.0
102.3	540.0	3	18.0	80.0	108.0	432.0	0.25	1.0
102.7	540.0	8	18.0	51.0	264.6	275.4	0.96	1.0
102.7	540.0	5	18.0	10.0	486.0	54.0	9.00	1.0
102.7	540.0	7	18.0	23.3	414.0	126.0	3.28	1.0
102.7	540.0	31	18.0	5.0	513.0	27.0	19.00	1.0
115.8	612.0	10	22.0	20.0	489.6	122.4	4.00	0.0
120.0	108.0	4	18.0	55.0	48.6	59.4	0.82	1.0
135.4	720.0	2	18.0	60.0	72.0	648.0	0.11	1.0
135.4	720.0	4	24.0	90.0	288.0	432.0	0.67	0.0
141.9	756.0	8	18.0	73.8	198.0	558.0	0.35	1.0
168.1	900.0	5	18.0	12.0	792.0	108.0	7.33	1.0
200.8	1080.0	7	18.0	75.0	270.0	810.0	0.33	1.0
200.8	1080.0	3	18.0	90.0	108.0	972.0	0.11	1.0

M_d^+	T_y^+	$N_b^\#$	$R_r(\%)$	$H_c(\%)$	NC^+	IC^+	NC/IC	D_r
266.3	1440.0	8	12.0	70.0	432.0	1008.0	0.43	1.0
400.0	1080.0	5	18.0	25.0	810.0	270.0	3.00	1.0
500.0	3600.0	13	18.0	20.0	2880.0	720.0	4.00	1.0
593.5	3240.0	22	24.0	7.0	3013.2	226.8	13.28	0.0
1000.0	1800.0	19	24.0	45.0	990.0	810.0	1.22	0.0

+ Rs in Million, # Number, % Percentage

Source : Field Survey, 1996

APPENDIX G : STUDY AREA

NEPAL					INDIA
S. No.	*Development Regions*	*Districts*	*Main Border Entry Areas*	*Adjoining Areas*	*States*
1.	***Eastern***	***Jhapa***	***Kakarbhitta, Dhulabari***	***Naksalbari***	***West Bengal***
2.	"	"	***Bhadrapur, Chandragadi***	***Galgaliya***	"
3.	"	***Morang***	***Biratnagar, Rani bazaar***	***Jogbani***	***Bihar***
4.	"	Sunsari	Bhantabari	Bhimnagar	"
5.	"	Siraha	Siraha bazaar	Jayanagar	"
6.	"	Janakpur	Jaleshwor	Bhittamod, Jayanagar	"
7.	"	Sarlahi	Malangawa	Sunabarsa	"
8.	Central	Rautahat	Gaur	Bairganiya	"
9.	"	Bara	Kalaiya	Raxaul	"
10.	"	***Parsa***	***Birgunj***	***Raxaul***	"
11.	***Western***	***Rupandehi***	***Bhairahawa, Belahiya***	***Sunauli, Nautanawa***	***Uttar Pradesh***
12.	"	Kapilbastu	Taulihawa, Krishna nagar	Kakarhawa	"
13.	***Mid-Western***	***Banke***	***Nepalgunj***	***Rupaidiya, Nanpara***	"
14.	"	Bardiya	Gulariya, Rajapur	Murtina, Katarniya	"
15.	***Far-Western***	***Kailali***	***Dhangadi***	***Gauriphanta***	"
16.	"	*Kanchanpur*	*Mahendra-nagar*	*Banbasa*	"

Source: Extracted from Tourist Map of Nepal, HMG, Ministry of Tourism, Development of Tourism, Kathmandu, Nepal, 1982.

BIBLIOGRAPHY

Adekunle, Joseph O. (1968)[a] "The Demand for Money : Evidence from Developed and Less Developed Economies," *IMF Staff Papers* 15, 220-266.

Adekunle, Joseph O. (1968)[b] "The Demand for Money : An International Comparison," *The Indian Economic Journal* 16(1), July-Sept., 22-33.

Aghevli, Bijan B. (1975) "The Balance of Payments and Money Supply Under the Gold Standard Regime: U.S. 1879-1914," *The American Economic Review* 65(1), March, 40-58.

Aghevli, B.B., Khan, Mohsin (1978) "Government Deficit and the Inflationary Process in Developing Countries," *IMF Staff Papers* 25(3), Sept., 383-415.

Aghevli, B.B., Khan,M.S., Narvekar, P.R. and Short, B.K. (1979) "Monetary Policy in Selected Asian Countries," *IMF Staff Papers* 26(4), December, 775-824.

Ahmad, Syed (1977) "Transactions Demand for Money and the Quantity Theory," *Quarterly Journal of Economics* 91,327-335.

Akerlof, George A. (1982) "The Short-Run Demand for Money: A New Outlook at an Old Problem," *The American Economic Review* 72(2), May, 35-39.

Akerlof, G.A. and Milbourne, D. (1980) "The Short-Run Demand for Money," *The Economic Journal* 90(306), 885-900.

Almon, Shirley (1965) "The Distributed Lag Between Capital Appropriations and Expenditures," *Econometrica* 33, January, 178-196.

Arango, S. and Nadiri, M.I. (1981) "Demand for Money in Open Economies," *Journal of Monetary Economics* 7(1), 69-83.

Arize, Augustine (1985) "Permanent Income, Inflation Expectations and Money Demand Function in Nigeria," *Indian Journal of Economics* 65(258), January,289-305.

Artis, M.J. & Lewis, M.K. (1976) "The Demand for Money in the United Kingdom: 1963-73," *Manchester School of Economic and Social Studies* 44, June, 147-181.

Artis, M.J. & Lewis, M.K. (1984) "How Unstable is the Demand for Money in the United Kingdom," *Economica* 51, 473-476.

Asian Development Bank (1995) *Asian Development Outlook:* 1995 & 1996, Asian Development Bank, New York: Oxford University Press, 149-154.

Bain, Andrew D. (1971) "Monetary Control Methods in the United Kingdom" in G. Clayton, J.C. Gilbert and R. Sedgwick (eds.), *Monetary Theory and Monetary Policy in the 1970s*, London: Oxford University Press.

Bain, Andrew D. (1978) *The Control of the Money Supply: Penguin Modern Economics*, second edition, Great Britain: Penguin.

Barari, Mahua (1996) " The Effect of Financial Market Activities on Money Demand: A Case Study of India," *The Indian Economic Journal* 44(1), July-Sept., 47-63.

Barrow, R.J. (1970) "Inflation, the Payments Period, and the Demand for Money," *Journal of Political Economy* 78, Nov.-Dec., 1228-1263.

Basu, Kaushik (1977) "Some Implications of Baumol's Theory of Transaction Demand for Money," *The Indian Economic Journal* 24(4-5), April-June, 402-413.

Basyal, T.R. (1994) "Development of Domestic Saving Mobilization in Nepal: An Overview," *Economic Review*, Nepal Rastra Bank, Occasional Paper N. 7, April, 14-41.

Baumol, William J. (1952) "The Transactions Demand for Cash: An Inventory Theoretic Approach," *Quarterly Journal of Economics* 66, November, 545-556.

Beenstock, Michael (1977) "Monetary Independence Under Fixed Exchange Rates: The Case Study of West Germany 1958-1972," Compiled by S.F. Frowen and et al., *Monetary Policy and Economic Activity in West Germany*, London: Surrey University Press.

Bhasin, Vijay K.(1988) "Demand for Money, Foreign Aid and the Non-neutrality of Money," *The Indian Economic Journal* 36(1), July-Sept., 76-91.

Bhattacharya, B.B. (1974) "Demand and Supply of Money in a Developing Economy: A Structural Analysis for India," *The Review of Economics and Statistics* 56(4), Nov., 502-510.

Biswas, Basudeb & Saunders, Peter J. (1990) "Money and Price Level in India: An Empirical Analysis," *The Indian Economic Journal*

38(1), July-Sept.,103-114.

Blejer, Mario I. (1978) "Money and the Nominal Interest Rate in An Inflationary Economy: An Empirical Test," *Journal of Political Economy* 86(3), June, 529-534.

Bomberger, William A. and Makinen Gail F. (1980) "Money Demand in Open Economies: Alternative Specifications," *Southern Economic Journal* 46, July, 30-39.

Bordo, Michael D., Choudhri, Ehasan U. (1982) "Currency Substitution and the Demand for Money: Some Evidence for Canada" *Journal of Money, Credit and Banking* 14, 48-57.

Boughton, James M. (1991) "Long-Run Money Demand in Large Industrial Countries," *IMF Staff Papers* 38(1), March, 1-32.

Bowles, Roger A. and Whynes, David K. (1979) *Macro Economic Planning*, London: George Allen and Unwin Ltd.

Branson, William H. (1997) *Macroeconomic Theory and Policy,* Second Edition, Reprint, Delhi: AITBS Publishers and Distributors.

Brunner, K. & Meltzer, A.H. (1967) "Economies of Scale in Cash Balances Reconsidered," *Quarterly Journal of Economics* 81, August, 422-436.

Brunner, K. & Meltzer, A.H. (1972) "Friedman's Monetary Theory," *Journal of Political Economy* 80(5), Sept.-Oct.,837-851.

Brunner, Karl. & Meltzer, Allan H. (1964) "Some Further Evidence on Supply and Demand Functions for Money," *Journal of Finance* 19, May, 240-283.

Cagan, Philip (1959) "The Monetary Dynamics of Hyperinflation" in M. Friedman (ed.), *Studies in the Quantity Theory of Money,* Chicago: University of Chicago Press.

Calvo, Guillermo A. and Rodriguez, Carlos A. (1977) "A Model of Exchange Rate Determination under Currency Substitution and Rational Expectations," *Journal of Political Economy*, 85(3), June, 617-625.

Cargill, Thomas F. & Meyer, Robert A. (1979) "Stability of the Demand Function for Money: An Unresolved Issue," *The American Economic Review* 69(2), May, 318-323.

Carr, J. and Darby, M.R. (1981) "The Role of Money Supply Shocks in the Short-run Demand for Money," *Journal of Monetary Economics* 8(2), Sept., 183-200.

Chakraborty, D. and Kulkarni, K.G. (1991) "The Relationship Between Desired and Actual Money Demand: Adjustment Coefficient in Case of India," *The Indian Economic Journal* 39, July-Sept., 87-95.

Chandler, Laster U. (1975) *The Economics of Money and Banking*, Fifth Edition, New York: Harper and Row.

Charemja, Wejciech W. and Ghatak, Subatra (1990) "Demand for Money in a Dual currency Quantity Constrained Economy: Hungary and Poland (1956-85)" *The Economic Journal 100*, December, 1159-1172.

Chen, Chau-Nan and Tsaur, Tien-Wong (1983) "Currency Substitution and Foreign Inflation," *Quarterly Journal of Economics* 98(1), February, 177-184.

Chow, Gregory C. (1960) "Tests of Equality between Two Sets of Coefficients in Two Linear Regressions," *Econometrica* 28, July, 591-605.

Chow, G.C. (1966) "On the Long-Run and Short-Run Demand for Money," *Journal of Political Economy* 74(2), April, 111-131.

Clark, Peter B. (1970) Demand for International Reserves: A Cross-Country Analysis," The *Canadian Journal of Economics* 3, Nov., 577-594.

Clinton, Kevin (1973) "The Demand for Money in Canada, 1955-70: Some Single-Equation Estimates and Stability Tests," The *Canadian Journal of Economics* 6, February, 53-61.

Coates, C. Robert (1976) *The Demand for Money by Firms*, New York: Marcel Dekker Inc.

Cooley, Thomas F. and Leroy, Stephen F. (1981) " Identification and Estimation of Money Demand," *The American Economic Review* 71(5), December, 825-844.

Corker, Robert and Tseng, Wanda (1991) "Financial Liberalization, Money Demand and Monetary Policy in Asian Countries," *IMF Occasional Paper* 84, 11-22.

Courchene, Thomas J. and Kelly, Alex K. (1971) "Money Supply and Money Demand: An Econometric Analysis for Canada," *Journal of Money, Credit and Banking* 3(2), May, 219-243.

Courchene, T. J. and Shapiro, H.T. (1964) "The Demand for Money: A Note from the Times Series," *Journal of Political Economy* 72(5), October, 498-503.

Crockett, Andrew D. and Evans, Own J. (1980) " Demand for Money in Middle Eastern Countries," *IMF Staff Papers* 27(3), Sept., 543-577.

Crowther, Geoffrey (1994) *An Outline of Money*, Reprint, New Delhi: University Book Stall.

Cuddington, John T. (1983) "Currency Substitution, Capital Mobility and Money Demand," *Journal of International Money and Finance* 2, August, 111-133.

Culbertson, John M. (1972) *Money and Banking*, New Delhi : Tata McGraw-Hill Publishing Company Ltd.

Cuthbertson, Keith (1988) *The Supply and Demand for Money*, United Kingdom: Basil Blackwell Ltd.

Daniel, Betty C. and Fried, Harold O. (1983) "Currency Substitution, Postal Strikes, and Canadian Money Demand," *The Canadian Journal of Economics* 16(4), November, 612-624.

Deadman, Derek and Ghatak, Subrata (1981) "On the Stability of the Demand for Money in India," *The Indian Economic Journal* 29(1), July-Sept., 41-54.

Dennis, Geoffrey E.J. (1981) *Monetary Economics*, London & New York: Longman.

Dillard, Dudley (1979) *The Economics of John Maynard Keynes: The Theory of a Monetary Economy*. Second Impression, Ghaziabad: Vikas Publishing House Pvt. Ltd.

Driscoll, M.J. and Lahiri A. K. (1983) "Income Velocity of Money in Agricultural Development Economies," *The Review of Economics and Statistics* 65, August, 393-401.

Edwards, Sebastian (1984) "The Demand for International Reserves and Monetary Equilibrium: Some Evidence from Developing Countries," *The Review of Economics and Statistics* 66(3), August, 495-500.

Erian, Mohamed E. (1988) "Currency Substitution in Egypt and the Yemen Arab Republic - A Comparative Quantitative Analysis," *IMF Staff Papers* 35(1), March, 85-102.

Faig, Mequel (1989) "Seasonal Fluctuations and the Demand for Money," *Quarterly Journal of Economics* 103, 847-861.

Fair, Ray C. (1987), "International Evidence on the Demand for Money," *The Review of Economics and Statistics* 69, 473-480.

Feige, Edgar L. (1967) "Expectations and Adjustments in the Monetary Sector," *The American Economic Review* 57, May, 462-473.

Feige, E.L. and Pearce, D.K. (1979) "The Causal Relationship between Money and Income: Some Caveats for the Time Series Analysis," *The Review of Economics and Statistics* 61, November, 521-533.

Fisher, Douglas (1968) "The Demand for Money in Britain: Quarterly Results 1951 to 1967," *Manchester School of Economic and Social Studies* 36, December, 329-344.

Foot, David K. (1977), "The Demand for Money in Canada: Some Additional Evidence," *The Canadian Journal of Economics* 10, Feb.-Nov., 475-485.

Frenkel, Jacob A. (1974) "The Demand for International Reserves by Developed and Less Developed Countries," *Economica* 41, February, 14-24.

Frenkel, Jacob A. (1977) "The Forward Exchange Rate, Expectations, and the Demand for Money: The German Hyperinflation," *The American Economic Review* 67(4), September, 653-670.

Frenkel, Jacob A. and Jovanovic, Boyan (1980) "On Transactions and Precautionary Demand for Money," *Quarterly Journal of Economics* 94, August, 25-43.

Friedman, Benjamin M. and Kuttner, Kenneth N. (1992) "Money, Income, Prices and Interest Rates," *The American Economic Review* 82(3), June, 472-492.

Friedman, Milton (1959) "The Demand for Money: Some Theoretical and Empirical Results," *Journal of Political Economy* 67(4), August, 327-351.

Friedman, M. (1968) "Money: Quantity Theory," Sills D.S. (ed.) *International Encyclopedia of the Social Sciences* 10, USA: The Macmillan.

Friedman, M. and Schwartz Anna J. (1970) *Monetary Trends in the United States and the United Kingdom*, Chicago: The University of Chicago Press.

Fry, Maxwell J. (1974) *Resource Mobilization and Financial Development in Nepal*, Kathmandu: CEDA &NRB.

Fry, Maxwell J. (1978) "Money and Capital or Financial Deepening in Economic Development," Journal of Money, Credit and Banking10(4), 464-475.

Gaudel, Yadav S. (1994) "Money Supply Determinants in Nepal: An Economic Analysis," *Economic Literature* 5(1), Tribhuvan University, P.N. Campus, Pokhara, Jan.-June, 18-24.

Ghatak, Subrata (1981) *Monetary Economics in Developing Countries*, London: The Macmillan Press, Ltd.

Ghosh, Alak (1971) *Control Techniques in Indian Monetary Management*, Calcutta: World Press.

Goldfeld, Stephen M. (1973) "The Demand for Money Revisited," *Brookings Papers on Economic Activity* 3, 577-638.

Goldfeld, S.M. (1976) "The Case of the Missing Money," *Brookings Papers on Economic Activity* 3, 683-730.

Gujarati, Damodar (1968) "The Demand for Money in India," *Journal of Development Studies* 5(1), 59-64.

Gujarati, Damodar (1978) *Basic Econometrics*, Tokyo: McGraw-Hill Kogakusha Ltd.

Gupta, K.L. (1970) " The Demand for Money in India: Further Evidence," *The Journal of Development Studies* 6, January, 159-168.

Gupta, Suraj B. (1995) *Monetary Planning for India*, Fourth Impression, New Delhi: Oxford University Press.

Gurley, G.S. and Shaw E.H. (1960) *Money in a Theory of Finance*,

Brookings Institution.

Habibulla, M.S. (1990) "Choice of Scale Variable and the Specification of Malaysian Money Demand Function: A Note," *The Indian Economic Journal* 38(1), 79-88.

Hamburger, Michael J. (1966) "The Demand for Money by Households, Money Substitutes and Monetary Policy," *Journal of Political Economy* 74. December, 600-623.

Handa, Jagdish (1977) " The Concepts of the Demand for Money to Hold and As the Means of Payment," *The Indian Economic Journal* 24(4-5), April-June, 390-401.

Hanson, J. (1965) *A Dictionary of Economics and Commerce*, London.

Haque, Mainul (1989) "Demand for Money in the United Kingdom: An Empirical Measurement," *The Indian Economic Journal* 37(1), July-Sept., 74-81.

Hart, Albert Gailord (1968)) "Money: General," D.L. Sills (ed.), *International Encyclopedia of the Social Sciences* 10, USA: Macmillan, 426-432.

Heerden, J.H.O (1981) " Income and Interest Rate Elasticities of the Demand for Money in South Africa: Comments and Extension," *The Indian Economic Journal* 41(1), July-September, 83-89.

Heller, H.R. (1965) "The Demand for Money-The Evidence from the Short-run Data," *Quarterly Journal of Economics* 79, June, 291-303.

Hester, Donald D.(1982) "On the Adequacy of Policy Instruments and Information When the Measuring of Money is Changing," *The American Economic Review* 72(2), May, 40-44.

HMG/N (1992) *The Eighth Plan* (1992-97), National Planning Commission, Nepal, July.

Hoffman, Dennis L. and Rasche, Robert H. (1991) "Long-Run Income and Interest Elasticities of Money Demand in the United States," *The Review of Economics and Statistics* 73(4), 665-674.

Hwang, Dennis B.K. (1994) "Money Supply and Economic Growth: A Causal Study on Taiwan," *Indian Journal of Economics* 75(297), October, 143-149.

ISD (1994)[a] "Balance of Payments Situation with India : A Medium Term Proposal for its Correction," Institute for Sustainable Development (ISD) for Nepal Rastra Bank, *Economic Review*, Occasional Paper N.7, April, 75-91.

ISD (1994)[b] "Inflation in Nepal," *Economic Review*, Nepal Rastra Bank, Occasional Paper N.7, April, 99-108.

Jacobs, Rodney L. (1974) "Estimating the Long-Run Demand for Money from Time Series Data," *Journal of Political Economy* 82(6), Nov.-Dec., 1221-1238.

Johnson, H.G. (1962) "Monetary Theory and Policy," *The American Economic Review* 52, June, 351-354.

Johnson, H.G. (1972) *Readings in British Monetary Economics*, H.G. Johnson et al (eds.), London: Oxford University Press.

Johnson, H.G. (1973), *Further Essays in Monetary Economics*, Cambridge: Harvard University Press.

Johnson, H.G. (1978) *Macro Economics and Monetary Theory*, Great Britain: Basic Blackwell.

Johnson, H.J. (1963) "Notes on the Theory of Transactions Demand for Cash," *Indian Journal of Economics*, 44(172), July, 1-11.

Johnson, H.J. (1993) *Financial Institutions and Markets: A Global Perspective*, Tokyo: Mc Graw Hill International Edition.

Joshi, Himanshu and Saggar, Mirdul (1995) "The Demand for Money in India: Stability Revisited," *Reserve Bank of India, Occasional Papers* 16(2), June, 79-97.

Joshi, N.C. (1978), *Readings in Nepalese Economy*, First Edition, Allahbad: Chugh Publications.

Kafka, Alexandre (1978) "The New Exchange Rate Regime and the Developing Countries," *Journal of Finance* 33(3), June, 795-802.

Kamaiah, Bardi (1984) "A Note on Demand for Money in India: Some Structural Estimates," *Indian Journal of Economics* 64(254), January, 345-351.

Kamath, Shyam J. (1984) "The Demand for Money in India 1951-76: Theoretical Aspects and Empirical Evidence," *Indian Journal of Economics* 65(257), October, 131-172.

Kaminow, Ira (1969) "The Household Demand for Money: An Empirical Study" *Journal of Finance* 24(4), September, 679-693.

Kaur, Gian (1995) "Monetary and Fiscal Policies in India- A Test of Their Relative Effectiveness," *Indian Journal of Economics* 43(1), July-Sept., 55-66.

Kavanagh, N.J. and Walters A.A. (1972) "The Demand for Money in the United Kingdom, 1877-1961: Preliminary Findings" in Johnson H.G. et al (eds.), *Readings in British Monetary Economics*, London: Oxford University Press.

Khan, A.H. (1982) "Permanent Income, Inflation Expectation and the Money Demand Function in Developing Countries," *Pakistan Development Review* 21(4), 259-273.

Khan, Mohsin S. (1974) "The Stability of the Demand for Money Functions in the United States, 1901-1965," *Journal of Political Economy* 82(6), Nov.-Dec., 1205-1220.

Khan, Mohsin S. (1975) "The Monetary Dynamics of Hyperinflation: A Note," *Journal of Monetary Economics* 1, July, 355-362.

Khan, Mohsin S. (1977) "The Variability of Expectations in Hyperinflation," *Journal of Political Economy* 85, August, 817-827.

Khatiwada, Yuba R. (1994) *Some Aspects of Monetary Policy in Nepal,* New Delhi: South Asian Publishers.

Khatiwada, Yuba R. (1997) "Estimating the Demand for Money in Nepal: Some Empirical Issues" Economic Review, Occasional Paper N.9, NRB, Jan., 1-43.

Koot, Ronald S. (1975) "A Factor Analytic Approach to an Empirical Definition of Money," *Journal of Finance*30 (4), September, 1081-1089.

Kremers, Jeroen J.M. and Lane, Timothy D. (1990) "Economic and Monetary Integration and the Aggregate Demand for Money in the European Monetary System (EMS) *IMF Staff Papers* 37(4), December, 777-805.

Krishnamurti, K. (1984) "Inflation and Growth: A Model for India," *Indian Economic Review* 19(1), 111-116.

Lahiri, Ashok K. (1991) "Money and Inflation in Yugoslavia," *IMF Staff Papers* 38(4), December, 751-788.

Laidler, David E.W. (1966)[a] "Some Evidence on the Demand for Money," *Journal of Political Economy* 74(1), February, 55-61.

Laidler, David E.W. (1966)[b] "The Rate of Interest and Demand for Money -Some Empirical Evidence," *Journal of Political Economy* 74(6), December, 545-555.

Laidler, David E.W. (1971) "The Influence of Money on Economic Activity: A Survey of Some Current Problems," in G. Clayton, J.C. Gilbert and R. Sedgwick (eds.), *Monetary Theory and Policy in the 1970s.* London: Oxford University Press.

Laidler, David E.W. (1972) "The Demand for Money" in H.G. Johnson and a Committee of the Money Study Group (eds.) *Reading in British Monetary Economics,* Great Britain: Oxford University Press.

Laidler, D.E.W. (1977) *The Demand for Money: Theories and Evidence,* Second Edition, New York: Dun Donnelley.

Laidler, D.E.W. (1981) "Monetarism: An Interpretation and An Assessment," *The Economi Journal* 91(361), March, 1-28.

Laidler, David E.W. and Parkin J.M. (1970) "The Demand for Money in the United Kingdom 1956-1967 : Preliminary Estimates," *Manchester School of Economics and Social Studies* 38, September, 187-208.

Lane, Timothy D. (1992) "Household Demand for Money in Poland: Theory and Evidence," *IMF Staff Papers* 39(4), December, 825-854.

Latane, H.A. (1960) "Cash Balances and the Interest Rate - A Pragmatic Approach," *The Review of Economics and Statistics* 42, 445-449.

Laufer, Nikolaus K.A. (1977) "Further Evidence on the Relative Importance of Fiscal and Monetary Actions in the Fedral Republic of Germany," Compiled by Frowen et al., *Monetary Policy and Economic Activity*, London: Surrey University Press.

Laumas, G.S.& Mehra Y.P. (1976) "The Stability of the Demand for Money Function: The Evidence from Quarterly Data," *The Review of Economics and Statistics* 58(4), 463-468.

Laumas, Prem S. (1978) "Monetization, Economic Development and the Demand for Money," *The Review of Economics and Statistics* 60(4), November, 614-618.

Lee, H.T. (1967) "Alternative Interest Rates and Demand for Money: The Empirical Evidence," *The American Economic Review* 57, December, 1168-1181.

Lee, H.T. (1969) "Alternative Interest Rates and Demand for Money-Reply," *The American Economic Review* 59, June, 412-417.

Lefton, Norman B. (1974) "The Demand for Real Cash Balances and the Expected Permanent and Contemporaneous Rates of Inflation-Abstract," Journal of Finance 29(1), March, 274-275.

Levhari, D. and Patinkin, D. (1968) "The Role of Money in a Simple Growth Model," *The American Economic Review* 58, 713-753.

Lewis, Arthur W. (1966) *Development Planning*, London: George Allen and Unwin Ltd.

Lewis, Kenneth A. and Breen, Francis S. (1975) "Empirical Issues in the Demand for Currency: A Multinational Study," *Journal of Finance* 30(4), September, 1065-1079.

Liang I.F. and Liu, Z.R. (1971) "Demand for Money in Asian Countries: Empirical Evidence," *The Indian Economic Journal* 18(4-5), April-June, 475-481.

Lieberman, Charles (1979) "Structural and Technological Change in Money Demand," *The American Economic Review* 69(2), May, 324-329.

Lodha, S.L. (1988) Determinants of Money Stock in India, Jaipur: RBSA Publishers.

Lothian, James R. (1976) "The Demand for High-Powered Money," *The American Economic Review* 66(1),March, 56-68.

Mahajan, Y. Lal (1980) "The Stability of the Demand for Money Functions: A Cross Country Analysis," *The Indian Economic Journal* 28(1), July-Sept., 18-30.

Mammen, Thampy(1970) "A Test of Friedman's Theory of Demand for Money with Indian Data," *The Indian Economic Journal* 17(4-

5), April-June, 494-499.

Mammen, T. (1991) "Supply and Demand for Money," *The Indian Economic Journal* 38(1), 58-67.

Mangla, I. (1979) "An Annual Money Demand Function for Pakistan: Some Further Results," *Pakistan Development Review* 18(1), 21-33.

Mathieson, Donald J. (1975) "Monetary Policy in an Inside Money, Open Economy," *Quarterly Journal of Economics* 89(1), Feb. 81-102.

Mckinnon, R.I. (1973) *Money and Capital in Economic Development*, Washington: The Brookings Institution.

Melitz, J. (1976) "Inflationary Expectations and the French Demand For Money 1950-70," *Manchester School of Economics and Social Studies* 44(1), March, 17-41.

Meltzer, Allan H. (1963) "The Demand for Money: The Evidence from the Time Series," *Journal of Political Economy* 71, June, 219-246.

Metwally, M.M. and Rahaman, A.M.M. Abdel (1990) "The Demand for Money in the Economy of Saudi Arabia," *The Indian Economic Journal* 38(1), 89-102.

Meyer, Paul A. & Neri, John A. (1975) "A Keynes-Friedman Money Demand Function," *The American Economic Review* 65(4), September, 610-623.

Milbourne, Ross (1983) "Price Expectations and the Demand for Money: Resolution of a Paradox," *The Review of Economics and Statistics* 65(4), November, 633-638.

Miles, Marc A. (1978) "Currency Substitution, Flexible Exchange Rates and Monetary Independence," *The American Economic Review* 68,428-436.

Miller, M. and Orr, D. (1966) "A Model of the Demand for Money by Firms," *Quarterly Journal of Economics* 80, 413-435.

Ministry of Finance (1993) *Economic Survey*, H.M.G., FY.1992/93, Kathmandu.

Ministry of Finance (1995) *Economic Survey* (Revised), H.M.G., FY.1994/95, Kathmandu.

Ministry of Finance (1997) *Economic Survey*, H.M.G., FY.1996/97, Kathmandu.

Mitchel, William E., Hand, John and Walter, Ingo (1974) Readings in Macroeconomics: *Current Policy Issues*, New York: McGraw-Hill.

Mookerjee, Rajen (1984) "The Demand for Money in Colonial India: A Secular Perspective," *The Indian Economic Journal* 32(1), July-September,49-60.

Motley, Brian (1967) "A Demand for Money Function for the Household Sector-Some Preliminary Findings," *Journal of Finance* 22(4),

September, 405-418.

Nelson, R.R. (1965) "The Constant Elasticity of Substitution Production Function and Economic Growth Projections," *The Review of Economics and Statistics* 47, 326-330.

NPC (1992) The Eighth Plan (1992-97), National Planning Commission (NPC) Secretariat, H.M.G., Kathmandu, July.

NRB (1988) *Multipurpose Household Budget Survey - A Study on Income Distribution, Employment and Consumption Pattern in Nepal*, Nepal Rastra Bank (NRB), Kathmandu.

NRB (1995) *Nepal Rastra Bank, Quarterly Economic Bulletin* 29(2), Mid-January.

NRB (1996) *Nepal Rastra Bank, Quarterly Economic Bulletin* 30(2-4), Mid-July.

NRB (1997) *40 Years of the Nepal Rastra Bank (1956-1996)*, Kathmandu..

NRB (1999) *Nepal Rastra Bank, Quarterly Economic Bulletin* 33(3 & 4), Mid-April -Mid-July.

Nyong, Michael O. (1993) "Income and Interest Rate Elasticities of the Demand for Money in South Africa: Comments and Extension," *The Indian Economic Journal* 41(1), July-Sept., 83-89.

Obstfeld, Maurice (1982) "Macroeconomic Policy in the Open Economy: Can We Sterilize? Theory and Evidence," *The American Economic Review* 72(2), May, 45-49.

Ojha, J.C. and Rajbahak, R.P. (1965) *Banking and Modern Currency in Nepal*, Kathmandu : Educational Enterprise.

Owoye, O., Coo, Akorlie, A. and Onafowora, Olugbenga A. (1995) "Another Look at the Evidence on the Efficacy of Monetary and Fiscal Policies in Developing Countries :An Application of the St. Louis Equation," *The Indian Economic Journal* 43(1), July-Sept., 127-139.

Pant, Bhubanesh (1993) "Selected Issues on Trade Liberalization," *Nepal Rastra Bank Samachar*, Annual Publication, 38th Anniversary, April, 33-38.

Pant, Hom M. (1978) "An Econometric Analysis of the General Level of Prices in Nepal," *Economic Journal of Nepal* I(4), Oct.-Dec,.68-89.

Pant, R.D. (1983) *Interest Rate Policy of Nepal*, A Study Jointly Sponsored by the Institute for Development Studies and International Development Research Center, Canada: Ottawa.

Pant, Yadav Pd. (1970) *Problems in Fiscal and Monetary Policy: A Case Study of Nepal*, Kathmandu: Sahayogi Prakashan .

Pant, Y.P.(1982) *Economic Development of Nepal*, Third Edition, Allahabad : Kitab Mahal.

Park, Yung Chul (1973) "The Role of Money in Stabilization Policy in Developing Countries," *IMF Staff Papers 20*, July, 379-418.

Pathak, D.S. (1981) "Demand for Money in Developing Kenya- An Econometric Study (1969-78)," *The Indian Economic Journal* 29(1), July-Sept., 10-15.

Patinkin, Don (1965) *Money, Interest and Prices: An Integration of Monetary & value Theory*, Second Edition, New York: Harper and Row.

Patinkin, D. (1972) "Friedman on the Quantity Theory and Keynesian Economics," *Journal of Political Economy* 80(5), Sept.-Oct., 883-905.

Patnaik, S.C. (1982) *Supply and Demand for Money: An Equilibrium Analysis*, New Delhi: Sterling Publishers.

Paudel, Danda Pani (1992) "Credit Planning: Theory and Practice," *Economic Review*, Occasional Paper, Nepal Rastra Bank (6), April, 50-61.

Paul, M.T. (1992) "Demand for Money, Inflationary Expectation and Stock Market," *The Indian Economic Journal* 40(1), 36-62.

Paul, R.R. (1992) *Monetary Economics*, First Edition, New Delhi: Kalyani Publishers.

Perera, Nelson (1988) " Demand for Money in Sri Lanka 1960-1984," *The Indian Economic Journal* 36(1), July-September, 18-32.

Peterson, Richard E. (1972) "The Permanent Income Hypothesis of the Demand for Money," *The Review of Economics and Statistics* 45(1), February, 364-373.

Peterson, Richard E. (1974) "A Cross Section Study of the Demand for Money: The United States, 1960-62," *Journal of Finance* 29(1), March, 73-88.

Poloz, Stephen S. (1980) "Simultaneity and the Demand for Money in Canada," *The Canadian Journal of Economics* 13, Feb.-Nov., 407-420.

Poudyal, Sri Ram (1989) "The Demand for Money in Nepal," *Economic Review, Occasional Paper* (3), Nepal Rastra Bank, April, 27-63.

Prasad, K. and Sampath, R.K. (1977) "Transactions Demand for Cash: The Indian Experience," *The Indian Economic Journal* 24(4-5), April-June, 381-389.

Prasad, Kampta (1969) *Role of Money Supply in a Developing Economy: A Theoretical and Empirical Analysis*, Bombay: Allied Publishers Pvt. Ltd.

Rajbahak, Ram P. (1992) *Nepal-India Open Border - A Bond of Shared Aspirations*, New Delhi: Lancer Publishers.

Rawat, P.C. (1974) *Indo-Nepal Economic Relations*, First Edition, Delhi: National Publishing House.

Reejal, Pushkar R. (1986) *Monetary and Credit Policies of the Nepal Rastra*

Bank and their Impact on the Nepalese Economy, Kathmandu: Ratna Pustak Bhandar.

Rodriguez, Carlos Alfredo (1993) "Money and Credit Under Currency Substitution," *IMF Staff Papers* 40(2), June, 414-426.

Roy, Hirendra Nath (1997) "What Classical and Neo-Classical Monetary Theory Really was," *The Indian Economic Journal* 44(1), July-Sept., 17-34.

Salam, Md. Abdus (1995) "The Balance of Payments as a Monetary Phenomenon: An Econometric Study of India's Experience," *The Indian Economic Journal* 42(3), January-March, 70-75.

Sampath, R.K. and Hussain, Zakir (1981) "Demand for Money in India," *The Indian Economic Journal* 29(1), July-Sept., 17-36.

Santomero, Anthony M. (1947) "A Model of the Demand for Money by Households," *Journal of Finance* 29(1), March, 89-102.

Santomero, Anthony M. & Seater, John J. (1981) "Partial Adjustment in the Demand for Money: Theories and Empirics," *American Economic Review* 71(4), Sept., 566-578.

Saravane, M. (1971) *The Demand for Money in India, A Sectoral Approach*, Delhi: Vikas Publications.

Sargent, Thomos and Wallace, Neil (1973) "Rational Expectations and the Dynamics of Hyperinflation," *International Economic Review* 14, June, 328-350.

Sayers, R.S. (1960) "Monetary Thought and Monetary Policy in England," *The Economic Journal* 70(280), December, 710-724.

Sen, J. (1977) *Indo-Nepal Trade in the Nineteenth Century*, Calcutta: Firma Klm Private Ltd.

Seith, T.T. (1992) Monetary Economics, Third Edition, New Delhi : S. Chand & Company Ltd.

Shahi, Musle A. (1977) "The Demand for Money: Some Empirical Evidence from Developing Countries 1960-1974," *The Indian Economic Journal* 24(4-5), April-June, 357-370.

Shapiro, A.A. (1973) "Inflation, Lags, and the Demand for Money," *International Economic Review* 14, February, 81-96.

Sharma, Gunanidhi (1987) *Monetary Structure of the Nepalese Economy: Policy Issues in Theory and Practice*, New Delhi: South Asian Publishers.

Sharma, K.K. (1968) *Indian Monetary Policy: A Study in Recent Developments*, Meerut: Meenakshi Prakashan.

Sharma, M.P. (1993) "Full Convertibility An Effort Towards Macro Economic Adjustment in Nepal," *Nepal Rastra Bank Samachar*, Annual Publication, April, 10-16.

Shrestha, B.P. (1965) *Monetary Policy in An Emerging Economy: A Case*

Study of Nepal, Kathmandu: Ratna Puatak Bhandar.

Shrestha, B.P. (1981) *An Introduction to Nepalese Economy*, Fourth Edition, Kathmandu: Ratna Puatak Bhandar.

Shrestha, B.P. (1990) *Nepalese Economy in Retrospect and Prospect*, Kathmandu: Himalayan Book Sellers.

Shrestha, G.K. (2000) "The Financial System and the Rural Micro-financial Services in Nepal," *Nepal Rastra Bank Samachar*, Annual Publication, April, 67-77.

Shrestha, S.P. (1993) "Economic Reforms for Sustainable Development in Nepal," *Nepal Rastra Bank Samachar*, Annual Publication, April, 2-9.

Siebke, Juergen (1977) "Price Expectations and Interest Rates in the Federal Republic of Germany," Compiled by S.F. Frowen et al, *Monetary Policy and Economic Activity in West Germany*, London: Surrey University Press.

Singh, Tarlok (1984) " Determinants of Demand for Money in India," *Indian Journal of Economics* 65(256), January, 83-97.

Singh, T. (1990) "Modelling the Demand for Money in India," *International Journal of Development Banking* 8, 33-41.

Singh, T. (1995) "Money-Prices Causality in India - An Empirical Investigation," *Indian Journal of Economics* 75(299), April, 425-428.

Slovin, Myron B. and Sushka, Marie Elizabeth (1975) "The Structural Shift in the Demand for Money," *Journal of Finance* 30(3), June, 721-731.

Spencer, David E. (1985) "Money Demand and the Price Level -Notes," *The Review of Economics and Statistics* 67(3), August, 490-496.

Sprenkle, C.M. (1967) "Is the Precautionary Demand for Money Negative?" *Journal of Finance* 22(1), March, 77-82.

Srivastava, N.N. (1989) *The Perspectives in Monetary Theory*, Delhi: Patriot Publishers.

Starleaf, Dennis R. (1970) "The Specification of Money Demand-Supply Models Which Involve the Use of Distributes Lags," *Journal of Finance* 25(4), September, 743-760.

Starleaf, Dennis R. and Reimer, Richard (1967) "The Keynesian Demand Function for Money: Some Statistical Tests,' *Journal of Finance* 22(1), March, 71-76.

Stevens, Stanley C. (1971) 'The Negative Precautionary Demand for Money Reconsidered," *Journal of Finance* 26(3), June, 749-755.

Subrahmanyam, G. (1977) "On the Nearness of the Time Deposits to Money: An Empirical Study," *The Indian Economic Journal* 24(485), April-June, 414-422.

Swamy, P.A.V.B. and Tavlas, G.S. (1989), "Financial Deregulation, the

Demand for Money and Monetary Policy in Australia," *IMF Staff Papers* 36(1), March, 63-101.

Swoboda, A.K. (1976) "Monetary Approach to the Balance of Payments Theory," in E. Claasan & P. Salin (eds.), *Recent Issues in Monetary Economics*, New York: North Holland Company.

Teigen, Ronald L. (1964), "Demand & Supply Functions for Money in the United States: Some Structural Estimates," *Econometrica* 32(4), October, 476-509.

Thapa, G.B. (1993) "Nepal Fully Floats its Currency on Current Account, *Nepal Rastra Bank Samachar*, Annual Publication, April, 27-32.

Thapa, Nara B. (1993) "Recent Monetary Developments in Nepal: Challenges and Implications for Monetary Policy," *Nepal Rastra Bank Samachar*, Annual Publication, April, 83-91.

Thapa, Nara B. (1997) "The Money Supply Function in Nepal," *Economic Review, Occasional Paper* N.9, Nepal Rastra Bank, Jan., 44-45.

The Economist (1995), Vol. 335, (22-28)th April, London.

Thornton, John (1989) "The Demand for Money in India: A Test of Mckinnon's Complementarity Hypothesis," *The Indian Economic Journal* 37(1), 82-86).

Tobin, James (1956) "The Interest Elasticity of Transactions Demand for Cash," *The Review of Economics and Statistics* 38, August, 241-247.

Tobin, J. (1958) "Liquidity Preference and Behaviour Towards Risk," *The Review of Economic Studies* 25, February, 65-86.

Trivedi, Mukund S. (1980) "Inflationary Expectations and Demand for Money in India (1951-1975)," *The Indian Economic Journal* 28(1), July-Sept., 62-69.

Trivedi, M. (1983) "Inflationary Expectations and Demand for Per Capita Real Balances: Evidences from Indian Economy," *Artha Vijnana* 25(1), 21-36.

Tseng, W. and Corker, R. (1991) "Money Demand and Financial Liberalization," *IMF Staff Papers* 84, July, 11-22.

Tsiang, S.C. (1969) "The Precautionary Demand for Money: An Inventory Theoretical Analysis," *Journal of Political Economy* 77(1), Jan.-Feb., 99-117.

Turnovsky, Stephen J. and Wohar, Mark E. (1984) "Monetarism and the Aggregate Economy: Some Longer-Run Evidence," *The Review of Economics and Statistics* 66(4), November, 619-629.

Upadhayaya, K.P. (1991) "The Efficacy of Monetary and Fiscal Policies in Developing Countries: An Approach of the St. Louis Equation,"

The Indian Economic Journal 39(1), July-Sept., 35-42.

Valentine, Thomas, J. (1977) "The Demand for Money and Price Expectations in Australia," *Journal of Finance* 32, June, 735-748.

Villanueva, Dalano P. (1971) "The Adaptive Expectation Model of the Demand for Money: Some Further Results," *IMF Staff Papers* 18, 183-188.

Vries, Casper G. de (1988) "Theory and Relevance of Currency Substitution with Case Studies for Canada and the Netherlands Antilles," *The Review of Economics and Statistics* 70(3), August, 512-515.

Walter, A.A. (1965) "Professor Friedman on the Demand for Money," *Journal of Political Economy* 73, October, 545-551.

Waud, Roger N. (1970) "The Demand for Real Money Balances and the Complete Keynesian System: A Graphical Exposition," *The Indian Economic Journal* 17(4-5), April-June, 438-452.

Waud, Roger N. (1974) "Monetary and Fiscal Effects on Economic Activity: A Reduced form Examination of their Relative Importance," *The Review of Economics and Statistics* 56(1), February, 177-187.

WDR (1994) "Trends in Developing Economies," *World Development Report* (WDR), New York: Oxford University Press.

Westaway, A.J. and Weyman -Jones, T.G. (1977) *Macroeconomics: Theory, Evidence and Policy*, London: Longman.

Whalen, Edward L. (1968) "An Extension of the Baumol-Tobin Approach to the Transactions Demand for Cash," *Journal of Finance* 23(1), March, 113-134.

White, William H. (1978), "Improving the Demand for Money Function in Moderate Inflation," *IMF Staff Papers* 25, 564-607.

Wilford, D. Sykes, and Wilford, Walton T. (1978) "On the Monetary Approach to the Balance of Payments: The Small Open Economy," *Journal of Finance* 33(1), March, 319-323.

Willms, Manfred (1971) "Controlling Money in an Open Economy: The German Case," *Federal Reserve Bank of St. Louis Review* 53(4), April, 10-27.

Wong, Chorng-Huey (1977) "Demand for Money in Developing Countries: Some Theoretical and Empirical Results," *Journal of Monetary Economics* 3, 59-86.

Zecher, J.R. (1976) "Monetary Equilibrium and International Reserve Flow: Australia" in J.A. Frenkel and H.G. Johnson (eds.), The Monetary Approach to the Balance of Payments, London: George Allen & Unwin.

INDEX

2SLS procedures 125

actual reserves 85
Adaptive expectations 116
adjustment coefficient 114
adverse balance of payments 164
Aghevli 89
agricultural 106
  Credit Fund 28
  income 106
Agriculture Development Bank 63
Alfred Marshall 37
Almon 171
  polynomial lag 119
  technique 119
appropriate definition of money 93
Arango & Nadiri 79
Asian Countries 168
autocorrelation in 102, 143
Autoregressive 112

balance of payments 12, 16, 75, 86, 171
bank
  liquidity 162
  reserves 155
banking
  operations 30
  rate 164
  system 29, 81
basic indicator 162
'basket' of foreign currencies 156
Baumol 42, 43
Baumol-Tobin's
  approach 45
  inventory theoretic approach 33
bond rate of interest 81
bonds 76
bottlenecks 124
Bowles 148
Bowles and Whynes 148
Breen 97
broad definition of money 10
broad money 68, 160
brokerage fee 43
budgetary deficit 12, 16, 89
business portfolio 135

Cambridge cash balance approach 33
capital
  flows 87
  gains 41

inflows 139
market 14
outflow 71
CES 'linearized' models 141
Chicago School 47
Chow test 97, 103
classical
approach 47
model 103
coefficient matrix 45
coins 68
column vector 45
Commercial Bank Act 63
commercial banks 23
complementarities 110
composite price index 84
constant elasticity of substitution (CES) 129
consumer price index 66, 84
Contemporaneous rate 92
continuous deficit in annual budget 164
control the money supply 160
Cooperative Credit Societies (CCSs) 28
coordination of fiscal and monetary tools 165
copper coins 26
cost of living index 84
credit
expansion 160
market 54
planning 167
policy 22
cross sectional 144
Cuddington 139
currency basket system 85, 156, 173
currency substitution 141
ratio 172
current
account deficit 74
income 94
interest rate 118
rate of interest 50
custodian 30
custom duties 145

deficit financing 158, 159
degree of autocorrelation 116
demand deposit 2, 3
depletion of foreign exchange 75
desired 85
real balances 51
determinants 77
devaluation 8, 67
Dh test 124
dichotomy 169
disbursements 61
discrepancy 118
diseconomies of scale 144, 172
disequilibrium in 163
domestic credit supply 162
domestic currency 135
double-digit inflation 88
dual
credit system 166
currency system 6
Durbin h Statistic 115
Durbin- h test 114
DW statistic 101
dynamic adjustments 98
dynamism in 153

easy monetary policy 165
econometric research works 96
economic
and financial reforms 27
fluctuations 21
growth with stability 163
stability 11, 165
stabilization 171
economies of scale 172
efficacy of monetary 163, 166

eighth plan *(1992-97)* 151
elasticity of substitution 172
employment 138, 172
equities 76
excessive liquidity 152
exchange rate 12, 85
exogenous variable 170
exorbitant rate of interest 27
expected
    price 118
    rate of inflation 85, 89
    real income 51
external balance in the economy 161
external shocks 157

fifth plan period *(1975-80)* 150
financial
    assets 14, 49
    deepening 115
    institutions 7
    intermediation 90
    liberalization 28, 63
    liberalization policy 156
    markets 81
    resources 145
    system 14
first five-year plan *(1956-61)* 150
fiscal
    deficit 89
    policy 163
Fisher, I. 35
    approach 33
    view 35
fixed exchange rate 145
    regime 85
    system 157
fixed or flexible exchange rate 4
floating exchange rates 157
Foreign Exchange Regulation Act (1963) 6
foreign exchange reserve 98, 107
fourth plan (1970-75) 150
free reserves 17
freely floating exchange rate system 157
Frenkel 51, 108
Friedman 95
Friedman, M. 33, 47
full convertibility 73
future income 94

general price index 84
geo-economic 145
geographical proximity 133
GNP deflator 84
gold standard 4
Goldfeld's 51, 79, 115
government bond 50, 83
    yield rate 96
government borrowings 69, 160
government securities 26
gross domestic product (GDP) 63, 64
gross domestic savings 65
gross national expenditure 79
Gujarati 116
Gurley 50

health hazard 145
healthy balance of payments 149
herculean task 162
high
    employment 148
    liquidity 54
    powered money 68, 95, 157, 167
higher employment 161
Hoffman 104
Hoffman and Rasche 104
homogeneity condition 107
homogeneous 50
human wealth 47, 50

Hume, David 34

identification 128
idle resources 174
illegal trades 174
implicit 77
implicit GDP deflator 77
income 12
    elasticity 55
    equality 148
income level 78
indigenous moneylenders 27
industrial development corporation 23
industrial finance 31
inflation 8, 12, 48
inflationary 69
    pressures 165
    target 160
insensitive 103
inside 2
insignificant 110
interest
    bearing assets 98, 123
    elastic 47
    elasticities 81
    elasticity 55
    rate 12, 160
        differentiation 26
        liberalization 173
        policy 71
interest-bearing assets 107
International Monetary Fund (IMF) 72
inventory management 46
investment 32, 65

Johnson 51
joint venture banks 11, 63, 86

Kamath 88
Kaminow 44
Keynes 38
Keynes-Friedman's model 56, 58
Keynesian
    effect 80
    framework 42
    liquidity preference approach 33
    theory 34, 51, 75
    transmission mechanism 42
Khan 89
Koyck model 116

labour mobility 87
lagged
    income 118
    money stock variable 114
    values of 119
Lahiri's 88
Laidler 41, 51, 98, 104
Laidler and Parkin 98
Latane 79
least developed countries 98
legal tender money 4
Levhari 45
Lewis 97, 147
Lewis and Breen 97
liabilities 16
liquid
    asset 9
    money 142
liquidity 110
    preference 139
    trap 39
long-term
    bonds 39
    economic stabilization 165
    securities 21
luxury 82

managed floating exchange rate 86, 166, 173

marginal propensity to hold money 98
market transparency 25
Marshall 33
Marshall, A. 35
Marshall-Pigou 38
maximum feasible output 149
maximum level of output 161
Mckinnon 110
McKinnon type 161
McKinnon's Hypothesis 97, 110, 171
measurement of the bias 172
Meltzer 49, 51
Meyer and Neri 51
Ministry of Finance 158
monetarism 87
monetary
  approach 171
  assets 167
  authority 173
  base 162
  control instruments 148
  development 153
  disequilibrium 89
  disquilibrium 158
  dualism 69
  equilibrium 87, 91
  expansion 166
  feedback 20
  flows 130
  management 9
  management 161, 173
  phenomenon 83
  planning 147, 167, 173
  planning 148
  policy 8, 93, 173
  shocks 87
  stability 90
  system 4, 19
  transaction 90
  money 35
  illusion 38, 98
  market 14, 29
  multiplier 159, 162, 167
    stock 95
  variables 119
  supply 9, 13
    analysis 154, 159
multicollinearity 78
multiplier 154, 159

narrow definition of money 10
narrow money 67, 160
narrow money balances 171
national income 14
National Income Accounting 64
near money 1, 36
neoclassical economist 37
Nepal Bank Limited 63
Nepal Housing Development Finance Company Ltd. 28
Nepal Rastra Bank (NRB) 6, 29
Nerlovian partial adjustment model 112
net
  domestic assets 18
  foreign assets 18, 69
  services 74
  transfers 74
ninth plan (1997-2002) 152
NNP deflator 84
nominal interest rate 70
nominal money balances 96
non-agricultural income 106
non-agricultural sector (YNAG) 106
non-bank financial institutions 28
non-borrowed reserves 17
non-human 47, 50, 146
non-monetized economy 7
non-neutral 45
NRB Act 1956 30

OLS procedures 125
open market operations 153, 154
open market policy 154
openness to India 165
opportunity cost of holding money 71
opportunity cost variable 48, 81
original CES model 143
ornaments
  bullion 30
  gold 30
  silver 30
outside 2
overdraft 8, 169

pace of monetization 152
pace of monetization 68
parameters 45
Parkin 98
partial
  adjustment 112
  mechanism 114, 119
  convertibility 73
Patinkin 35, 45
payments, adverse balance of 74
pegging 162
per capita nominal money balances 103
permanent income 51, 76, 80, 94
permanent rate of inflation 92
permanent wealth 76, 80
persistent inflation 148
physical assets 49, 110
physical capital 161
Pigou, A.C. 35
Pigous 33
pivotal variables 98
policy-controlled variables 158
political instability 169
polynomial lag 171
poor indicator 162
population 12, 89
portfolio
  adjustment 50
  shift 140
positive
  bias 172
  monetary feedback 169
  serial correlation 142
Prasad 55
precautionary 38, 76
price hike inflation 89
price level 12, 77
price stability 148, 165
price taker 145
primary market 25
proxy 76
proxy variable 114
prudent monetary policy 157
public credit programmes 150
public debt 31

qualitative instruments 153
quantitative 153
quantity theory 34
quasi money 1, 68

Rasche 104
Rastriya Banijya Bank 63
rate of
  inflation 160
  interest 14, 77
  monetization 12, 90
  population 64
return 48
real
  assets 14
  balance effect 42
  balances 96
  income 89
  interest rates 70
  money balances 161
rate of interest 71, 111

receipts 35, 61
refinancing 167
    of commercial banks 153
region-wise interest rate 140
regression model 143
relevant determinant 83
remittances 30, 149
reserve money 16, 67, 95, 107
resource gap 158
restrictive indicator 162
return to scale parameter 144
Rudimentary 88
Rupee 68
Rural Micro Finance Development Centre 152

sales 35
Sampath 55
satisfactory balance of payments 148
savers 164
savings 32
savings gap 5
Sayers 161
scale variable 78
Schwartz 95
second plan *(1962-65)* 150
secondary market 25
second-degree polynomial 119
security market 24
seventh plan period *(1985-90)* 151
Shaw 50
short-term
    funds 155
    securities 21
    stabilization 174
silver coinage 26
simultaneous
    equations model 123
    equations system 120, 125
single equations system 97
sixth plan period *(1980-85)* 151
sluggish growth 90
social insecurity 169
South-East Asian Countries 54
special drawing rights 4
speculative 76
    demand for money 39, 103
    motives 38
speed of adjustment 115
Sprenkle 46
stability test 103
standard error 116
static price expectation 110
statutory requirements 26
statutory reserves 155
Stevens 46
stochastic process 46
stock exchange 32
store of value 57
strategic role 72
structural model 87
structuralism 87
suitable monetary policy 166
surplus 75

target oriented monetary policy 166, 173
target-threshold model 47
Tejarath system 130
temporary abode of 49
purchasing power 10
third plan (1965-70) 150
time
    deposits 3
    lag 165
    series 74
        data 88
Tobin 42, 44
trade
    deficit 74, 75
    liberalization 73
    transaction 38, 76

and precautionary purposes 11
demand 164
income 172
variable 46
transmission mechanism 4, 81
of monetary 161
transmitted inflation 90
treasury
bill 83
market 155
rate 96
Tsiang 46

unemployment 54
unrequited transfers 75
upsurge in inflation 54

velocity of money 90

Waud 40
weighted average 48
Whalen 45
wholesale price index (WPI) 84, 88, 94
Whynes 148
Wicksell effect 80
Wong 108
World War II 131

yield on assets 38